Refuge

Chronicle of a Flight from Hitler

Studies in Austrian Literature, Culture, and Thought

Biography, Autobiography, Memoirs Series

Egon Schwarz

Refuge
Chronicle of a Flight from Hitler

Translations by Philip Boehm,
Hildegarde and Hunter Hannum,
and Caroline Wellbery

ARIADNE PRESS
Riverside, California

Translated from the German
Keine Zeit für Eichendorff
©Büchergilde Gutenberg, Frankfurt

Felix Pollak "Refugee" reprinted
with the kind permission of Sara A. Pollak

Library of Congress Cataloging-in-Publication Data

Schwarz, Egon, 1922-
    [Keine Zeit für Eichendorff. English]
    Refuge : chronicle of a flight from Hitler / Egon Schwarz ;
    translations by Philip Boehm ... [et al.].
        p.   cm. -- (Studies in Austrian literature, culture and
    thought. Biography, autobiography, memoirs series)
    ISBN 1-57241-104-X
        1. Schwarz, Egon, 1922- 2. Exiles--Austria--Biography.
    3.World War, 1939-1945--Refugees--Biography.
    4. Germanists--United States--Biography. 5.College teachers--
    United States--Biography. I. Title. II. Series.

    PT67.S.36 A3413 2002
    830'.9--dc21
    [B]   2001041329

Cover:
Art Director, Designer: George McGinnis

Refugee

He was born in Vienna
he died in Auschwitz
he is living in New York

He still believes
all men are brothers
under the skin

but he also knows
they'll any day
skin each other alive

so they may be
brothers

Felix Pollak

Acknowledgments

First I would like to thank the Alexander von Humboldt Foundation for their generous support, without which the English edition of this book might never have seen the light of day. A number of people have worked piecemeal over the course of several years in preparing the translation: fortunately all of them are (and remain!) close friends. In particular I would like to thank Hildegarde and Hunter Hannum for their careful labors, my daughter Caroline for overcoming an initial familial reluctance to work with these texts, and to Philip Boehm for translating many new passages and finding a voice for the whole. Finally I would like to dedicate this book to all my friends who either cannot or will not read German.

Prefatory Note

Writing is communicating, and anyone setting out to write an autobiography must first consider for whom the narrative might be of interest. In general it is either the person or the events themselves that make a life worth telling. A famous name can lend even the most banal account a certain market value, but when someone who has lived outside the public view wishes to attract an audience, his[1] experiences must be in some fashion exemplary. They must in some way reflect the spirit of the age, and speak to readers whose own lives were molded by similar forces. As I cannot claim to fit the former category, it is this latter ambition which I hope to accomplish, for despite its share of fantastic or grotesque features I regard my life as typical. Its course was shaped by the same historical tendencies that determined the fate of my entire generation.

But writing is not only communicating with others; it is also an act of self-examination, so I shall add my own personal reasons why I think my story is worth telling. In so doing I shall have to simplify the myriad shades of feeling into three main categories, the first of which is a common psychological impulse to account for one's life. As my fellow Austrian Arthur Schnitzler wrote in his diary: "Nothing is more moving than one's own life – " and by that I believe he meant more than a childish infatuation with whatever happened to befall a person. This urge to render account is probably an innate metaphysical need, an inborn questing for the meaning of an individual's existence.

This very personal reason for writing my memoirs leads promptly to a historical one. Starting with Albert Speer, over the past several years one prominent National Socialist after the other has published his autobiography. As I have already hinted, the public devoured these memoirs with great curiosity: even the less

---

[1] I am aware that women also write autobiographies. But since I have my own case in mind I will use the masculine pronoun.

4

than profound thoughts of the least attractive individuals acquire significance if their authors once strutted about on the world stage. History is not only made by the powerful; it also tends to be interpreted in their favor, rather than from the point of view of their subjects or victims. But even in our present-day pluralistic world there remains reason to give voice to the other side. In any event I feel a strong desire to show how someone fared whose life was thrown out of orbit because these fellow travelers, these half and whole Nazis were allowed to hold the reins for a while.

My final motivation for doing this might be called a philosophical one: because I have been a plaything of historical forces, because the first two decades of my life contain practically nothing that was spontaneous or self-induced, I have a particularly intense interest in the issue of free will. Reflecting on my career, I hope to learn how to distinguish more convincingly between what was imposed upon me by circumstances and what I myself did to shape my life.

CHAPTER ONE
Childhood and Youth in Vienna

I was born in Vienna, the Imperial City, equipped with that highly prized golden heart of the Viennese, a people who take a proverbial delight in song, love, and food. Unlike restless nomadic nationalities such as the Italians and the Swiss, who frequently forsake their homeland, never to return, the Viennese, we are told, are a people in love with their native soil who make much of their *Gemütlichkeit* and eagerly hurry home when their summer vacation is over. Why is this so? Because nowhere else on earth are there such crisp *Kaisersemmeln* or "Kaiser rolls" and such good mountain spring water as in Vienna. In Vienna, the light-footed city of the waltz and of carefree sybaritic amusements, every girl was sweet, every gentleman a charming baron, every janitor a connoisseur of grand opera, and every meal a succulent *Wiener Backhendl* or Viennese roast chicken. Even the relationship of the despised minorities to the alien soil on which they struggled to find a footing was prettified in the popular couplet:

Wía da Moses de Judn hot g'fiehrt iebers Meer,
Do wóan in da Leopoidstodt die Kafféeheiser leer
[When Moses led the Jews across the Sea,
The cafés in Leopoldstadt all became empty].
(Leopoldstadt, for the uninitiated, is a district of Vienna where many Jews lived.)

Even today, when nothing more exists of these delights but the ghosts conjured up for purposes of tourism, the eyes of travelers grow a bit moist when they hear you come from Vienna. The name conjures visions of *Torte* and whipped cream; evidently many must imagine that this is a place where the most intimate dreams of a rather prosaic imagination can still come true.

It is true that I was born in Vienna, but it was not in the Vienna of legend. If there were an element of choice in these matters, I would have to add that the time of my birth was poorly chosen:

it was a few years after the First World War during an economic crisis which virtually obscured the blinding radiance of the legend. Vienna, until recently the great capital of a polyglot empire, had just been demoted to the status of a wobbling enlarged head on a body formed by a small, backward country still haunted by the ambitious dreams of yesteryear which stood in glaring contrast to present-day social reality. Today, in the last quarter of the twentieth century, whoever admires the pristine, museum-like facades of the old Viennese palaces and sundry baroque edifices will have a hard time picturing the gray, depressed Vienna of my childhood. And anyone who encounters the bustling prosperity of the Austrian provinces will have an equally hard time imagining the once rampant unemployment of the capital. The same traveler would be amazed to learn that the Austrian state of Vorarlberg, now so prosperous, at that time petitioned to join the Swiss Confederation, on the grounds that their local dialect was more Swiss-Alemannic than German-Bavarian like the rest of Austria. (Naturally the petition was rejected.) Among my earliest frightening memories are visions of cripples, blind men, and war-disabled who stood on every corner stretching out begging hands, caps or tin cups to the passer-by. I can still see the homeless who slept in parks and under the bridges crossing the Danube, the many fiddlers, the organ grinders and street-singers who performed in rear courtyards, catching the ten Groschen wrapped in paper thrown down to them from the windows above. The doorbell would ring several times a day, even more on Saturdays, as if by some tacit agreement. Through the peephole you could glimpse grotesque figures claiming to be university graduates out of a job, or simply "Ausg'steuerte," people whose unemployment compensation had run out; through the opening provided by the safety chain you would then hand them some food and a few small coins.

In hindsight, the apartment where these unfortunates received their alms (after climbing several flights of stairs) appears unbelievably primitive and confined: a narrow hall, an old-fashioned kitchen, a living room where I slept at night on a sofa, and a small bedroom for my parents, called a "cabinet" for reasons unknown to me. There was no bathroom. One washed at the water tap. The weekly ablutions took place in a vat in which cold water was mixed with hot. My selective memory of early childhood registers the transformation of our latrine-like toilet into an "English water closet" which the family greeted ecstatically as a great technological innovation. Proof of our backwardness was also the fact that our street, until then unpaved, received a coat of asphalt one day. Perhaps I remember this particular improvement because my mother, averse to anything pleasurable, had trouble keeping me from bending down to inhale the fresh scent of tar deep into my lungs. Our street, Geologengasse, owed its name (which remained enigmatic to me for a long time) to the Imperial Institute of Geology around the corner. At about the same time electrical street lighting was introduced. Before that a uniformed man went from one gas lamp to the next with an enormously long pole to ignite the incandescent mantles which emitted a ghostly light, greenish and pale but nevertheless heartwarming. The result, unfortunately, was that the gas lamp above our dining table, surrounded by colorful coral fringes, also disappeared, making way for what seemed to me a much more impersonal electric fixture. Among the irreplaceable things lost together with one's childhood are the intense pleasures derived from light and color as well as taste and other sense perceptions. No intellectual development, however liberating, can fully compensate for the loss of such sensations that are the delight of the first years of life. For me they had the power of temporarily brightening the gloom that enveloped Vienna when I grew up there. My Jewish parents were born in the old Austro-Hungarian provinces. My father came from distant Bukovina in the east, my mother from Pressburg, located on the Danube only sixty kilometers downstream from Vienna. Despite its proximity to the capital it belonged to a very different world.

Anchored in its dynastic traditions as it was, Vienna was also infected by a kind of commercial fever, the consequence of capitalism having been introduced relatively late. As a result the city served as a magnet for members of eastern Jewish communities who had been practically untouched by the modern

Western world. These people often had only the dimmest of notions of the possibilities offered by the great Hapsburg capital, but it was for this very reason that they found it irresistibly attractive. Lured by indistinct hopes of social advancement, and repelled by the orthodox intolerance, poverty, and stagnation of his own background, my father had come to Vienna as a young man. But no one hailed the arrival of an unskilled shop clerk who very quickly discovered that the Viennese cobblestones were not made of gold. His main meal in those impoverished times consisted of a loaf of bread which he and a similarly unfortunate fellow worker consumed in the archways of the inner city where they would withdraw in embarrassment to escape the glances of the crowds of passers-by.

It was not economic success but the Great War that put an end to his first period of privation in Vienna. For four years my father defended the Hapsburg monarchy as an artilleryman on the battle-swept Italian front. As a child I often listened in amazement to his tales of wartime adventures which I had a difficult time visual-izing; descriptions of air battles, gas attacks, dangerous river crossings, heavy bombardments, and long stays in overcrowded field hospitals. Sometimes I was allowed to play with the contents of a cardboard box full of distinguished service medals attached to gaily colored ribbons, of silver medals awarded for bravery, and of yellowing photographs showing soldiers grouped around large guns. The last time I caught sight of these treasures was as a young emigrant in South America, on the Feast of St. Rochus, the patron saint of animals. An embittered group of former frontline soldiers – my father among them – who had been driven from their homeland pinned their war decorations on dogs and, to the astonishment of the native Indian population, chased these animals through the streets and marketplace of a little town high in the Andes.

But I am getting ahead of my story. During the First World War when he was visiting relatives, my father met my mother, who was a distant cousin of his. In 1921 they married, and in 1922 I was born. Together they tried to make a decent living in the impoverished Vienna of the days of the Republic, but the times were not auspicious. They changed their line of business often, yet this flexibility still didn't bring them the prosperity they sought. I have prized memories of the pens and pencils, the smooth glazed paper, the various fascinating types of colored inks in their stationery shop, which we forsook one day – I have no idea how or why – never to return. My father's next venture was a dairy, which I was sometimes allowed to visit. The heated milk flowed over a large corrugated sheet of metal, where it cooled off before being poured into big, sour-smelling aluminum cans. These were then transported on horse-drawn wagons that were kept ready and waiting in nearby barns. The great brown horses were my favorite part of the whole operation, as they stood before their troughs grinding away their hay and oats and idly switching their tails, completely oblivious to my own delight at being lifted onto their broad backs.

But evidently the milk business led no closer to that elusive "easy street" my parents so often discussed, for one day the good butter, cottage cheese, and whipped cream which had so abundantly graced our table suddenly disappeared as if swept away by an unseen hand. And the next time I was allowed to visit my father at work it was in a factory for manufacturing earmuffs. It was his own patent: a bent metal band with oval flaps of fur or velvet affixed to each end and worn over the head so that both ears were covered. I doubt that a large percentage of the Viennese population made use of them; I certainly didn't see many people sporting this practical invention. Nevertheless, all the ears of our immediate family stayed comfortably protected during the severe cold spells that plagued Vienna in those days. I vividly remember one such winter – it must have been 1927 – so frigid that the Danube froze over, and to my boundless amazement I watched a team of horses pull a wagon across the broad, ice-covered river.

Useful as they were, the earmuffs failed to fulfill the hopes that had been placed in them, and they, too, gave way to another product. My father rented some very spacious rooms in the Schüttelstrasse, and soon the place was crowded with thousands and thousands of berets, in every color and size. Although these head coverings are known in the German-speaking world as "Baskenmützen" or "Basque caps," my father packed, shipped and sold them under the name of "Pullman caps."

At the same address, in a back room as dimly lit as an alchemist's cell, a man in shirtsleeves – who was often referred to as my father's "partner" – was busy pouring oils and essences into all kinds of test tubes. These liquids were sometimes cold and sometimes hot, but they were always heavily scented, for this partner was laboring to produce by chemical means a sweet-smelling but very affordable hair tonic or mouthwash, which he planned to distribute throughout the civilized world at an enormous profit. But the result can only have been a further disappointment, for these interesting wares – caps as well as cosmetics – followed their predecessors into the oblivion of history, and after domi-nating the daily conversation for some time, they and their laud-able qualities were never mentioned again. I, on the other hand, had to wear my ridiculous "Pullman caps" to school for years while my classmates sported their much more fashionable visor caps or were even allowed to expose their uncovered hair to the winds.

Once again my father changed his line of business, remaining true only to his general metier of merchant. He now moved to a commercial building in Vienna's First District, where in one room sharp knives cut patterns of silk or cotton, which were then transformed into readily recognizable shapes by ladies in an adjoining room busy treading the pedals of sewing machines. My father had become an underwear manufacturer and remained one until our emigration. Despite this steady occupation, however, our family's circumstances hardly showed any change, let alone improvement. But I didn't pay as much attention to this last phase of my father's European career; these matters lost much of their magic for me as I began to be occupied with my life at school.

It would be wrong to conclude from these repeated changes that they were due to other causes than a lack of commercial aptitude and above all the depressed state of the economy. My father was a quiet and methodical man, perhaps somewhat phlegmatic and unimaginative. He performed his daily chores industriously, meticulously and regularly. He rose at the same early hour, washed and shaved, ate the same simple breakfast, walked on foot to his place of business and showed up again for the midday dinner, the main meal of the day. His afternoons displayed the same inalterable uniformity, and he ended each working day with the same precise routine: after a modest supper he would read the newspaper, then listen a while to the radio he himself had constructed. He went to bed early, a reliable, unpretentious man who never lost his equilibrium. I am convinced that these stable habits contributed to my parents' longevity. Both died in Los Angeles at a venerable age, my father in his mid- eighties, my mother well over ninety. And yet their lives could hardly be called uncomplicated; on the contrary, they were full of disappointments, deprivation, persecution and danger. But they overcame them all – World War I, inflation, Austro-fascism, emigration, the long years in various Latin American countries, renewed uprooting and immigration to the United States. Despite all adventures and adversities certain things always remained the same: the way my father brushed his teeth, tied his shoes and hung his pants over the back of a chair, carefully protecting the crease. Perhaps there was a measure of pedantry in these routines. On the other hand, in situations where mindlessness would have been fatal the same unruffled constancy often saved the day. My father was no gambler; he did not venture and did not gain, but perhaps he survived by not taking unnecessary risks.

The only unusual thing about him was that he drew and painted. With pencil or brush he covered countless sheets of paper and canvases which I admired from early on. I did not inherit this talent but I owe to it the many, almost weekly visits to the Viennese picture galleries, art collections and museums, far beyond what was customary in our social circles. Even though I was frequently bored on these endless excursions, they did provide me with an early awareness of the visual arts. Gradually I developed an eye for them and they significantly enriched my education. There is another thing for which I am grateful to my father: the enjoyment of mountains, fields and forests. In the warmer seasons we often took the streetcar to the outskirts and started hiking on one of many well-marked trails in the Vienna woods, fortified by fruit and sandwiches carried in our knapsacks. Without this example and early introduction I might never have acquired my lasting pleasure in the outdoors and might never have traveled through the Andes, the Himalayas, or explored the wildernesses of Iceland, New Zealand and the North American continent, which I count among my best experiences.

In many respects my mother was the exact opposite of my father. Nervous, excitable, often ill-humored, suffering from indeterminate illnesses and ailments, she was overanxious in protecting me, her only child, and she resisted any sign of independence on my part, relinquishing her control only reluctantly as I grew up. But I am thankful to her, not only for many acts of motherly kindness, but also for bestowing upon me a powerful gift; I owe to her my acquaintance with a potent, liberating force that influenced my life fundamentally. In contrast to my father, my mother liked to read all kinds of novels and stories, and she saw to it that I, too, was provided with books from the earliest possible age. With this magic she opened up a fantastic world for the lonely child without siblings, a world into which I escaped not only from an annoying overindulgence but from my entire monotonous petit-bourgeois environment. I quickly devoured the Grimms' and Bechstein's fairy tales as well as those by Andersen and Hauff, Gustav Schwab's classical legends and Brehm's animal stories, Münchhausen's tall tales and *Gulliver's Travels*, Cooper's *Leatherstocking*, many volumes of Karl May and the few German classics that were kept in a small book case. To these must be added a number of cheap Reclam paperback editions of world classics and the contents of entire lending libraries in which my parents enrolled the insatiable reader they had spawned.

Despite their differences, my parents' marriage was relatively harmonious, partly due to the fact that my mother was endowed with the stronger will power, which she wielded quite effectively. My father was disarmingly good-natured and conciliatory; he chose to avoid arguments whenever possible, which left me to my mother's notions of upbringing, ideas that were often arbitrary and suffused with scurrilous bits of superstition. This was a common division of labor among middle-class families: the father performed as breadwinner while the mother raised the children and ran the household.

I should also mention that despite our restricted finances we always had a maid. These would mostly be girls from the country who served our needs indefatigably, for very little remuneration and practically no comfort, in the kitchen, at the market, in the cellar where the laundry was washed and in the attic where it was dried. They would also double as my "governess," for this too was part and parcel of our bourgeois lifestyle.

Beyond that, however, I am unaware of any luxuries. From my present perspective I regard our life as one of almost monastic seclusion. My parents confined their indulgences to the odd meeting with friends in a coffeehouse or a Sunday visit to the movies. Occasionally we would go for a walk in the Prater – the famous Viennese amusement park and nature preserve – where we stopped at a teashop for a *Kracherl* as the soft drinks were called in antediluvian Vienna. We hardly ever entertained guests at home. It may have happened once or twice a year that business acquaintances or friends came to dinner. These very rare festive occasions wrought havoc with our frugal habits, and caused a great deal of excitement. Hitherto unseen dishes suddenly appeared, crystal bowls emerged into full view from their encased captivity, alcoholic beverages graced the table. But the ultimate delicacy was a square loaf of "Sandwich bread" – a mysterious, foreign word at that time – that my father cut into thin slices and garnished with exotic morsels such as anchovies, salami, smoked salmon and olives. I scarcely remember the conversations or even the faces of those present at such feasts. But I do recall the sensation of elegance and big-world sophistication evoked by a wisp of cigarette smoke hovering around the lamp. With the exception of the museums my parents participated little in Vienna's cultural life. Once in a great while they visited the opera, a theater or a

14

concert. These rare urges could have easily been satisfied in a less extravagant hometown. This abstention had as much to do with my parents' intellectual frugality as with their perennially precarious finances. Their strength lay in the realm of character, in their human compassion, their ability to mourn, their sense of humor. They had each gone to school only a few years, and what they had learned seemed to have left no impression, or at least it was never mentioned. In conversation they seldom mentioned politics or historical events and never discussed intellectual problems. The linguistic level on which my parents operated was by no means elevated. My father's German still bore traces of his native Yiddish in syntax and pronunciation, so that it differed audibly from the colloquial Viennese, whereas my mother, linguistically more adept, never lost the accent of her Hungarian mother tongue. That I outgrew this background is due more to my parents' social ambition than their intellectual aspiration. As far as I can remember they expected me to become a "doctor." It was a miracle that I ultimately fulfilled this expectation, even though not in the medical sense they obviously had in mind, and I believe this was the direct result of their faith in me. The slightest sign of intelligence on my part was greeted with enthusiasm; every spark of talent was fanned with care. Long before I went to school, even before I knew there was such a thing, they had spread rumors of my exceptional gifts. As a result, the extended family treated me like a certified genius, with the patronizing benevolence of people who have legitimate claims to the fulfillment of a sacred vow. How in the normal course of things I would have satisfied or disappointed such enormous expectations I dare not even think about. But surely all this goodwill contributed to my later development.

To this very day the thought of my Austrian Gymnasium evokes intense, and strongly ambivalent, feelings in me. I sometimes remember it as a kind of barracks where sadistic sergeants drilled their charges under the threat of lashings, or as a torture chamber where defenseless inmates were subjected to fiendish torments that had no other purpose than to break their will and rob them of any individuality. In other moments, I am able to recognize other aspects of this grotesque: the larger-than-life torturers swinging whips over the emaciated bodies of helpless, half-grown pupils fade into fainthearted figures easily intimidated by the daily confrontation with that collective beast always poised to spring, which is known in ordinary parlance as a classroom full of young boys. From this perspective, I realize that my tormentors were in reality a lot of nervous, underpaid, poorly dressed petty officials, simply exacting revenge for the many humiliations of their existence by misusing their ludicrous power, by unfairness, favoritism, and nasty little acts of cruelty. And yet this school was where we journeyed day after day, rain or shine or even snow. It was home to many formative impulses, to all sorts of suffering but also numerous joys. Important human contacts were made and broken, and friendships were forged, some of which have managed to survive even the wildest cataclysms of fate. Despite everything this was the place where the mind was awakened and where, at least in some rudimentary fashion, the first intellectual attitudes were molded which played such an important role in how we later would view the world. The Gymnasium was where our fantasy was tamed and our character emerged from a seething chaos of emotions and began to acquire recognizable shape. It was the place where, almost imperceptibly over the course of what seemed like endless years, childhood gave way to the turmoil of puberty and ultimately to adulthood. No matter how much our reason struggles against the sentiments, we have to admit that an aura of youth surrounds this institution in our memories, shedding a warm glow even on the irrational and mean aspects of the life one experienced within its walls. And when after twenty years of exile, I revisited the city of my birth, I found myself walking through its streets in a dreamlike trance, deeply moved. As if drawn by some magnetic attraction I suddenly found myself standing in front of the heavy large oaken door of my school. There was the same unmistakable smell – a mixture of mildew, urine and disinfectant – that assaulted my senses, the same wooden benches, so small I could scarcely believe we had actually sat in them. And after all the immense personal and historical changes I had witnessed, I realized that the

Gymnasium had for a time been life itself, an impetus which cannot be ignored as it reaches deeply and overpoweringly into one's inner self with the serene impartiality of a natural force. And hence my ambivalent feelings.

For people of my family's social background, having their child attend the gymnasium was not something to be taken for granted. But my performance in the public elementary school was above average. I was considered good in arithmetic and reading, but it was really my German compositions that attracted my teachers' attention and won me the support of the school authorities. And without their recommendations even my parents' most ambitious desires to see me enter the realms of higher education would have been in vain. I was even permitted to take the entrance exams for a well-known school outside my district that counted the famous writer Karl Kraus among its former pupils, and after a few weeks of anxious waiting for the results I was accepted.

Nothing in later years brought home to me the profound differences between times and cultures more strikingly than my surprising discovery that children in America like to go to school. I *hated* my school. Not that I didn't have a high regard for learning or didn't feel the tense expectancy with which you encounter a mysterious new subject. After all, it was exciting to re-enter the familiar building for the first time after the summer vacation, equipped with a higher status, as a pupil in a more advanced grade. Even the scholarly ring of the Latin designations for the grades themselves – tertia, quarta, quinta, sexta – in Austria the order is the reverse of that in Germany – made you feel a shudder of awe. And the physics room, so unlike the other classrooms, with its graduated rows of seats rising back as in an amphitheater. The first time you took your seat in that room and looked down at the teacher's table laden with all manner of scientific paraphernalia, you felt true wonder and a genuine thirst for knowledge. But the stupefying routine and brutal suppression that characterized the daily life of the school stifled such pure desires at the very outset. Teachers and pupils were caught up in an abiding mutual hostility. Threats, severe admonitions, even outbreaks of rage and corporal punishment were the order of the day; the pupils reacted to all this with sullenness and spite, dishonesty, apple-polishing and tattling, rebelliousness, and a widespread system of cheating. Whatever the cause, this Austrian Gymnasium was pervaded by an authoritarian atmosphere that became positively poisonous after the rise of Austro-fascism: in other words, soon after my matriculation. Every little infraction of the rules was reported to one's parents to be "acknowledged" by them, in writing beginning with the formula: "I acknowledge that my son reported to me that despite repeated warnings he...." More serious infractions were punished by entering the offender's name in the dreaded "class book" or by summoning the parents, and even by detention and expulsion. Thus, for instance, when some of my classmates were caught passing erotic pictures they had drawn themselves – which made it even worse – a major scandal ensued, leading to their expulsion from the Gymnasium. What the regime most demanded and what these severe punishments enforced was not respect for faculty and curriculum, but submission and unquestioning acceptance of the system. No value was placed upon the amount learned or the efforts expended; the only things that mattered were examinations and grades, censure and admonitions, promotion and advancement.

This joyless and loveless state of affairs has etched night-marish scenes onto my memory, such as the Life Sciences teacher interrupting his lecture to lash out in a thick Viennese dialect at an inattentive pupil in the top row: "You gray pig up there, why are you always turning around? If you don't stop this instant, I'll smash you against the wall so hard your mother'll have to scrape you off with a ladle." I still see this brutal giant rushing over to the poor boy and pulling him by the hair. Nor can I forget how the Latin teacher, with his paranoid fear of being ridiculed, once singled out a poor fellow, dragged him the entire length of the schoolroom and flung him out the door. I still see the man's face, swollen and red with rage and exertion, as he screamed at the poor boy: "You little brat, I'll teach you to grin while I'm trying to bring the class to order. Just wait, you're going to pay for that." A symbol for me of the school's atmosphere was the new principal whom the Dollfuss government had appointed in place of a more civilized predecessor. This man, who always peppered his speech with the words "Christian" or "Christianity," would occasionally stalk through the building, hurling threats with outstretched arm and wagging index finger. "Aha, a piece of paper," he would shriek in a breaking falsetto, "and there's another; all this vicious student Bolshevism – we know where it comes from and we're going to take care of it." You can entertain people for a whole evening with school stories like these, and I have often succumbed to this temptation. But to give my amused listeners the impression that these absurdly humorous scenes form the substance of my schoolboy experiences is to gloss over the facts. For these ludicrous episodes demonstrate that the ideal of humanistic learning, which had been losing ground for a long time, had become a grotesque totalitarian farce. No wonder that in that atmosphere no one thought of learning, but at the most of "cramming," which meant thoughtless memorization of the assignment. Schoolwork was based upon a thoroughly corrupt system of whispering and copying answers, on the use of forbidden aids such as scraps of paper inscribed with mathematical formulas, and on cribs known as *Schmierer*, as we called the contraband translations from Latin which were passed from hand to hand. For their part, the teachers were either unsuspecting or unconcerned about this deception; they simply persevered in their fossilized methods of lecturing and hearing students recite and despotically meting out their favor or displeasure. While there were some exceptions, most were neither intellectually or pedagogically equal to the difficult demands of their profession. I have never determined whether this was due more to the political situation or the recent war – many of our teachers had been soldiers and came back with mental problems. Or perhaps it was simply the psychological reflection of a country that had been conquered, divided and stricken with one economic disaster after another. In any event, sixty years after the fact my judgment remains the same: that we pupils were in the care of a group of severely neurotic men and were therefore in great psychological danger ourselves.

Somehow I managed to muddle through this morass, although my grades declined as my disappointment and indifference increased, and I ultimately lost the status I had earlier enjoyed as an excellent pupil. Even so, according to the prevailing standards I was not a bad student; my report cards remained above average. But I cannot say in good conscience that in all those years in the Gymnasium I learned anything really worthwhile. I still know that Gaul was divided into three parts, and that Caesar had to cross a river called the Rubicon; I can still quote Cato's "Ceterum censeo Carthaginem esse delendam" and other gems of Roman wisdom articulated solely to spite future generations of Gymnasium pupils. I might be able to solve a binomial equation, if I had to, and I still know many German and Latin poems by heart – although in the eyes of the institution, poetry was useful only in punitive assignments of rote memorization. Latin and French consisted mostly of exercising grammar and memorizing vocabulary; we learned nothing about the Classical World, for instance. Any subject involving recent world events was taught with a gross nationalistic distortion. The severe upheavals that were shaking Austria as we sat warming our benches and that finally led to Nazi troops occupying that very school for weeks were never even mentioned. Evidently the building's thick walls were designed to keep the real world shut outside.

Since those days I have become acquainted with many schools in different countries, and have seen my own children grow up and go to school, but I have remained a skeptic. I suspect that schools, as they are run in our so-called civilized world today, are all too frequently based on false values, that they stultify the human mind, and oppress the youth who are their defenseless victims. Be that as it may, in my case my initial enthusiasm for school turned first into indifference and finally into an unceasing aversion. And by the time the historical events alluded to above put an abrupt end to my Gymnasium days before my graduation, I left that institution with no regrets – in fact, I even felt a distinct relief.

In all fairness to the Gymnasium I should say it was not the sole cause of my alienation, as this was sharpened by another force whose power not only permeated the school but reached far beyond it as well: the force of anti-Semitism. Although we lack a precise instrument to measure such a force, I can say that from my perspective Vienna was the most anti-Semitic city I have ever lived in. Hatred for the Jews is as old as the Christian world, and perhaps even older. What contributed to Vienna's special position among European cities in this regard was its large proportion of Jewish inhabitants – in my day there must have been about 180,000, or approximately ten per cent of the city's total population. Up to the time of the collapse of Austria-Hungary there were also large numbers of Jews in the eastern provinces. Basically this Empire, made up of many ethnic groups, was still a dynastic feudal state which had resisted capitalism and modernization longer than the other Western and Central European powers. In the long run, of course, these twin processes could not be halted, and when the inevitable Industrial Revolution finally did engulf the Danubian monarchy, new collided with old with tremendous force.

The resulting explosion catapulted the Jews out of their Eastern world into the ongoing maelstrom. At one time they were lured to the capital by the promise of opportunity, and driven from the country by growing insecurities, the result of overpopulation, cholera, and famine.

The first wave of Jewish emigration was met by a state policy that cleverly combined tolerance and enforced assimilation, the goal of which was to make out of these new arrivals useful members of the state. This "Germanization" set off a second tide of immigration that refused to ebb. The autonomy granted the Polish nobility helped complete a process already begun; serfdom was abolished and a "national" industrialization of Galicia and other Polish regions of the empire was set into motion.

These developments spelled the end of the Jewish shtetl or ghetto both economically and culturally, by depriving them of their livelihoods, which were for the most part preindustrial. This in turn placed tremendous pressure on the Jews of these areas to migrate to Vienna or even further West, sometimes all the way to America.

Their high degree of intellectual instruction (although not the traditional European schooling), their long acquaintance with economic hardship, and the adaptability this had taught them, enabled many of them to attain quick success within the constantly expanding opportunities offered by nascent capitalism. Nonetheless, the majority could never achieve a significant change in their social status.

The following progression was repeated so often that it became a practically unavoidable paradigm, although of course any one individual might get stuck at any one of the stations along the way, according to his own particular talents and fortune. First came the departure from the eastern shtetl, followed by the entrance into some trade, business or industry. This gradually led to a state of affluence, and ultimately the move to Vienna – with occasional stopovers in Bohemia, Slovakia or Hungary – and marriage to the daughter of an already emancipated family, who, more educated than her husband, would instill in her children a passionate love of German culture. The offspring of these unions would later work to expand their fathers' businesses, become professionals or else turn to the arts and literature.

Of course this sequence is accompanied by a series of intellectual developments: the loss of orthodoxy, indeed of almost the entire Jewish cultural heritage, the abandonment of Yiddish as the spoken tongue and of Hebrew as sacred language, a refinement in manners, and adaptation to the Western world.

This powerful process of secularization took two, three or sometimes even four, generations to accomplish. As a result, the Jews in Vienna occupied the most diverse levels of assimilation, ranging from new arrivals who maintained the old traditions in all respects – even in matters of dress and hairstyle – to those who had been established there for generations and whose families were often long since baptized. For these latter Judaism was no more than a vague family memory they were eager to forget.

The influx of masses of Eastern Jews – unique in its dimensions – into a society which was essentially still a traditional Christian one gave rise to a new type of virulent anti-Semitism which displayed an enormous range of pyschological symptoms including every shade of fear, hatred and envy. This new anti-Semitism combined traditional religious and economic prejudices with modern pseudo-Darwinian ideas to form an entire political *Weltanschauung*. What good does it do to know that the Yiddish, which the common Viennese man so mocked and hated, stemmed from the same Middle High German dialect as his own? Or that the black caftan he so feared as to demonize its wearer was actually the same dress his own forefathers had worn centuries before? All that may be of concern to the historian, but hardly for the young man growing up in such surroundings. All he senses – and from an early age on – is that he is "different," that he doesn't "belong." Member of a despised and persecuted minority, he is forced to come to terms with these basic existential facts of his descent and his peculiar position. A whole gamut of possible reactions, ranging from self-hatred to ethnic pride is open to him: assimilation and baptism; defiant insistence on religious and nationalistic Judaism; militant self-assertion, Zionism and emigration; even suicide out of disgust or despair at his hopeless existence. But one must not picture these choices as conscious, rational alternatives. Many possibilities exist side by side, and the youth accepts them all simultaneously, experiencing each psychological stage to a greater or lesser degree. Each leaves its mark on him, and only gradually, in conjunction with his whole character, does he develop a position toward Judaism that conforms to his own individuality and is in harmony with his general outlook on life.

A child's experiences are marked by their immediacy and spontaneity. A seven or eight-year-old, as I was then, who is chased all the way home after school by belt-swinging urchins howling "Jew, Jew, you're a Jew," doesn't care about the social background of his tormentors, the ideological source of their hostility, or the political stand of their parents. I knew nothing of these things; I experienced the persecution as something elemental, something indivisible, something one had to accept like the laws of nature.

Everywhere there were signs of the creeping hatred for Jews that had so suffused our milieu. Fights among children, verbal derision or hateful epithets shouted in the street, newspaper articles and pamphlets, pointed allusions in conversations – all saw to it that anti-Semitism could not be forgotten for long. One day it was the teacher calling the noisy class to order with the remark, "It sounds like a Jew school in here," the next day it was graffiti such as "Let the Jews rot" or "Jews back to Palestine" scribbled on walls or printed on posters. All these things set off a feeling of being despised and ostracized.

But it didn't take the outside world to evoke this consciousness in a child – his own family, his own circle was perfectly capable of doing that. Typical gestures, knowing glances, spoken apprehensions, moral admonitions such as "A Jew doesn't do a thing like that," Jewish jokes, the constant stream of conversations: "Is it true that he had himself baptized?" "But she doesn't look a bit Jewish." "He has a miserable Jewish nose, but otherwise he's pretty good-looking." "His mother doesn't want him to marry a Christian." "Don't act like a 'Schegez' (Christian boy)." Hour after hour the tensions of the Jewish minority surfaced in such seemingly insignificant remarks.

My grandparents in Pressburg (Bratislava), though touched by emancipation and Western enlightenment, for the most part still lived in undisturbed harmony with the Jewish community. My parents, on the other hand, distanced themselves considerably from their point of origin. While they had progressed quite a bit along the tortuous path from orthodoxy to assimilation, they had bogged down somehow about halfway. This road can be painful, even tragic – not only because it requires abandoning so many psychic and cultural values, but also because it does not necessarily lead to that hoped-for destination of integration. Adapting to the Christian world was no guarantee of acceptance – at least not in Austria and Germany.

As for myself, I found myself swept along by these same currents, without any exertion or conscious effort on my part, purely as an accident of birth. Raised in Vienna, educated in Viennese schools, familiar with every social level of Viennese dialect, I was indistinguishable by my speech from the rest of the

population. Unlike my parents, I was to all appearances completely at home in the Austrian capital. But because of the historical
circumstances that soon forced my life in quite a different direction, my higher level of assimilation turned out to be of no
importance.

To more fully understand the situation of the Austrian Jews at
that time, it is necessary to examine Judaism, a major force
working against their assimilation. What the Jews call religion
contains, beyond its purely theological aspects, many customs,
popular superstitions, and historical-nationalistic reminiscences,
and is therefore not nearly so easily separated from Jewish
collective identity as the religions of other national groups. If a
Swede converts to Catholicism or a Mexican becomes a Protestant
nothing changes in relation to his nationality. A similar step taken
by a Jew in prewar Vienna meant a radical change in his existential
situation. The examination of a Jew's religious consciousness is
thus no idle enterprise. It is difficult to accurately determine what
other people believe in their heart of hearts, including even our
parents whom we have observed for years and whom we have
"seen through" intuitively before we are able to subject them to
more rational analysis. Today I believe that my parents "felt
Jewish" through and through, although they were essentially non-
believers. They continued to observe a minimum of Jewish rites as
a kind of religious insurance, following the principle "Maybe
there's something to it after all," but above all as an expression of
their unshakable ethnic solidarity. They went to the synagogue
only twice a year, for the High Holy Days Rosh Hashanah, the
New Year, and for Yom Kippur, the Day of Atonement, when we
even observed the strict fast prescribed by custom. But the manner
in which we celebrated these holy days was an unmistakable
expression of our degree of secularization. Evidently there were
not enough temples to accommodate all the Jews in our district
who remembered their religious affiliation only once a year, so an
old Viennese palace, the so-called Sophiensäle was rented. These
rooms had once been used for balls and other worldly entertain-
ment; now the classic nudity of the Greek statues which adorned

them was decorously draped; rabbis and cantors were brought in, and the service of worship on this holiest of Jewish holidays was conducted according to the Reformed rite. The place filled up with Jewish businessmen – small merchants and big-time operators, salesmen, agents and clerks – as well as doctors and lawyers, who sat there in seats they had paid for as if in a theater. From morning until night they would read or sing Hebrew prayers, psalms, hymns, laments for the dead, and blessings, reflecting upon their ineradicable Jewishness, which they had neglected or even intentionally forgotten throughout the previous year.

We, however, continued to celebrate the Sabbath, at least after a fashion. But even lighting the wax candles proved too cumbersome for my mother, and I watched with secret disapproval as she directed blessings at the electric lamp hanging above the living room table. That was all. Considering how complicated and demanding the Jewish cult of Sabbath is, such a hypocritical gesture can only be regarded as the puny remnant of a once holy rite. The dietary laws were treated similarly. The dishes for milk and meat were kept apart – without undue strictness, I am sure – and meat was purchased at ritual butcheries, all of which did not prevent ham and other forbidden tidbits from entering the household. Once there, they were eaten from special plates with otherwise unused cutlery.

I was given to understand that these concessions to tradition were made for my grandmother's sake, who would otherwise have refused to visit, let alone share a meal with us. Such a half-hearted abandonment of centuries-old traditions, coupled with a similarly lukewarm adaptation to the modern Christian world, resulted in a double estrangement, perhaps not so much for the adults, who underwent this process more or less consciously, but very much so for the child. Thus, although this particular child hardly ever saw a real synagogue from the inside, he was also told that churches were horrid pagan haunts not to be entered under any circumstance.

Meanwhile Austrian law mandated that religion be taught in the schools, even to Jews. This instruction consisted solely in recapitulations of Old Testament stories and in the most elementary study of the Hebrew alphabet, with no true examination of Jewish theology.

And while it was surely more than a matter of religion, even these pitiful remnants of an exotic rite sufficed to isolate us from the Christians and caused us to have only the most superficial relationship with them. Most other tenants in our house were Christians, with whom we exchanged polite greetings when we met them in the stairwell. The corner grocer, the owner of the delicatessen store, sundry tradespeople all were Christians. But there was no close friendship with any of them. My parents' friends and acquaintances were Jews, the doctor and dentist were Jews, and the confessions separated even in school as if by a law of nature. But there was little traffic even with other Jews; most families kept to themselves, and there was certainly no sense of community. Perhaps in retrospect I am exaggerating this isolation; perhaps I felt it more acutely as a single child. If we had lived in the second district, where there was a large Jewish population, my impression might have been quite different. Much depends on one's perspective, the precise location where one experiences things. It is also possible that I am describing a condition endemic in the modern capitalist world at that time. After all, a lot has been said about alienation. But I still believe that phenomenon was felt more deeply by Jews of a certain social stratum who belonged to one group only loosely and to the other not at all.

On my magical visits to my grandparents I found that things could be quite different. Pressburg was only one hour away by train, and three by streetcar (!), which we took because it passed near our house. So we traveled to my mother's relatives several times a year, including the annual spring visit to celebrate Passover. The mere fact we had to cross a border, with passport control and custom inspections, was tremendously exciting. Equally extraordinary and even more enjoyable was the reception upon arrival: all of a sudden we would find ourselves surrounded by an entire clan of relatives. Uncles, aunts, and cousins of every conceivable degree of kinship, related either by blood or marriage, would suddenly appear, each with his own set of jokes and anecdotes, his own way of talking, his own eccentricities, personality, career, biography. And I, as my grandparents' only grandchild, was positively showered with attention and general admiration. Even the neighborhood children looked on me with flattering envy, as the boy from the big city, the sophisticated inhabitant of the unattainable metropolis.

The mix of cultures and languages in this border region was fascinating. What we called Pressburg was known in Hungarian as Pozsony: for generations the Hungarian monarchs were crowned there during the Turkish occupation. For Slovaks it was the capital Bratislava, since 1918 a part of the newly established republic of Czechoslovakia. On all sides you could hear a wild profusion of German, Yiddish, Czech, Hungarian, and Slovak – each with its own class nuances and regional dialects – a veritable Babel which outdid even Vienna, where snatches of many different languages were left over from the days of the monarchy. For me Pressburg was a true fairyland, with its ruined fortress and the broad Danube – which you could cross on a propeller boat – its meadows and bathing beaches, its baroque buildings and quiet parks. Excitingly new, kaleidoscopically varied, it was an exotic complement to my experiences in Vienna, a richly instructive new school.

And although I only realized it many years later, what impressed me most of all was the intact ethnic identity of the Pressburg Jews, and particularly the Jewish district. Despite the poverty and dirt, this latter was an invaluable example of *Gemeinschaft* or community – that oft-invoked lost paradise which had almost universally fallen prey to the Industrial Revolution. Jews lived together here in a densely populated section of the city that was swarming like an anthill, teeming with activity from morning until night. With its spice shops and trade stores, its food stands and markets, the wild assortment of characters and dress, its streets which were at once noisy and intimate – the whole place reminded me of the oriental bazaars I knew from *The Thousand and One Nights*.

But the mysterious thing about this world was that under its

apparent chaos there reigned a binding spiritual order that permeated and determined life down to its smallest, most insignificant
aspects. This order was the creation of the Jewish religion, whose
influence could be encountered at every turn; and no one there
dreamed of withdrawing from the community it created. Many
men still wore their hair in ringlets at the temple, their heads
constantly covered with black hats or little round caps called
yarmekel. Married women on the other hand wore a kerchief, or
else a *sheitel* – an unmistakable wig – over their short hair as a
sign they no longer wished or were meant to be physically
attractive. Here and there you could see *bocher*, boys recognizable
by their dress and bearing as Yeshiva students, budding scholars
of the Scriptures. And walking the streets you might pass the *mikve*
or women's ritual bathing place, the bloody *shechter* where
animals were slaughtered and bled according to kosher custom, or
else the baker, in whose sour-smelling shop the *tsholent* was left
in pots covered with cloths on Friday afternoons. This was the
tasty Sabbath meal of beans and meat, which could not be heated
at home because one could not light a fire on the day of rest. Here
one could look from the street into the crowded *cheyder*, where a
man wearing a caftan was drilling children in the basics of
Hebrew.

And in the middle of all this was the building where my
grandparents lived, a huge, multiunit tenement with many stories
and winding staircases, countless courtyards and passageways,
attics smelling of wood, and moldy coal cellars. Everything
resounded with a constant clamor: children roughhousing, mothers
scolding, men haggling over prices and peddlers hawking their
wares. People were constantly coming and going, chattering away
in their foreign accents and punctuating their speech with colorful
gestures. This was a different life: new, strange and utterly fascinating. Here there were no secrets, everyone knew the most
intimate details about his neighbors; the closeness was so great and
the personal life of each individual so accessible that most things
took place in the public eye, so to speak. The center of this world
was undoubtedly the *shul*, the orthodox synagogue, where there

was always at least a *minyen* – the requisite ten adult male members of the congregation – assembled for each of the many daily prayers prescribed for the Jews. In the cavernous rooms of this house of worship I observed the impassioned rites and listened to the ancient chants, not without a shudder of awe. I witnessed the shaking and sobbing ecstasies of petty merchants and artisans who transformed themselves like lightning into mythical herd owners and desert dwellers. Wearing their *tefillin* or phylacteries and wrapped in their *tallesim* or prayer shawls, they poured out the age-old sorrow of their race in powerful lamentations. This fervent worship put to shame the insipid ceremonies I had experienced back in the Sophiensäle.

Most striking of all were the Pesach, or Passover, observances which lasted a whole week and which were the purpose of our annual spring pilgrimage. These began with the burning of the *chometz*, or crumbs and leftovers from the previous year, and with the first breaking of the *matzoth*, the unleavened Passover bread, and reached their climax in the sacred Seder ceremonies celebrated around a festively decorated table. All the members of the family sat around the elevated platter bearing the symbolic foods – the salty and bitter dishes recalling the Captivity in Egypt, the Haggadahs with their colored illustrations that were read from in the course of the ceremony. And on this special occasion even I was allowed to sip the Palestinian wine. My grandfather, in everyday life a modest clockmaker, presided over this table as a venerable patriarch, with a flowing white beard and a beautiful silk cap trimmed in gold. As the youngest male present, mine was the time-honored task of reciting – in Hebrew and by heart, of course – the *mah-nishtano*, the traditional questions about the meaning of this evening and why it is different from all other nights of the Jewish exile. My questions elicited lengthy liturgical explanations and, in the pauses between them, comment from the older members of the family. Everything was so different, so special, with the singing of hymns and the opening of the door and the filling of a cup for the Prophet Elijah. (It always seemed to me that a bit of the wine in that cup disappeared as if the holy man were taking invisible sips). But the dramatic highpoint came when my grandfather, an ardent Zionist, solemnly proclaimed the ritual pronouncement: "This year still in exile, but next year in Jerusalem."

My grandparents were kind people and I felt sheltered and protected in their home. I know now – and sensed it even then – that the fascination their presence exerted on me came not only from their simple personalities, but also from the Jewish community as a whole, from the culture they represented. But I would be overstating the case to say that this world was better or more harmonious than the Western civilization surrounding it, to which I actually belonged and in which this particular enclave was merely an anachronistic relic. In actuality this Jewish way of life was imperiled and oppressed, and it would soon disappear completely, victim of a brutal annihilation, although of course no one realized that at the time. It was a society marked with poverty and disease, conflict and crudity, envy, madness and superstition, slander and malice. But it was also a society distinguished by unquestioned solidarity and by a communally shared fate, such as I have never rediscovered in half a century of wanderings. Its wondrous secret was that here you didn't have to inquire about the meaning of life – the answer was still decreed from above. Despite the keenly sensed menace always threatening from without, the Jewish community was a world of inner imperturbability and existential security.

By comparison my Viennese background seemed empty, and all my Latin and other *Gymnasium* learning only made me feel a spiritual outsider in Pressburg as well as a temporary guest. Moreover, at the age of thirteen or fourteen I was just embarking on my search for self, just beginning to look for the meaning of life – so all of a sudden I decided to become a good pious Jew myself. I had not yet learned you can't borrow an isolated feature from one culture and transplant it into another without changing its character or distorting its effect. So every week I began to visit the *aguda*, an association of orthodox Jews, in order to learn the myriad commandments and prescriptions that fill the day of the devout. I insisted on every detail, and much to my parents' dismay, I made them reintroduce all the rituals of our religion, which they had mostly discarded. My father's old prayer pouch came out of the drawer where it had been gathering dust, and I pestered him until he agreed to get up an hour earlier and commence each toilsome day by donning his phylacteries and performing with me the *shemono essre*, the long Jewish morning prayers. The Sabbath regained its rightful place, properly sanctified with *kiddush* at dusk on Friday and *havdala* after sunset on Saturday. All holidays and days of fasting had to be observed; even the least important rituals had to be performed. I demanded strict adherence to the dietary laws; obviously that meant an end to any and all ham. The more I learned from my weekly study of the liturgy, the more tyrannical I became, punishing even minor infractions, for example by threatening to disassociate myself from such a lax and godless household.

During Sukkoth I went so far as to refuse to sleep under our hitherto trusted roof, and my father had to petition the city school board to excuse me from writing in school on Saturdays. The request was granted, and with the moral satisfaction of an ascetic and true martyr I spent my Sundays copying the lessons I had missed and making up my homework; after all, the assignments had only been postponed.

Looking back on all hardships I imposed on my poor parents, the only thing I can say on my behalf is that they were the ones who started it. Inveigled by my fanatically religious grandmother, who was terrified by the prospect of my growing up as a heathen or even – perish the thought – as a bare-headed, lederhosen-clad Christian, they decided to send me to summer camp at an orthodox Jewish orphanage, instead of to the usual secular camp in the mountains. Over my indignant remonstrations I was shipped off to a place outside Vienna called Baden, where I spent my summer in strictest imaginable adherence to Torah and Talmud. But like most thirteen-year olds, I was impressionable and easily swayed. Despite my initial resistance, I gradually fell under the spell of the ghosts to which my parents had so carelessly entrusted me, and which I brought back into their lives when I returned.

Obviously this rebellion against my entire surroundings couldn't last, and the inevitable ultimately occurred; my zeal slackened more and more under the pressures and persuasions of a totally opposite environment. At first, however, I did not dare confess my change of view, nor give up the rituals I had so rigidly enforced. Instead I had to suffer the just but painful punishment of having to cling to a practice I no longer believed in, solely in order to save face. As a result I was more than glad when the deterioration of the political climate so deflected all attention from myself that I was able to drop the entire bothersome routine, under the cloak of the approaching catastrophes, without being noticed or repri-manded. That's just how paradoxical things sometimes turn out to be. Whenever I recall this adolescent episode, I am still surprised – as well as simultaneously embarrassed and amused – by how short-lived my attempt to forge a religious attachment to Judaism really was. The faith that once seemed alive and strong was simply lost, like an old umbrella left behind in some remote railroad station: the loss is irretrievable but scarcely mourned. Since that time I have lived my life without any need for religion, as an incorrigible atheist.

I proved even stauncher in my resistance to another Jewish temptation: Zionism, which at that time was impossible for any young Jew in Vienna to avoid. Due to various ideological schisms there existed all kinds of groupings and tendencies, each of which had its own "youth club," housed mostly in modest rooms in basements or back courtyards. These clubs labored without cease in their efforts to recruit members of the "rising generation." Consequently I found myself invited to the premises of numerous splinter groups – all of which were at loggerheads with one another.

To say I was completely unable to wax enthusiastic about any shade of Zionism is merely to simplify a complicated psychological and ideological process. After all, it was easy enough to agree with the one tenet they had in common, namely that the future awaiting the European Jews was far from rosy, and that violent storms were already breaking on the horizon. Hitler's rise and the National Socialist seizure of power among our mighty neighbors had cast a shadow across our border ever since I could remember, so it was little wonder that emigration was discussed with increasing frequency. Australia, America and of course Palestine were mentioned, but few people if anybody were desperate or courageous enough to go through with such a plan, and even fewer had the necessary means to do so.

However, Zionism rested on other tenets as well, and it was with these that I had my quarrel. The more religiously minded groups held little appeal as I was in the process of giving up religion. The Zionist Revisionist movement, commonly known as Betar, which was led by the charismatic Vladimir Jabotinsky, repelled me profoundly with its authoritarian and militaristic pretensions. The only Zionist group that might have attracted me at all was the one that leaned towards socialism; perhaps by using it as an example I can best explain my rejection of the movement as a whole.

I began exploring socialist ideas early on, at a point when my political orientation, just like my personality, was only beginning to take shape. Nothing could be more natural. Having grown up in modest circumstances, I felt, even as a small child, the sting of compassion for the many destitute people encountered everywhere in Vienna; early on I developed a keen sense of justice and human dignity. As a rule, Jews of our social class were not confronted with a confusing array of political choices. This became clear to me in the case of my apolitical father, who for lack of alternatives always cast his ballot for the Social Democrats. Practically speaking there were only two choices available: one of which, the Christian-Social Party, was fundamentally anti-Semitic – so what was left for Jewish voters?

Thus when I mention my socialist tendencies, as vague and

unreasoned as they were, I have a little more in mind than this identification imposed by necessity. Those were not only the years of Hitler's expanding powers but of Fascist triumphs in almost all European countries. As can easily be imagined, in their struggle against Dollfuss, my sympathies had been with the Viennese workers, although I was too young to understand the political intricacies. Naturally I could hardly be expected to be a fervent supporter of Austro-fascism, but my dislike for this homegrown variety was somewhat mitigated by the fact that it remained the only obstacle to the country's total Nazification.

My political watershed came, as it did for many others, with the Spanish civil war. The desperate defense of the Spanish Republic against Franco and the Falange mirrored for me the epochal struggle of good against evil. I embraced the Spanish cause with youthful ardor, waiting for news from Spain with feverish anticipation, listening to the Republican broadcasts every day, discussing the far-off events as though they were taking place in the suburbs of Vienna. Place names like Teruel and Burgos were no more alien than Sankt Pölten or Klosterneuburg. It was in debates about the Spanish civil war, both among us adolescents and with the adults, that my political philosophy began to take shape. I have to confess that it included a streak of anarchism, and ever since then a constant element in my view of the world has been a suspicion of the nation-state and all movements that play on nationalistic feelings, including socialist ones.

This is precisely what I held against the Zionists, including even the left-wing ones. In my opinion the last thing the world needed was yet another nation-state: the peace was being threatened well enough as it was by the ones that were there already. Jewish militarism, Jewish power, Jewish ethnic superiority – all were no less repugnant to me than the same notions applied to non-Jews. In the heated discussions we carried on night after night I passionately defended the rights of the Palestinian Arabs. I still do. In this I was influenced by an uncle who had emigrated to Palestine and returned disappointed by what he saw there.

Of course I cannot claim with these scanty remarks to have exhausted a subject of such historic dimensions such as the Arab-Jewish conflict. The Jews' right to asylum, their historical connection with Palestine, the guilt of the Arab ruling classes, the responsibility of the world powers, the clash of two religions and of two incompatible economic systems – all these problems require deeper consideration. An abstract anti-nationalistic bias is hardly enough by which to judge Jewish efforts to survive as a nation-state in an era where there seems to be no viable alternative. Israel has proven its worth by granting asylum to multitudes of refugees threatened by deadly persecution. And besides, what sense is there in moralizing about struggles that take place in the context of power politics? My intent was simply to explain in credible fashion why as an adolescent I refused to join any one of the Jewish organizations, why years later I did not hail the founding of Israel with greater enthusiasm, why today I feel justified in my skepticism by developments in Israel, and why in the future I will have nothing to do with Zionist chauvinists.

All this begs the question whether, in the early years of my life, I was acting according to what might be called a free will. The question is a thorny one; it is in fact my point of departure for these autobiographical reflections, where I hope to examine to what extent a given individual is master of his own fate and to what degree he is subject to forces beyond his control. Clearly I could have become a pious Jew or a Zionist, or else I could have completely ignored my Jewishness while emphasizing my Austrian identity; I might have gone so far as to convert as did some of my schoolmates. But nothing of the sort happened and none of this would have changed the course of events. Any of these decisions might have been possible at one point or another, but I took another path. I never denied my Jewishness, on the contrary I regard it as a formidable force in my life, but more a historical influence than a religious, nationalist or especially a biological one. But I have not made a central concern out of this Jewishness.

I married a non-Jewish German woman. For my children Judaism is a distant phenomenon, a social fact without psychological complications. In them the process of assimilation into which I was born has reached an irreversible stage. That one half of their ancestors lived in a Jewish ghetto and the other half were Westphalian peasants is no more remarkable in America than any other family background. They seem neither handicapped nor advantaged by this in their endeavors. One of my grandchildren has not only a Jewish but also a Native American grandparent and assorted other ancestors – Norwegian, English, and German. Such things always have some importance in your life and yet you have no control over them. Looking over my own career as a professional intellectual, I cannot say I *adopted* it, since that would preempt my reflection on the causes that led to it. At the risk of seeming less than logically correct, I prefer to say I *experienced* a zigzag course that ended with a professorship in the humanities at an American university.

Of course through the years outside forces and inner impulses become inextricably entwined. It would be small-minded on my part to deny that personality played a part or that certain existential choices affected the outcome. But in my youth the alternatives were severely limited. External pressures left so little play that it would be ludicrous to ascribe very much to any free agency or will. As a result I have to turn to various imponderables such as luck, fate, coincidence – for want of more precise concepts – to account for what actually happened.

Moreover, as I attempt to reconstruct my past, I am forced into making one simplification after the other. Merely by my putting them in words, events acquire a certain logic, a deceptive consistency that fails to acknowledge the subtle interplay between inner psyche and external reality. No matter how much the autobiographer wishes to stick to the unadulterated "truth," he cannot overcome the distance between the writing and the events them-selves, between the seasoned man he is and the young soul he once was. In reality the vacillations were probably more pronounced, the psychological determinacy of the acts less so. The inescapable feeling that "things could have been different" deprives the end result of much of its glory.

As I am unable to disentangle this web I will simply state what I believe to be true: that in Austria I never felt like a free agent, that the turbulent events I will next recount overwhelmed any and all feeling of free self-determination. Summarizing the influences on my first fifteen years, I can point to many varied experiences that shaped my mental development. Growing up in an Austria that had been diminished by war, as a member of a lower middle class family, meant living in the constant shadow of economic catastrophe, both national and individual. My Viennese environment was marked by social and political instability. In addition to the economic uncertainties, the plague of racism was reaching a poisonous intensity in the 1920s and 30s, and any child of Jewish extraction had to confront this on a daily basis. The more general threat of National Socialism in neighboring Germany troubled my entire childhood until the invasion of the German army put an end to it altogether. In order to find my way among these confusing realities I could choose between Judaism and Zionism on the one hand, and traditional European culture and socialism on the other – and somehow I drifted towards the latter.

While this analysis is inevitably over-schematized, I believe it to be correct – with one correction. As I began writing I felt it necessary to stress that Austria after the First World War had little in common with the Hapsburg myth of the "Blue Danube." And while I had good reason to contrast the reality of daily life in Vienna with the legend, the latter did have its effect even on me. In spite of everything, Vienna was home. Words such as Prater, Schönbrunn, or Neuwaldegg retained their magic. No water tasted better than the water from the tap in our Viennese kitchen when I came home sweaty from playing soccer and drank directly from the spigot – despite my mother's repeated rebukes. And to this day, whenever I eat a roll I always compare it – consciously or not – with Vienna's Kaisersemmeln, and the latter always come out on top. For years as a refugee, high in the Andes or deep in the rainforest, I had a recurring bittersweet dream in which I was walking down the Kärntnerstrasse, once again back "home" – from which I would wake to a decidedly un-Viennese day.

I shall not retract any of the harsh expressions with which I characterized the place of my birth, for they are true. However, what is equally true, if also somewhat absurd, is that I was deeply attached to the city; it was a long time before I was able to forget it. When the feared but expected events took place and Austria was taken over by the Nazis and suddenly ceased to exist, I was thunderstruck, and not only because this event shook my life to its very foundations, and sent me hurtling on a dangerous new course.

CHAPTER TWO
Anschluss

In early 1938 the Austrian chancellor Kurt von Schuschnigg found himself treacherously abandoned by Mussolini and pitilessly hounded by Hitler. In a last-ditch effort to rally support he called for a plebiscite, in which the Austrian people themselves were to decide whether Austria should remain independent or not. The simple yea-or-nay ballot was planned for the 13th of March. The government did everything to assure a favorable outcome, going so far as to attempt some reconciliation with the Social Democratic workers. But history happened differently; Hitler refused to wait for the election, and the Wehrmacht occupied the country on the 11th of March – a sequence of events that is already very well chronicled.

What does not appear in the history books, however, is my own encounter with Schuschnigg thirty years later. By then we both held academic positions, he at the Jesuit St. Louis University, myself at Washington University, where I taught until recently. We met at his house. The intervening decades had done much to cool our temperaments; as Ferdinand Raimund, the popular Austrian dramatist, once put it: fate is a carpenter who planes all men alike. In any event we spent the whole evening reminiscing on our experiences in Austria – he from the mountaintop, I with a view from below.

Before continuing my specific chronicle, however, I would like to make two more general historical observations.

The first is that the Nazis' seizure of power in Austria was by no means a replay of Hitler's takeover in Germany five years before. His regime was now established, its confidence boosted by diverse political and social triumphs. When it extended its supremacy to the small republic next door, everything that had taken the Nazis five years to achieve was imposed all at once, with well-rehearsed severity. Overnight a new set of rules and racial codes – including the Nuremberg statutes of 1935 regarding Jews – became the law of the land, changing the entire political and social life of the subjugated territory.

My second observation concerns my deep-seated skepticism towards a well-established myth, according to which Austria was an early, innocent victim of German fascism, a nation assimilated into the Third Reich clearly against the will of the people who were always ready to resist rather than completely acquiesce. Since 1945 this particular retelling has been of enormous advantage to the Austrian government, a myth that was propagated for under-standable reasons until it finally became official doctrine. Naturally Hitler couldn't know for sure how the population would have voted, but it's likely that many Fascist sympathizers and even outright Nazis would have cast their ballot for an independent Austria – or else he had no need to interfere. But it's also true – as every disinterested observer has stressed – that huge numbers flooded the streets to welcome Hitler with unbridled jubilation, and that a large majority cheerfully reconciled themselves to the *fait accompli* of annexation. Only small, isolated segments of the population dissociated themselves from the events – privately of course, since active resistance was unthinkable. An amusing anecdote may say more about the political inclinations of the Austrians than the available statistics: in order to ascertain how voters in the provinces might be leaning, a high government official is sent to a small town, where he asks the mayor various leading questions:

"What percentage of the local population considers itself Social Democrat?"

"About half."

"And how many Nazis?"

"Also half."

"My God, man, where does that leave the Front for the Fatherland?"

"Oh, Excellency, don't worry about that, we're all every last one of us for the fatherland."

On that famous 11th of March, I myself was sitting by the radio listening to Schuschnigg announce that the Germans were marching in. The chancellor ordered everyone not to resist "so that no German blood be shed."

I was only fifteen years old. But I was profoundly shaken; I sensed that something was collapsing, that life as I had known it was coming to an end; I felt imminent danger and impending uncertainty. And of course all my worst suspicions were later confirmed, and all at once the two most important spheres of my existence were thrown into enormous confusion: my life at home and at my school.

As she often did throughout the year, my mother had traveled to Pressburg a few days before the election, fully prepared to return in time to cast her ballot for an independent Austria. The German annexation changed these plans abruptly: over the phone my father convinced her to postpone her return until further notice. As it turned out she never saw Austria again.

From that point on I lived alone with my father, a fact which naturally altered our domestic routine and emphasized the abnormality of the situation. While this brought its share of discomforts, the experience also helped strengthen and prepare us for future difficulties. As for school, that had temporarily come to a halt, since German troops were being quartered in the building.

A strange and dangerous new life began. Even as the country was in the throes of jubilation, with the population welcoming its new leader and savior, brutal actions were being carried out against those denied admission to the new world order: political opponents and ethnic minorities, especially Jews. The methods of oppression varied greatly, from bureaucratic trickery to physical torment. Certain scenes, however, repeated themselves with astonishing regularity throughout the city. Every day you could encounter a man or a woman equipped with only the most rudimentary bucket or brush, laboring to remove some trace of the recent campaign, scraping posters off walls and columns, or else scrubbing away political graffiti someone had scribbled onto a wall or sidewalk in white paint. Vienna seemed to boast an inexhaustible supply of these occasions, as well as about two hundred thousand Jews who could thus be put to work. These unfortunate people were selected by brutish overseers in or out of uniform, who set their victims to the task at hand, urged on by a pack of jeering onlookers. From that moment on there was no safety from the rancor of neighbors nursing a grudge, or from the envious or hostile who needed only to drop off a postcard or make a quick phone call in order to cool their tempers at the expense of whomever they pleased. The doorbell might ring at any time of day or night, and one could be dragged off to a school, an office or onto the street to polish windows, scrub stairs, or remove some remaining trace of the recently deposed regime. No place was safe. One could be snatched up on a walk about town, although we had all reduced these outings to a minimum. Before you had time to turn around a whole block could be closed off, and anyone caught would be questioned and forced to present identification papers. Whoever wasn't "Aryan" was ordered to step aside. Troops of bearded Jews were seen being herded through the streets, and at the Danube a motley heap of people was made to perform ridiculous calisthenics under the watchful eyes of the Storm Troopers, whose inventive-ness at thinking up such torments seemed boundless. Some of the indignities they plotted were unbelievably imaginative. Once the posters had disappeared, along with any and all Christian or Socialist emblems, the boycott of Jewish-owned businesses began. Anti-Semitic slogans were pasted on the storefront or else signs were tacked up to warn passersby not to shop there. Few could muster the courage required to defy these injunctions and squeeze past the stalwart Storm Troopers. But even all this wasn't as bad as the crushing uncertainty, the dehumanizing constraints and humiliations. People were always asking when it would be their turn. Or else wondering bitterly how it was possible that their oppressors could act with impunity, while they, the victims, could neither protest nor defend themselves. It was as though the ground were torn from under my feet and the roof snatched from over my head – quite literally as I shall soon explain. Betrayal lurked everywhere: a neighbor next door, a fellow clerk at the office, an employee, a business partner or classmate could denounce you to the authorities without warning. Friendships suddenly broke apart, old acquaintances wanted nothing to do with you and would avert their eyes or cross to the other side of the street if they happened to run into you. The media, and in particular the newspapers, launched a massive campaign, accusing Jews of all kinds of scandalous behavior. The *Kronenzeitung* ran a popular series under the title "How I came to be an anti-Semite," which I read with morbid curiosity. In it I learned how one man had turned against the Jews because a Jewish merchant had sold him bad wares; another because he had seen a Jew eating a slice of bread and a piece of cake all at once. There was no office where one could find protection, no authority where one could lodge a complaint, no legal redress for even the basest of affronts and bodily assaults. On the contrary, these things were sanctioned by the law, or at least clearly condoned by the highest authorities. We were outside the law, free game in an open season.

An officially administered economic dispossession compounded our woes. Apartments were "repossessed" under the pretext of "Aryanization," and Jewish firms were handed over to so-called provisional managers.

But this visible persecution was relatively harmless compared to the terrible things which were taking place behind the scenes, in basement rooms of the police, in jails and prisons, and in the Hotel Metropol, where the Gestapo installed its headquarters, replete with lockup cells and torture chambers. Chilling stories started to leak out of these places, and horrible rumors began to circulate. People disappeared from their apartments or places of work and were sent to Dachau – the preferred concentration camp at that time – or else to places deeper in Germany, where the once harmless names of villages became lasting, fearful symbols of unbelievable human degradation: Ravensbrück, Sachsenhausen,

Oranienburg and all the others.

Friends of my father were torn from their families and never returned, others showed up weeks later with mangled faces and crushed limbs, and the frightening thing about it was that they didn't dare open their mouths to explain what had befallen them. From now on I was terrified, not only for my own sake; I also feared for my father's life. What would become of me if one day he didn't come home? We felt helpless and betrayed, utterly at the mercy of evil powers.

These fears were compounded when we were thrown out of our own house. Obscene notes began appearing on the door of our next apartment, where a former colonel from the Imperial Army lived with his young granddaughter. Night after night (so they claimed, though I myself never saw anything of the sort) these notes would appear on their door and I, as the only young Jew in the house, was held to be the perpetrator. After all, lascivious longings and obscene sexual acts were considered to be typically Jewish aberrations. Just a few weeks earlier, the old officer had assured my parents of his sympathies: he was an inveterate monarchist, he said, and would vote for an independent Austria. But now he told me to my face that he had seen me sneak across the hallway during the night in order to post my repulsive missives. When asked what possible motives I might have, he answered simply: "We're Nazis, and you're a Jew." The block warden – who had been a Nazi even when that was illegal – was summoned. He ordered us to clear out at once, claiming that this was a kindness for which we ought to be grateful, considering the seriousness of the case and his duty to turn me over to the Gestapo. But he would be lenient, he added, because my father had known about his illegal party affiliation for years and had never turned him in.

We moved out helter-skelter that very same day. Today such precipitous changes affect me less, since I have since made many moves, sometimes because I chose to and sometimes because I was forced, with the result that by now I have lived in many different countries and on several continents. But in those days things were different. This was my home, the place where I had grown up, where I had lived as long as I could remember. My concepts of family, of stability, of permanence were anchored in these walls, these stairs, these landings. Quite apart from the unfair accusation and the deep injustice of our eviction, I felt as though we were being driven into exile. I moved in with a friend of the family, while my father set up quarters at work. All this added to my disillusionment, to the feeling that I was experiencing the dissolution, even the destruction of the life I had thus far known.

In the meantime school had resumed its session. Here too, the rising currents were leaving their indelible mark. A few weeks after the annexation, an announcement appeared on the entrance to the school, informing us that because the buildings had been occupied by the military, all students would be moved to the Akademisches Gymnasium. Classes were to be held in two shifts in order to accommodate the sudden overload of students. This alone would have been enough to thoroughly disrupt the familiar regimen: the strange walk to a new school, unfamiliar rooms, and an entirely alien schedule replacing the routine once so pedantically observed. To all of us accustomed to an intractable Austrian bureaucracy, these changes seemed nothing short of subversive, well suited to the violent climate of the times.

As it happened the new circumstances paralyzed every effort to instruct and to learn. Time in the classrooms passed with little or no attention to the courses of study; a tacit agreement seemed to reign whereby the students did not prepare their lessons and the teachers did not call on them to do so.

However, the school did stay true to a time-honored tradition of active disinterest in current events, and although these were foremost on everyone's mind, there was never any open discussion of what was going on outside the walls of the Gymnasium. The teachers only revealed their various positions through silent expressions and hidden movements, obscure hints and whispered asides. A teacher who called class to order with an exaggerated

46

execution of the mandatory Hitler salute was showing his solid Teutonic convictions, while one who – like our class teacher – barely kept his hand raised was signaling more than a simple embarrassed reluctance. These were the only signs we had to go by, and yet they were essential in what they revealed. In those days one developed an extraordinary sensitivity to understatement and nuance, which had replaced concrete facts and honest, straight-forward assertions. Once, when we learned that the father of a Jewish schoolmate, a well-known lawyer, had committed suicide, the teacher who announced the news mumbled a reference to the "harshness of every new age." This cautious concession, this bare hint of sympathy was enough to classify that particular teacher as a freewheeling liberal and potential opponent of the changes underfoot. Others paraded their utter conformity to the present climate by making openly anti-Semitic jokes: one of our teachers, for example, announced his unquestioning approval of a proposal to send all Jewish students off to a separate school. It was high time, he said, to put an end to the "Chinese teahouse," the "chaotic synagogue" which we had made of the place.

The anti-Semite's wish was soon granted. Of course in some sense it had already taken place, since with few exceptions the "Aryan" pupils kept their distance from the Jewish ones, and – either out of opportunism or genuine distaste – would have nothing to do with us. To my horror one of them, an older pupil who had repeated a grade, even came to school in a brown Nazi uniform. This sudden turnabout, this dissolving of all sense of fellowship overnight, formed one of many unforgettable lessons I had to learn in those days.[2]

Despite this the split between Jew and non-Jew was not as

---

[2] More than sixty years later the students of this same school staged a moving memorial ceremony honoring those who had been driven out. The school authorities happened to learn that I was in Vienna at the time and invited me to attend: among the many hundred attending parents, guests and politicians, I was the only eyewitness.

easily effected as might have been expected, since it first had to be determined who was a Jew and who wasn't, according to the statutes imported from Germany. But this wasn't always easy, especially in Vienna. Of course we knew exactly what religion everyone belonged to because the class was divided for religious instruction. But in addition to the Jews who emphasized their affiliation by belonging to various Jewish institutions and who made up ten percent of the population, there existed countless others who lived beyond the grasp of statistics. Some had been baptized as Protestants or Catholics, others were without any religious affiliation at all, and very many came from utterly mixed backgrounds but nonetheless classified as Jews according to the Nuremberg statutes. Considering the demographic facts, the Nazis were absolutely right when they underscored the extraordinary "Jewification" of Vienna. It turned out that the percentage of Jews enrolled in the school was much higher than anyone had imagined, and although this should have come as no surprise, it came as a shock to many, including many who were immediately affected. The principal had us review a brochure explaining the new statutes regarding Jewishness in clear and simple prose, with the result that more than one pupil made the unpleasant discovery that his veins carried more than a tolerable amount of Jewish blood. I can still see one of my classmates holding the open pamphlet in his hand, comically stalking through the room shouting, "Half my kin is Jewish, but what am I?" Nothing illuminates more crassly the grotesque uncertainty faced by any number of Viennese than the fact that this particular boy was classified as an 'Aryan' and did not have to join us in our exodus.

Even though we had realized the arrangement was a temporary one, it seemed that our guest appearance at the Akademisches Gymnasium – which counted Erwin Schrödinger, Arthur Schnitzler, Hugo von Hofmannsthal and many other luminaries among its alumni – had no sooner begun than it was over. Those of us officially declared Jews had to report to a Gymnasium in Vienna's Jewish sector, where at least we no longer had to hear how our presence was defiling the Aryan purity of the high school where knowledge had hitherto been imparted to us. But even here, in this ghetto of a school, no one so much as thought of actually teaching us, and the school year ended after only a few weeks of barely disguised inactivity. We received report cards that had been arbitrarily filled out and were summarily dismissed, in most cases forever. And that spelled the end of my formal education for many years to come; it would be years before I again resumed study at an officially regulated institution of learning.

My life in Austria was also coming to a rapid close. Like most people in our situation, my father kept busy making feverish efforts to wind up his business affairs and to prepare for departure: we had already decided to rejoin my mother and our other relatives in Pressburg as soon as possible. Vienna had become uninhabitable for people like us and the question was not whether to leave, but where to go and how.

This was the great difference between German Jews and their Austrian counterparts. When Hitler came to power in 1933, only a small group actually thought of emigrating, consisting mostly of political activists who were extremely vulnerable and others who were exceptionally farsighted. But the overwhelming majority of German Jews could scarcely contemplate the idea of relinquishing their language, their home, their livelihood and property, a whole network of links between the family and the national culture, all just because of a change of government, however suspect the new leaders seemed. They might have saved themselves if they had thought differently, early on, when the world was still open to their plight. But Hitler's regime proved durable, the persecutors of the Jews gradually revealed their full fanatical agenda, and the situation became intolerable. By the time many realized that leaving Germany had become a bitter necessity it was too late; the Nazis had passed measures by which anyone wishing to emigrate had to leave behind everything he owned. Those who could get out were no better off than beggars, and in the meantime most other countries had closed their doors to further refugees.

The Austrian Jews had taken note of these developments, so

that when disaster struck they were generally without illusions. I
don't believe that there were many who thought they could save
themselves without emigrating.

But History had advanced all too rapidly. Fascism had cast its
shadow across the globe; the people of Europe both sensed and
feared the coming of war; governments refused to grant asylum to
the hundreds of thousands seeking entry, by making conditions,
raising obstacles or else by barring them outright. Once again only
the wealthy were able to help themselves. Lacking both money and
the necessary network of foreign business associates, the little man
was left to rely on good luck and other, equally unpredictable
factors such as the sympathy, good will and responsiveness of
others, as well as his own energy, endurance and shrewdness.

Long lines formed at the foreign embassies and consulates of
Vienna, everyone seeking safety, often waiting entire nights for
nothing more than the preprinted forms of an indifferent
bureaucracy. Questionnaires were filled out and handed in and that
was all. Anyone with a valid visa was looked upon as one of the
great and mighty of the earth, and an American affidavit – a
prerequisite for entry into paradise – was the equivalent of a
country estate in more peaceful times. Stamps and seals, sailing
permits and exit visas became the stuff of legend; people discussed
these things as though they were events of world historical import.
Rumors abounded; entire novels were concocted from the
inexhaustible stories of emigration, both legal and otherwise. A
sudden report, no matter how unverifiable or unreliable, for
example that Panama had made a certain number of visas
available, could cause hundreds to rush to the Panamanian
consulate, and the inevitable disappointment would last only as
long as it took for the next miracle to appear. A brand new
economy sprang fully grown from out of the earth, with its own
new breed of businessmen: agents who smoothed the way to the
various revenue and passport offices, guides who purported to
know secret passages to Switzerland, operators who claimed they
could procure certificates to Palestine. How easily the world could

have saved all these people – so persecuted, so threatened, so in need of shelter. But it chose instead to content itself with suspicion, hatred and egocentric greed, and so it shares the responsibility for the horrible fate that awaited so many. Caught like mice in a trap, the victims had no choice but to submit to their torment, without escape and without defense, until they either encountered a miracle or else succumbed to the violence inflicted on them. And where in all this can we find the much-sung freedom of the individual?

CHAPTER THREE
Human Freight

We were lucky; through a narrow opening we managed to slip into freedom. We acquired our exit permit, paid our emigration fees and dealt with whatever other chicaneries the authorities had invented to hamper the departure of those they were ostensibly so anxious to get rid of. All formalities were taken care of – save one.

The bane of all emigrants was a thing with a name so ghastly that in all these years I haven't forgotten it: the *Steuerunbedenklichkeitserklärung*, which might translate as "unexceptionable tax status declaration." This document appeared to be as difficult to obtain as it was necessary to present. People waited in lines literally for days, clogging the buildings where the necessary forms, stamps and receipts were issued; naturally no fewer than a dozen authorized signatures were required. But the day came when we had overcome this hurdle as well. We wound up our business matters, closed the factory premises, bundled up the few possessions we hadn't sold off or given away, said a few last good-byes – and presently I found myself sitting beside my father aboard a train that was steaming towards the Czechoslovak border.

I can't say exactly what was going on in the heart of that forty-five-year-old man who was leaving behind everything he'd ever had and was now heading towards an uncertain future, evicted from his home, bereft of possessions and lacking any means of support. But I very clearly recall the mix of feelings that welled up inside the sixteen-year old adolescent. And even if I might not have been able to put a name to that tumult of sensations, I did understand that at that moment, in that short ride, my childhood was coming to its end. Fraught with threat and charged with promise, this realization stood before me with unmistakable clarity. Even so, it would take years before my thoughts could free themselves from a past which was becoming more and more

52

irrevocably shut off: school, friends, the many faces of Vienna I had known since early childhood, everything that was or might have been and now would never be. Among the many conflicting emotions surging inside me, I felt a passionate yearning for what I had lost, shame and outrage at how my own country had forced our departure, and finally the relief in knowing we had managed to escape just in the nick of time.

The future also began to impose itself, one very different than what I had imagined, full of concrete fears and vague hopes. These latter were nebulous intimations of a 'better' life somewhere in a freer world, where people like us would be tolerated and would even be able to pursue our own happiness without obstruction.

The fears, however, were far more definite. Would we be able to cross the border? We were missing that one essential ingredient, that elusive essence, the very elixir of life – a visa, and however inconceivable it seems to most people today, our entire existence depended on it.

But we had taken what precautions we could and everything went without a hitch. Our passports were checked and we quickly passed through Austrian customs; after all, our documents were in impeccable order. I walked behind my father, frozen with fear, my heart pounding. Slowly we stepped over the wooden barrier and into Czechoslovakia, towards a waiting group of blurred figures. I immediately recognized my uncle, but at the same moment I was shocked to discover the others were border guards. We kept going. All of a sudden the guards turned away and let us pass without asking to see our documents, as I had every reason to assume they would. My uncle grabbed my elbow and hurried me off to a car that was waiting for us nearby, doors were opened and closed, the motor cranked to a start and we were on our way. A certain amount of money and a few soft-spoken words had enticed the customs officials into a momentary dereliction of duty – which in turn allowed them to fulfil their human obligation, as I realized at the time. The whole thing had lasted only seconds. We were saved.

Or so we thought. We couldn't know then that we were driving in the wrong direction, that safety from Hitler lay to the west. After all we weren't clairvoyant.

We spent the next few days enjoying our newfound freedom, in a euphoric frenzy of reunion: with my mother, my grandparents, and with all the extended family and friends. We were paraded around like circus animals and asked about everything and everybody. We were made to describe our ordeals in endless detail: what we had seen with our own eyes, what we had experienced, what we knew only from hearsay. We were asked about the persecutions, the arrests, the concentration camps, the violence, the cruelty, the jubilation of the inhuman oppressors, as well as acts of resistance and signs of possible unrest. Everyone was obsessed with politics, optimists and pessimists alike. As for us, we were regarded as heroes who had escaped a horrible hell.

Soon enough, however, a new routine set in. People seemed to have heard enough. In fact, I soon observed, much to my astonishment – and thousands of refugees experienced the same thing – that after a brief flicker of curiosity, no one wanted to know the least thing about "Aryanization" or the Gestapo, about visas or passports – and so they left us to our own devices.

This new routine, however, had little substance; it was without activity, without firm holds, or hope. We had no money, and having entered the country illegally, we could not apply for work permits. The authorities weren't supposed to know anything about us and we had to watch whatever we said. Everyone around us had their own affairs to mind; we had none. Even though we were a thousand times better off than other emigrants who were biding their time in far off lands with neither contact nor connection, it soon became apparent that our presence in Pressburg was quite superfluous.

By and by we arranged to do a few odd jobs for friends or friends of friends who didn't insist that their new employees be registered with the authorities. I embarked on a brief career as a milkman, rising at dawn to make my deliveries. I would deposit two bottles at No. 4 on the third floor, one bottle at No. 8 on the fourth floor, with an occasional bottle of cream, and proceed down the list of subscribers until I had covered every building in the blocks that comprised my territory.

On another occasion I became an accountant. Sitting in the back of a small grocery store I added up long columns of sales figures and entered the totals: 1.40 for cucumbers, 3.70 for ham. It's hard to conceive of this in an age of automatic price scanners and cash registers. For a haughty student of the Gymnasium these activities were a little humiliating, but for a young socialist there was a certain pride involved in being an active member of the "working class."

My self-respect was better served by my position as a language tutor. I had spent my last months in Vienna learning a little Spanish, partly with the help of a dictionary, partly under the tutelage of a medical student, who in his turn had been instructed by his South American friends. I now passed on this useful knowledge for a fee. My clients were mostly people of modest means for whom taking a language – and especially one as exotic as Spanish – would have been a luxurious frill. But now, under the pressure of the times, it seemed more prudent than extravagant. I quickly abandoned all talk of participles and gerunds for the sake of a less lofty pedagogical parlance. As it turned out, I was to have many similar opportunities to replace the high-flown theories I had learned in the Gymnasium with more down-to-earth methods born of practical necessity.

While most people sensed the country's vulnerable position, the more optimistic placed their faith in the excellent state of the national defenses and the preparedness of the Czechoslovak army. Or else they found comfort in the friendship pact with France, the holy promises of the Allies, and the frequent reassurances of Russian goodwill. The pessimists, on the other hand, toyed with the thought of emigration, and those who were very clever and courageous actively prepared for departure. But all without exception had some stance; in those days everyone was a coffeehouse strategist and politician.

My Pressburg relatives followed without exception a more confident line. Hitler wouldn't dare, the West would never allow,

Slavic solidarity would prevent, the Nazi regime would break down under the weight of its own excesses. "You'll see," said the same uncle who had smuggled us in, "come autumn you'll be back in Vienna."

My mother's siblings had outgrown the Jewish quarter; one brother had become a lawyer, a respectable gentleman who sported pince-nez, another was a partner in a dairy business, a third had learned his grandfather's trade making watches and jewelry, and the fourth had gone into business. Everyone was doing well, two already had families, and I had lost long ago my privileged position as only grandchild. No one could seriously contemplate the misery of flight all because of some 'chimera' (as my much-admired uncle the 'Doctor' called it). When one of us expressed our own doubts or fears, they were brushed aside as paranoid hallucinations.

However their opinions may have diverged in other matters, there was one thing with which they all agreed: something would have to be done with me. If against all expectations the uncertain state of affairs were to continue, I would have to keep up my schooling there. So once again I found myself back inside a musty schoolroom, chewing my pen as I took the exams to enter the seventh grade of the Pressburg German Gymnasium – and this just when I was beginning to feel grateful that the turbulent times had at least spared me such tortures.

As it turned out history again interceded and I was unable to make any more intimate acquaintance with yet another Gymnasium. On the very day when I was to enter the venerable institution, I was rudely turned away by a group of pupils who had stationed themselves outside. They were on strike and classes were suspended until further notice. My puzzlement was soon clarified by a large hand-painted placard bearing the words: "School won't start/ Till the Jews depart," one slogan announced with indisputable clarity. Affected by the spirit of the times, the fanatical students had decided to expel their Jewish classmates.

But by then events were moving so precipitously that no one paid any attention to my personal fiasco. Lord Runciman had sent his report to the English government, which as is now known had long since abandoned its ally; next came the talks at Bad Godesberg and the Munich Conference, and the country where we had hoped to find asylum was callously partitioned. And then one day we looked up and saw the dreaded red, white and black flag with its swastika waving at us across the Danube from the Pressburg Au, a park with forests and meadows not unlike our own old Prater. It was no longer possible to cross the river. Now we were completely surrounded. My own life's course was again swept up by the historical tide – which is after all the reason for writing this book.

Slovakia was particularly affected by these developments. Hitler had been quick to take advantage of the longstanding tension between the Slovaks and their Czech cousins, and helped install a Fascist government in the new Slovak state, under the leadership of the cleric Tiso. A paramilitary group, the Hlinka Guard, was formed on the model of the SA or SS, which gradually began to unleash the terror it had long been plotting. One of the first orders of business involved the persecution of the various minorities living in Pressburg: Czech officials were sent "home" to Bohemia, Hungarians were extradited to Hungary, and Jews were subjected to a new set of special rules and regulations. As a token of gratitude to Hitler, the benefactor who had placed them in this enviable position of power, the new authorities paid particular attention to the refugees who had fled the ever-expanding Third Reich and had sought safety within what was now Slovakia.

The police carried out systematic raids: uniformed officers as well as plainclothesmen made nightly rounds, moving from house to house, apartment to apartment. Anyone affected by the new decrees was dragged out of bed and onto the streets, where they were loaded onto waiting trucks that sped off with their human cargo into the night. It hardly mattered to which endangered species we belonged: the fact we had no residence permit meant we could count on being shipped away the moment we were discovered.

We did what we could to forestall this fate. We ventured

outside only after dark, and one of my uncles would serve as a scout, walking fifty meters ahead, peering around corners and signaling us to follow if the coast was clear. In this way we actually managed to escape detection during a midnight raid of my grandmother's building, where we were sheltered.

I can't say how long we could have kept up such a lifestyle, sleeping by day and slinking through the streets at night – we never got the chance to find out. After only a few days the disaster we had hoped to avoid finally caught up with us.

Around midnight everything had seemed peaceful enough, except for a few groups we had seen in the distance, functionaries of the state and their victims – men, women and children with the wrong passport, language, religion or race, whatever that meant. No one really knew for sure exactly what it was or how it could be determined. Even if the authors of the Nuremberg laws would have happily abandoned all religious criteria for making this determination, they could not dispense with it. After all, according to them any person with four Christian grandparents qualified as a non-Jew, although this criterion scarcely proved anything about one's racial background: it merely focused the issue of conversion two generations up the ancestral tree.

We thought we were safe, since the devilry usually ended around one or one-thirty, when all of a sudden a door swung open right in front of us and we walked smack into the middle of a patrol. Thanks to the protests of my Slovak-speaking uncle we were allowed to go home and throw together a few belongings. The officers accompanied us, of course. A little later we were standing in an open truck together with other unfortunates, and off we drove into the night.

Our ears were abuzz with all kinds of rumors and speculations on our fate, in Yiddish, German, Hungarian and any number of Slavic dialects. Where were they taking us? Prison? Would we be deported to Germany? Sent to forced labor? Placed in a concentration camp?

Dawn came and some people recognized various landmarks. We were heading towards the southwest, and more and more people surmised that we were being transported to the land that had been ceded to Hungary in accordance with the Munich Accords.

This view soon proved to be correct. From the truck we could see occasional Hungarian troops marching or else camped out beside the road.

We passed through one village after the next. Then all of a sudden the truck stopped, and we were quite unceremoniously unloaded. Our guards jumped back onto the truck and drove off hurriedly in the direction from which we had come. That was the last we saw of them.

We found ourselves in the marketplace of a little town, and from curious onlookers crowding around us we learned its name: Dunaszerdahely. Two days earlier it had been known by its Slovakian name, Dunaeskastreda, but now both the town and its name had become Hungarian. Hungarian slogans were everywhere, such as "Haza felé vonolunk" – "We're heading home" – which was how this transition had been officially poeticized.

But what was to happen with us? A few other trucks had deposited their human cargo on the same marketplace, so that by now there were about eighty or a hundred of us – a fairly sizable crowd considering that we were in a totally unfamiliar region without food or shelter. Despite our extraordinary situation, everyone still observed the decorum of polite behavior. Little did we know that our unauthorized perch on the marketplace of a Slovak-Hungarian town foreshadowed an even more precarious future.

To this day I am grateful when I think back on the townspeople. Without any orders (after all, the Slovak authorities had already left and the Hungarian ones had not yet arrived) they brought food and blankets, shovels and tents – who knows where what supplies they scrounged – in order to feed and house their uninvited, helpless guests. The tents were pitched with great commotion; huge cauldrons of goulash were brought to our campfires. Soon the pots were simmering, and the steam drifting invitingly from the hearty soup, which warmed our bodies that had been numbed by the long ride. At last our spirits rose, and the gloom that had taken hold of most of us dispersed. New friendships were made, jokes were shared, and people bantered back and forth as happily as at a picnic, as though everyone had been on the friendliest of terms for years. Experiences such as that have taught me that it takes little to spark the love of life. A bit of warmth, a plate of food, a sense of solidarity and soon even the greatest hardships are forgotten.

Before long a lively exchange had begun, and some individuals were taken home by the townspeople and given myriad little tasks to perform. My job was to saw wood for two women, to split the logs and stack the pieces in a shed, where they were kept on hand for the winter. I hope they kept cozy in their tiny rooms: I can't say I was particularly adept at this unfamiliar task, my hands soon blistered and muscles ached I had never known I had. But in return I was fed well, and slept better on the hard floor of my tent than in the softest feather bed. For all its lack of amenities, this interlude now strikes me as a peaceful idyll. Of course today I realize that there were many others, older than myself, whose responsibilities for their nearest and dearest would not let them forget their fears even in the relative calm of these six or eight days. (Our group included pregnant women, frail old men, and even a retarded person.) But viewed from the carefree eyes of youth, everything seemed charged with adventure, and this perception magically transformed our stay in Dunaszerdahely – and even the terrible things that happened later – into something fantastical and epic. Had I been wiser or more experienced, I would hardly have been able to pretend that camping out in the marketplace of a small Central European town could be anything but a precarious interlude.

What was bound to happen happened all too quickly. Soon after our arrival, the Hungarians moved in, first the military, then the civilian authorities. Thanks to our central position we had a good view of history taking place right before our very eyes. The vacated offices filled up, desks which had recently served Slovak bureaucrats now served Hungarian ones – at least that's how I see it. Naturally the new management could hardly be expected to approve of the tent city that had taken over the town square and the constant ruckus going on outside the windows that were newly theirs. Helpless as we were, our fate was sealed, and presently the familiar scenario was repeated with only slight modification.

A number of gendarmes appeared: what did it matter that their uniforms were different and that the rudely shouted orders were in Hungarian rather than Slovak or German? We were told to dismantle the tents, to clean and collect whatever we had borrowed and to gather our own belongings. Then we were once again taken into custody.

My mother made use of the ensuing commotion to run to the mayor's office to plead for her family in her most eloquent Hungarian (as she put it). But all her linguistic prowess fell on deaf ears; we were marched off to the railroad station like everyone else four abreast and bundled with bag and baggage onto a waiting train that was impatiently snorting steam. Before long we were on our way towards a new and totally obscure destiny.

We could extract no information from our guards, even when the train stopped one or two hours later and we continued our journey on foot, along a rough country road, loaded down with all sorts of backpacks and trunks and boxes. Again the question, where to? Again the bootless speculation, the imagined terrors, the near-hysteria. The mood infected the children, half a dozen or so of whom were soon weeping and wailing in concert. We would have presented a macabre sight to any passing traveler, but there was none.

We continued on this strange pilgrimage for over an hour, until first dusk fell, then night. At last we arrived at an abandoned farmstead, which turned out to be our temporary destination. Packed together worse than animals into two tiny rooms, we spent the night not so much lying next to one another as heaped together on tables, benches and floors. Our jailers made themselves more comfortable in separate quarters.

At dawn, after the most Spartan ablutions at a well, we assembled in the courtyard. There was no breakfast; in fact no one had eaten a thing since we started, except for those who had hurriedly managed to pack a few provisions. The captain of the gendarmes gave a brief address, the gist of which was promptly translated: we were to hand over any money still in our possession – anyone failing to comply would be shot! This command, not to mention the fear of what was to come, unleashed a terrible commotion. In a small side pocket of my pack we had hidden a few bills, the last remnants of a once orderly existence. Timidly, my mother showed it to the guard who was rummaging through our belongings, and he pocketed the banknotes with an unforgettable smirk. In retrospect it is impossible to know whether this act really saved my life or whether my mother had unnecessarily forfeited our last savings. The fact was that we no longer had anything left in the world but our naked selves. How could we hope to survive?

When everyone had been searched, we set off as on the previous day. But after only a short while our guards stopped behind some bushes along the road and signaled us to continue on alone. Reluctantly we started up again. The road had become a path that led us through open fields, dotted with haystacks and an occasional shrub, but no trees. As far as the eye could see there was not a single human habitation.

No sooner had we advanced two or three hundred feet into this landscape than a group of bleary-eyed figures emerged and started towards us. Others soon joined them until we were completely surrounded. In the ensuing hubbub we learned these were fellow victims whom the Hungarian military or police had abandoned in this spot a day or two earlier. After we exchanged questions and answers, they asked us for food and we distributed what little we had left.

A few hundred meters ahead of us we could see the border of Slovakia; behind us, a chain of Hungarian soldiers blocked the way back. We were stranded in what amounted to a broad line of demarcation – the technical term for a border zone that has resulted from international accords. For all practical purposes we had been banished to a no man's land.

Next followed one of the most absurd episodes in my life, utterly different from anything I had ever known. Poverty and unemployment, strikes and protests, wars and revolutions, even the inhumanity with which one person torments the next – these things still seem 'normal' by comparison, belonging to the realm of past or at least possible experience. But the idea that some people could be declared so unwanted as to warrant their complete expulsion from society, that they could be denied even the most rudimentary status of citizenship and deprived of the most basic right to live – that was something unheard of. Especially in that time and place, in the middle of Europe, from states whose leaders paid constant homage to the achievements of Western civilization, to Christian values, manners and mores. This was truly beyond comprehension.

Over the next few days a number of newcomers straggled in from the Hungarian side. Like us, they had been ferreted out of their homes, placed under arrest and transported here. But apart from them there were no other arrivals, and our group stayed at about five hundred. We were a crowd of exiles with little or nothing in common: Hungarians who had spent their entire lives in Pressburg, Slovaks who had lived just as peacefully in Hungary, German and Austrian Social Democrats who had escaped to Czechoslovakia. There were Jews from Vienna, Berlin, Cologne and Breslau, some educated, some not; some were highly assimilated, others wore caftans and sidelocks. There were people of every age and both sexes, married and single, whole families with little children, people who had been torn away from their relatives and knew nothing of their whereabouts, a Babel of German and Yiddish, Slovak and Hungarian. Some people had falsified documents; others had none at all. The only thing this motley group truly shared was their fate; in some way or another, all had been swept up by the wave of fascism spreading across Europe.

But life went on, even here, in our extreme privation. A few clear-headed persons began to organize the group. The first priority was to scare up some provisions. Several people were sent to comb the fields, which stretched for miles on both sides. Soon some potatoes, turnips, corncobs and whatever had been left over from the last harvest were roasting over small fires. We found water in a pond. It was November; the weather was autumnal, cold and damp. A few drops of rain fell and the orthodox Jews began praying loudly, raising their voices to heaven, begging for a respite. But hardly anyone else still expected help from that quarter.

I don't know how long we continued this way – it may have been a few days or many. But after all these years I remember one scene with the vividness of a hallucination, a single episode breaking the general monotony. All of a sudden a military vehicle – some kind of jeep – came rolling towards us from the Slovakian side, carrying an officer of evidently high rank and a single family; father, mother and two bluish, half-frozen infants, one of whom actually died a few hours later. These unfortunate people had been found on an island on the Danube, where they had fled to escape the brutalities of their persecutors. By virtue of our sheer numbers we were able to offer them some semblance of friendship and protection. But the spectacle we presented was evidently too much even for this hardened soldier. When he saw so many homeless human beings camped in the middle of the civilized world, the obvious misery, the tattered clothes, the worn faces staring at him in mute entreaty or accusation, he was overcome with pity. He covered his face and looked away, his body shaking with sobbing. Touched by this display of emotion, hundreds of outcasts cried with him.

However much it seemed to transcend tremendous social barriers, this wee bit of human sympathy remained nothing more than a private reaction, one which could not be translated into official leniency. At the officer's request, a Viennese doctor we had chosen as our spokesman presented a list of things we needed most: food, tents, medicine, the right to send women who were obviously pregnant into town and to have the corpses removed there as well. As it was, several people had died already, and the oldest and frailest could not possibly be expected to survive such hardship. A few days later we received our answer: all but one of our demands was denied. The corpses were removed.

In the meantime, however, help had arrived from another source. The Jewish community of Pressburg had caught wind of our plight and had obtained permission to send provisions. Before we actually became desperate, the first truckload passed through the border guards and arrived at our encampment carrying priceless delicacies. Unloading became a kind of festivity. Bread and sausage, milk and fruit disappeared the moment they were discovered. It was incredible how quickly five hundred starving individuals could consume a seemingly inexhaustible supply of food. Finally, even a small barrel of wine was rolled out, and when its contents had gone the way of the rest, our good spirits reached a peak. Everyone relaxed; we exchanged stories and bits of news deep into the night, as though we had just become acquainted and yet were already the best of friends.

From then on our situation improved. The deliveries from Pressburg arrived every day, there was no lack of things to eat and drink; even bits of money began to appear here and there. A modest fraternizing began with the border guards, giving rise to an ongoing trade; soon pipe tobacco and cigarettes found their way into the camp, and an occasional bottle of brandy helped cut the chill of the frigid nights. Here, too, human beings showed their amazing ability to adapt.

My parents and I didn't have to rely on these comforts very long, as the prospect of escape arose almost immediately. One evening we discovered to our amazement that the driver of the 'grub truck' was none other than the same enterprising uncle who had earlier smuggled us across the border. His presence in this no man's land, disguised as a truck driver, could mean only one thing, and we immediately took the cue. When no one was looking we slipped onto the back platform of the vehicle, a pile of empty baskets and burlap bags came flying on top of us and off we rode towards the border.

Everything went as smoothly as if we were out on a Sunday drive. Only our hearts, pounding underneath the piles of empty potato sacks, bore witness to the dangers of the undertaking.

The truck had to stop at several checkpoints; the guards were so close we could make out what they were saying. But the driver's permit easily satisfied the bored and unsuspecting soldiers.

The danger was over; half an hour later we arrived back at my grandmother's. The abduction had been successful; we were free. Once again we were safe – at least for the nonce. I can't say with any certainty what became of the others. For a few months we kept hearing rumors: the camp had been dissolved, the inmates had been taken into town and put in prison. However that may be, given the subsequent fate of both the Slovak and Czech states, it is unlikely that very many of those who had been there escaped alive[3].

Hot water, soap, a bed – that night I learned the meaning of luxury. Since then I've learned more: that every sense of belonging, justice and human community rests on an illusion, that these things have been loaned until further notice by those in power, to be revoked at their whim. Thus far I had managed to hold on to some hope, even when people turned their backs on us, when Austria collapsed and our ties with that country were dissolved. Somehow I had still been able to place the blame on a single nation, a single government, or even – if I really wanted to make it easy for myself – on a single man. At the same time I had imagined I could find elsewhere what I had lost at home. But the events of the previous weeks instilled in me a total disillusionment, one which has stayed with me up to this very moment and which I wouldn't give up for anything. Ever since then, even in the best of times, I have always felt as though I could feel the earth spinning beneath my feet, that everything I possessed was mine for only a moment. The feeling is by no means an uneasy one; on the contrary, this shaky ground has its own security, there is no small comfort in such detachment. Which is precisely why the Christian

---

[3] Years later I was very surprised to find a report on our very camp had been sent to the US Department of State by George F. Kennan, then a young diplomat at the American legation in Prague.

religion has sought to awaken this sense in its followers – though often in vain. Not having been blessed with the joys of a Christian upbringing, I had to acquire this knowledge along a detour through a no man's land between the two Christian states of Hungary and Slovakia.

The euphoria we felt after the success of our daredevil flight was soon gone. In the dreary, sobering light of autumn, 1938, it was only too clear that although we had escaped one calamity, we were a still a long ways even from our status quo ante. After all, we were now in greater danger than we had been before our arrest. More than ever we had to avoid the attention of the authorities: not a soul, and this included our most intimate acquaintances, was to know of our whereabouts. But how long could a whole family remain hidden in such close quarters, where everybody knew everything about everybody else and where gossip was a favorite pastime? Whenever anybody came to call on my grandmother, or even so much as rang the doorbell, we removed all traces of our existence and crawled into the darkest corner of the furthest room. Leaving the house was out of the question, not to mention finding a job.

And the political horizon was continually darkening. The optimists quietly yielded the floor to the prophets of doom, and they, of course, would be proven right. But no matter how you looked at it everything pointed in the same direction: away from Pressburg. But what safe passage was there out of the swelling sea of fascism? We discussed the matter from various angles and decided to go to Prague, at that time still an antifascist island that could offer us temporary asylum. After that, "we'll see" – a new stock phrase that stressed the general lack of open prospects. No step we took was guaranteed to be the right one.

This was true of Prague as well. Moving to the besieged capital of a country that was partitioned and in deadly danger was an act of desperation. But like everyone else in our situation, we *were* desperate.

The trip alone provided ample proof of how hemmed in we really were. We had chosen to travel by train, since that seemed to us the most unobtrusive means available. Fortunately we made it through the station without getting caught. But the ride itself was harrowing enough; following the German occupation of the Sudetenland, the Pressburg-Prague line now passed through enemy territory, so that we were separated from National Socialism only by the fragile walls of the coach. Through our windows we could see the Nazi emblems decorating houses and city squares, flitting by in nerve-wracking proximity. The trip seemed endless, and when the train finally did arrive in the Prague station, we once again felt as though we had escaped by the skin of our teeth.

Prague itself was thronging with people fleeing their pursuers like game running before the beaters and hounds, a last stand for cornered prey. There were refugees of every description: Jews from the four corners of the earth, as well as political opponents of the Nazis – Communists, Social Democrats, Austrian monarchists. Every group had its own rescue station. Even the relatively small numbers of Christians of Jewish origin had an aid program; I believe it was called Gildemeester.

Hopeless, helpless and penniless, we joined the already swollen ranks of the officially unwanted. For the first time we really came to know the misery of emigrants, the daily scenes being repeated a thousand times over in European capitals not yet overrun by the Nazis – from London to Belgrade, from Warsaw to Paris. We now realized how good we had had it in Pressburg, with our wide circle of relatives and acquaintances, compared to the impersonal wretchedness of this claustrophobic city where we didn't know a soul.

For the first few days we found refuge in the emigrant hotel "Flora," already known throughout half of Europe, in the Vinohrady suburb. There, for the first time in my life, I was "interviewed" by a journalist, a reporter for a Swedish newspaper. How this person singled us out, I don't know. The fact is he made me give him an elaborate account of our sojourn in the no man's land. These events still seemed sensational to a public not yet completely inured, not yet acquainted with other, impending atrocities. A few days afterward I was the proud possessor of a

Swedish article on my fate, although all I could make out was my own name scattered throughout the article and the large red "J" which was stamped over the entire front page. This "J" was to become increasingly familiar.

One of my father's first efforts brought him to the over-crowded rooms of the HICEM, the Jewish aid agency, where needy human beings kept the benches warm for hours just in order to present an overworked official with an impossible request. Practically everyone came here to obtain financial assistance and some means to travel to a safer place, preferably overseas. I now believe, paradoxically, that our stay in the no man's land is what saved us. We were given some clothing – used but warm (by then it was decidedly winter) – and an inexpensive place to live, a small back room on the top floor of the "Sektpavillon," a favorite wine and amusement hall on the Jakubská ulice. To get there you had to steal through several rooms of spoon-packed waiters sleeping off the night's fatigue. But for all that it was a place to stay, and we had long ago stopped worrying about convenience.

Soon we had even procured our official residency permits. Although these were only valid for three months, we were assured that they could be renewed. In this respect the Czechs were incredibly generous; after all in the Europe of 1938, as we had learned, it was no small privilege for the likes of us to be allowed to simply *be* someplace, with legal status and stamps and sanction. More than anything else, the people in the aid agency, roused from their usual lethargy by our story (corroborated, of course, by the Swedish newspaper, with which we never parted) gave us new hope. Considering our "extraordinary situation," they promised to leave no stone unturned in their attempts to find a visa. But first we needed new passports, since our old Austrian ones had expired, and these could be obtained only in the German Consulate.

The building stood on enemy territory, which I entered with a terror I still recall today. But the bureaucratic machine churned smoothly: we submitted our photographs, paid the requisite fees and sooner than we imagined possible we each received a brand new German passport.

These passports differed noticeably from our Austrian ones in two respects. The first page was now adorned with the obligatory "J", printed in provocatively large, glossy red ink.[4] In addition, the new German state had been so generous as to equip us each with new middle name: my mother was called Erna Sarah, my father Oscar Israel, while I became Egon Israel Schwarz.

The aid agency took these passports in order to send them to the HICEM headquarters in Paris, where the visas were distributed. We began the dreadful waiting. Zlata Praha – golden Prague – how unreceptive we were to your celebrated beauty! My father and I pored morosely over a homemade chessboard for hours; or else we studied the newspapers, which invariably contained nothing but depressing news. Occasionally we would leaf through an English or Spanish grammar or repeat absurd sentences out of an English phrase book: "When does the bank open?" and "At what time does the train leave?" These activities were interrupted only by the meager, cold meals we ate in a corner of the room. For these frugal repasts we depended on the small but welcome weekly allotment provided by the Jewish aid service. Even when we did venture onto the wintry streets, we could not escape our tattered clothes or the odd stares from passersby, for whom our German language had become anathema. As a result we hardly paid any attention to the myriad sights of that wonderful and ancient city. Fear and poverty make for bad tourists.

One night a fire broke out in the "Sektpavillon." A gas range had exploded somewhere in the building, tearing the tenants from their sleep and sending them racing into the street. We were there too, in threadbare coats hastily thrown over our night-clothes, shivering from the cold, watching with fright as the flames and smoke leapt from the windows, as we waited for the firemen

---

[4] It was only much later that I learned whom we had to thank for this distinction, namely the Swiss and Swedish immigration authorities, who had asked the Germans to make it easier for them to tell at a glance which of their visa applicants were Jewish!

to come and put out the fire so we could go back to bed. In retrospect this scene seems emblematic of our situation in Europe: homeless and helpless, poor and afraid we watched our native continent go up in flames.

But we would not stay for long. Soon after the fire, in early February 1939, my father came back from one of his frequent visits to the aid agency, triumphantly waving some documents as he came bursting through the door. The passports had returned from Paris, and on each one, in one of the first pages, high up in the left-hand corner – I still see it exactly – was a visa from Bolivia. Now where was that again?

The boat was scheduled to leave for South America from La Rochelle-Pallice, a provincial French port. Obviously we had a number of things to do before then, not the least of which was getting to France. At that time the only one way of leaving the isolated city without passing through fascist territory was through the air. And so my first plane ride was doubly adventurous; flying free was more than just a metaphor. As the airplane bore higher and everything on the ground became smaller and more distant, I again sensed that combination of anxiety and eager curiosity, of power and magic which adolescents so often feel as they go out into the world. It really must be magic, I thought; out of all the thousands who had to stay behind, I was lucky enough to be lifted out of my affliction. The tilled acres of central southern Germany stretched out peacefully below me, crossed by rivers and roads and dotted with towns and villages. What was it that prevented a harmless traveler from making this crossing by land? And then there was Paris, the City of Lights, capital of the cultured world.

But alas, we hardly did Paris any more justice than Prague. I had dreamed of its splendors ever since I began studying French in school. And now there I was among the monuments with no time to explore, no chance for any real contact with the city's essence. The few days we spent in the French capital were far too short, my French far too unreliable for that. Besides, we were all too busy with very un-Parisian tasks. For us, it seemed that all roads led to the aid agency.

This one was located in a stately building. We had to report there to procure our lodgings and obtain a daily allowance, since we no longer had a penny. We also had to find the "Pacific Steam Navigation Co." to obtain our berths, middle-deck to the North Chilean port of Arica, and from there to a travel agent for our train tickets from Arica to La Paz. Finally we had to apply to the Chilean Consulate for a transit visa, which was stamped in our passports only after we had filled out endless forms and produced the requisite documents. And while these arrangements took up most of our short time in Paris, I can say with pride that I had a croissant with coffee in a real Parisian bistro, and that I went for a ride in the famed Metro. I even went so far as to address a passerby, who had no idea of the heroic effort I was making, with the question: "Comment va-t-on au Boulevard des Capucines?" This meant a lot to me, and it would have to last for many years, a savored memory of a Europe that was free and yet untrammeled by war.

Finally everything was done. We paid a last visit to the aid agency, where we each received good wishes, a handshake, and eight dollars to cover our arrival in the New World. Before long we were in the train heading for the port. The boat was the *Orduña*, whose gigantic black hull rose endlessly out of the softly moving water as we made our way up the swaying ladder. At last the moment arrived when this colossus of twenty thousand tons set into motion and we gradually made for sea. Soon Europe was nothing more than a streak of gray, barely distinguishable from the gray sky and the gray Atlantic, until nothing was left except the ocean itself, bordered by a remote horizon. It would be seventeen years before I again laid eyes on the continent of my birth, the mainspring of so many decisive forces in my life.

The crossing itself consisted of the most diverse impressions, which can be loosely grouped into two categories of perception. The first involved the adventure of sea travel itself, which I – not quite seventeen – found particularly exciting. I marveled at our tiny, self-contained steamer, this tiny molecule of civilization at the mercy of the elements, which soon showed how unruly and wild they really could be. A storm brought raging high seas in the notorious Bay of Biscay, and the giant vessel was tossed by the waves like a nutshell. Surges high as houses swept the top deck. Lifelines were rigged for the crew, and passengers weren't allowed to leave the innermost rooms. Proudly I lorded over the empty dining room, my appetite unfazed by the yaws and pitches. I explored the ship without cease, day in, day out, from the boiler room to the bar, from the galley to the recreation room, held back only by the insurmountable barriers that separated the second class quarters. Then the weather let up, the ocean became smooth, the sun shone again and became hotter with each nautical mile.

Tropical waters, unimaginable temperatures, flying fish... and finally, after ten days, the first land – the Bahamas. Although we kept our course far offshore, the dark-skinned natives paddled over and dove into the crystal green water to retrieve the coins being tossed from above. Their cupped hands sweeping through the water and the pale soles of their feet made them seem strangely foreshortened in the water, until they captured the glittering silver and returned to the surface.

The first port where we were allowed to disembark was Kingston, the colorful capital of Jamaica, with its strange black men (until just recently the only black man I had seen was the uniformed porter of the Vienna Meinl Coffee Company). Next came the Panamanian port Cristóbal Colón, where the business district seemed more like an Eastern bazaar, with Hindu proprietors hawking silk shirts for a dollar apiece – if you had that much. Another district – said to rival Marseilles in sinfulness – housed business of another sort, and girls of all complexions proffered unmistakable invitations to the young man who responded with a mix of agreeable shudders, although he unfortunately had to decline.

Apart from these adventures, there was another, unrelated side to our voyage. It became all too apparent that our brave vessel had very recently served as a freighter, and that to meet the recent growth in demand she had been refitted as an emigrant-transport ship, although as such she was barely up to the task. We were traveling third class and not allowed to forget it for a moment: the food was virtually inedible, the cabins and sleeping quarters were crammed deep in the hull and became boiling hot as soon as we entered tropical waters. The personnel treated us with undisguised disdain. Rumor had it that the captain himself said he pitied the countries where his ship would be unloaded.

Evidently many of the governments at several ports of call shared this feeling; as a rule only the first and second class passengers were allowed to disembark, while we had to stay on board, like so many tons of human cargo.

Thus when we arrived at La Habana, all I could do was stand on the deck, burned by the sun, and look longingly. The shimmering "pearl of the tropics" held little welcome for the exiled beggar. Decades later, when Castro took over the government, this one memory sufficed to give me deep satisfaction, for the heyday of the third class had begun at last.

But at that time we were constantly reminded that our *Orduña* was not a typical passenger liner, but a barge freighting exiles and outcasts. There were oppressed refugees from every corner of the Third Reich; some had been in concentration camps, some had had their stores looted by the SA, others who had watched their pianos being thrown from the windows during *Kristallnacht*. There were Spaniards and Latin Americans who had fought in vain for the Spanish Republic against Francisco Franco, under circumstances of incredible loss and sacrifice and who were now returning home or seeking asylum in a place where their own language was spoken.

I never again saw such a motley assortment of people jumbled together. There were the Chileans, smoking and speaking unbelievably rapidly, the chess-playing Cubans, each one a miniature Casablanca, and the well-bred Jewish matrons from Cologne and Frankfurt. North German doctors and university professors with finely polished speech and Bavarian boys with broad dialects who – God knows how – had managed to come into conflict with the Nazis. Merchants from Tauentzienstrasse, the Fifth Avenue of Berlin; Eastern Jews from the Galician shtetl; impoverished

Austrian aristocrats clinging to pitiful vestiges of elegance and luxury. Many had intimate acquaintance with barns and makeshift shelters of every sort, with dirty prisons and merciless police and immigration authorities from many countries. Some even had ties to the Parisian underworld. And everyone had not just one, but many tales to tell. The *Orduña* was my first university – the only one for years to come – and by no means the worst.

Fortune had it that an educated Spanish engineer from Bilbao took me under his wings; I would like to honor his memory by entering his name here: Mariano Perea. There's little more I can do for him; I have no idea where he may be or whether he is still alive. Much to his wife's displeasure, he allowed me to spend many evening hours in his company – in a small circle of admirers who gathered around him to listen to the magical strains of his classical guitar. At first we communicated in French, but he soon switched over to his mother tongue, anticipating that I would need that language a great deal more where I was headed. This intelligent, experienced man not only honored me with his instructive conversation; he also helped me improve my very rudimentary Spanish, clarifying its various subtleties. I was quick to incorporate what I heard, and began to sense I might have a genuine talent. After just a few days, I was chatting away with my mentor fairly well, as he continued to teach and correct me. And by the time he went ashore at Callao three weeks later, I was able to express my farewell and heartfelt sorrow at our parting, in a Spanish which was both fluent and – at least I think – grammatically correct. During the remainder of the trip I gave an intensive course for those emigrants who wanted to practice the new language, and when we landed I played the part of official interpreter, helping a number of passengers through customs.

The most memorable moment of this lively and instructive crossing arrived one day in the form of a telegraphed news report posted on a bulletin board. Among a number of random trivial announcements, one brief statement caught our eyes: Germans occupy Prague. Of the hundreds of thousands for whom this event was nothing less than a death sentence, we had been chosen to survive. No rhyme, no reason: we had hardly done anything to deserve this distinction; in fact, *we* had hardly done anything at all.

And so the question of will arises once again. By this point no one should be terribly surprised to hear that in the face of such fundamental interference from the outside, I am less prone to stress the role of human agency and individual self-determination. And yet surely *some* agency, some degree of individual initiative helped to save us. Perhaps no one single action but a whole mechanism of carefully constructed cogs and wheels, which proved quite solid once events had set it into motion. Or perhaps our own efforts mattered less than the care and compassion of others. For even during times seemingly governed by chance and circumstance, it is possible to distinguish between deliberate acts of succor and support, and the lawless forces of oppression.

CHAPTER FOUR
New World

South America – what adjectives can do justice to that place where I spent more than ten years of my life, in hostile love and intimate estrangement? Exotic? Dreamlike? Brutal? Bewitched? Enchanted? Relict of the prehistoric past or realm of a promising future? Chile, Ecuador, Peru, Colombia – all descriptions pale in the face of the continent's incomparable diversity, its inexhaustible wonder, its overwhelming otherness. Eager as I am to deliver my account, I despair at the impossibility of the task.

Neither angelic eloquence nor even devilish persuasion would suffice to describe the seclusion in those times of Bolivia, home to the Quechua and the Aymara, and foster-home to a boy from halfway around the world. High in the Andes, the wild, rugged country seemed an unremittingly harsh place to live; constant sandstorms lashed the *altiplano*, a tundra-like plain 4,000 meters above sea level. And the Tibetan solitude was intensified beyond belief following the loss of any access to the sea, and thus to the world, as a result of senseless wars.

The incredible isolation struck us even in Arica. Upon landing we discovered we had just missed the train to La Paz; the next one wouldn't leave for another five days – more frequent contact with the magical land of Bolivia simply did not exist.

Arica itself seemed utterly and hopelessly un-European, especially compared to the winding streets and crooked buildings of Prague; here the town had been laid out with geometric precision. And while the Czech capital was still battling the winter cold, here we faced a merciless sun that beat down on us without so much as a cloud to soften its rays. Japanese barbers were snipping hair inside the salons, while a saw was cutting gigantic fish into thick slices at the concrete-floored marketplace. And everywhere our nostrils were assaulted by a foul stench, which drifted in from offshore, where hundreds of thousands of birds hovered above the guano islands that stood out chalky white against the glistening blue sea.

The entire city could boast only a few half dried-up trees and shrubs; whatever was to grow had to be tended with water fetched from far away, because it virtually never rained. This meant that the nitrates occurring in the earth's surface could not be washed away, and were easily obtained through open mines, an important – and famous – source of income for the entire region, and especially the port city Arica.

But none of this wealth could console the eye of the visitor, to whom the whole area looked as oppressive and barren as a lunar landscape. And so, despite the ominous shrugs and frowns with which people answered our questions about Bolivia, we were impatient to continue our journey.

The railway to La Paz is one of the highest in the world, a technological wonder, built by some English engineers in the nineteenth century. The train slowly winds its way from the coast into an increasingly impassable mountain terrain, climbing slopes so steep that with each new turn you think it can go no further. But on and up it goes, undaunted, over 5,000 meters above sea level. A nimble official scurries from compartment to compartment with an oxygen mask to relieve those overcome by *soroche*, an altitude sickness causing shortage of breath. At last the highest pass has been crossed, and the train descends until it reaches the *altiplano*, which stretches endlessly between the huge chains of mountains that make up the Andes. This high, arid plain supports only the most unassuming scrub brush, unbroken but by a few Indian lodgings, far-flung and forlorn.

We have arrived in a region cut off from the rest of the world, surrounded by the impregnable walls of the second tallest mountain range on earth. The train keeps descending, slowly spiraling down into a depression. First huts, then houses, and finally, the station. After sixteen hours we have reached our destination.

La Paz is built on a moraine, 3,700 meters above sea level; the edges of the town extend up to 4,000 meters. The air is thin and dry; it parches the throat and all mucous membranes. You can never inhale enough of it. For the first several days you feel no hunger, just a constant thirst, and an iron vise painfully pressing against your forehead, until finally your body slowly becomes acclimated to the lower air pressure.

Of course that's not the only adjustment we required: there was almost nothing familiar in either the natural world or the social one. The new sights and experiences could not be measured by central-European standards, or even understood. And yet we had no other background, no other system for perceiving and analyzing, no other choice than to apply the ideas and expectations we had acquired in one culture to a completely different one. That was our dilemma. It took me years to synthesize what I had brought to South America and what I found there into a broader awareness, a more comprehensive understanding of human experience.

We spent the first night in a simple hostel where we had to share the room with various strangers. A single dollar went amazingly far; even so, we had just about used up what scanty reserves we had, and would soon have to find some way to earn money. But first we had to come to terms with this world where everything was foreign, from the odors that betrayed the primitive hygienic conditions to the smoke from the many open fires fed with llama dung and brushwood from the tundra. Or the infinitely melancholy strains of the indigenous music, which at first seemed so monotonous it grated on the nerves. Later it began to sink in; and once you've listened to it night after night for several months, it never leaves you. Nor were we prepared for the inconceivably poor dwellings built of adobe and corrugated metal, which stretched out far beyond the center of the city, where the better houses were clustered, down into the canyons and up along the cliffs.

Nothing, however, seemed so foreign as the people themselves. Almost all were Indians, typically dressed in colorfully striped, coat-like ponchos that reached the knee, short linen pants with bare calves, and thongs made of leather and old tire rubber. The men wore llama wool caps with rounded earflaps, while the women sported hats that resembled men's bowlers. They also wore layers of broad skirts, and almost every one of them carried a child on her back, tightly bundled. We learned that 95% of the population belonged to two Indian nations, each with a different language: the Aymaras who had settled in and around La Paz, and the Quichuas or Quechuas, who lived everywhere else. The latter were descendants of the Incas. Most spoke little or no Spanish, many had no concept of "Bolivia" – those who lived far from the cities had never even heard the word. Even though serfdom had been abolished in theory, it remained in practice. Many of the indigenous people toiled away on vast haciendas, whose size was measured by the number of families living there: the acreage itself had never been surveyed. Any Indian who dared to flee risked being caught by the military, returned to the landowner and subjected to severe punishment. If he wanted to marry he needed the consent of the patrón, to whom he was always in debt, despite his constant hard labor. Nor did he feel free in the city. When he encountered a white man he would step respectfully off the sidewalk. And if a member of the upper classes signaled for him to approach, he would do whatever task was required, without grumbling, and be grateful if he received a tip instead of a kick in the behind.

Almost everyone was dismally poor, with the exception of a few tycoons whose large land holdings and rich mines brought them fortunes which they preferred to squander in Paris. (The Bolivian tin monarch Patiño was one of the ten wealthiest men in the world.) A fledgling middle-class consisting of merchants, teachers, civil servants, military officers, and professionals in the private sector could be found scattered throughout the towns, which were very small and extremely provincial – only La Paz had more than 100,000 inhabitants.

No government could remain in power without the consent or support of the army. The president, Germán Busch, of German descent, was a lieutenant colonel and the hero of the Chaco War, which had recently been lost. Throughout its hundred years of independence, Bolivia had warred with each of its neighbors with disastrous consequences. First it lost the rich, but still unexploited Mato Grosso to Brazil in the Rio-Acre War; next the indispensable coast, with its port city of Antofagasta in a war with Chile. Finally it lost the Gran Chaco during the recent war with Paraguay, although this conflict was said to have really been a war between Shell and Standard Oil.

The military was also on constant call to cope with the frequent civil unrest. Revolutions were frequent, although fortunately they seldom caused much disruption in everyday affairs. Various political and economic factions fought bitterly among themselves, and whenever one of them managed to win over a few higher-ranking officers or a regiment stationed in the capital, a *revolución* was declared, accompanied by a successful or unsuccessful coup d'état. A few shots would be exchanged, and people would be warned to avoid certain streets on days when revolutions were occurring. The army, incidentally, had been trained by Ernst Röhm, who later returned to Germany, where he became a friend of Hitler and the head of the SA.

For the uninitiated it was virtually impossible to understand exactly what was going on politically. In retrospect, one might consider Germán Busch the first "modernizer" of "under-developed" Bolivia. Evidently the Chaco War opened his eyes to the tremendous needs and terrible inequities of the South American continent. As a young officer he witnessed firsthand the unfathomable incompetence and corruption of his superiors. At the time of my arrival, stories about how the war had been waged and lost were still making the rounds. One of them told about a drunken feast organized by officers on the front lines, during which a girl was carried in on a shield, naked except for mounds of caviar under her arms and between her thighs. They say that half of division headquarters was taken prisoner that night, drunk to the point of unconsciousness. Of course anyone with any insight realizes that this war was not fought in the interests of Bolivia or Paraguay. Neither country possessed the means to develop the territory under dispute; no matter how many riches it might conceal. In fact as far as I know the Gran Chaco remains unexploited to this day.

It seems that Busch, returned from this debacle, decided to put Bolivia's name on the map by building roads, dams and irrigation systems, by establishing industries, by teaching the Indians to read and write and by incorporating them into the machinery of state. He also intended to reduce all foreign domination – partly by taking control of foreign capital – and to unlock the country's vast riches, while involving massive numbers of indigenous people in the process. I'm not claiming that these were easy goals; I'm not even sure they were possible. Not even the revolution of 1952, which undertook the same program with broader mass support and with incomparably greater energy, managed to make much more than a start. But it's safe to assume that Busch was thinking along similar lines. The word "nationalism" comes to mind, but this is a decidedly European term, born of a completely different experience and applied to different circumstances. When we say "nationalism," we automatically think of the linguistic and cultural unity, as well as the historical continuity that marks the development of a people who sense they belong together. The South American countries, however, developed out of arbitrarily drawn districts administered by the Spanish colonists, until they achieved "independence" about a hundred years ago – if "independent" is at all applicable in view of the tyranny exercised by foreign companies supported by their governments. What sense of belonging could there be between the thin urban population, which aspired to live according to the European model, and the indigenous masses, who lived in conditions so primitive they seemed prehistoric, who had been robbed of their own culture and could barely communicate in the official language of state? No, European-style "nationalism" has little to do with the hatred the natives bore the arrogant Europeans who came to Bolivia to enrich themselves, and who looked down on the local population with unspeakable disdain. Nor do the concepts of "left" and "right", so inextricably tied to European history, apply to the political arena. They fail to describe the strivings of a few intellectuals and young officers – including some who had studied abroad – who dreamed of a national industry, of wresting the mines from the foreign companies, of bridling the local oligarchies that were exploiting the people. Inadequate as they are, however, these concepts are still invoked – not only to describe these countries but also to justify superpower policy directed against South America, as is proven by the failure of political scientists to comprehend and explain such phenomena as Perón or the Bolivian National Revolutionary Movement.

It would have been far more accurate to speak of "colonialism" or really "post-colonialism," since the wars for independence which put an end to Spanish rule played a great role in shaping the consciousness of many South Americans. These terms would have explained so much of what my family went on to experience: the widespread xenophobia we had to endure, the unchecked exploitation of Indians and lower-class mestizos by the ruling classes, and the extreme radicalization of students and academicians. We would have better understood the indifference to and ignorance of the events in Europe that were so important to us, the developments that determined our fate as well as our own self-perception. Perhaps we would have even coped more easily with the primitive living conditions, the rampant corruption, the general unreliability that drove us to despair – and all those things which set us apart and made it impossible for us to ever feel at home among the Bolivians.

But it was too early for words like "colonialism" and "underdevelopment"; they did not yet exist, nor did the entire conceptual apparatus to which they belonged, and which developed in the aftermath of World War II. And so nobody at the time really understood what was going on, least of all those immediately involved. It seems that Germán Busch came too soon as well. The reason I make so much mention of him is because he was in power when I arrived, but I am more concerned with a certain type, who since that time has been ruling South America, and even other parts of the world. His policies, such as freezing foreign assets and imposing trade sanctions on foreign capital, were considered the abuses of power by a leftist despot. The fact that he had one of the three leading tin tycoons, Mauricio Hochschild, sent to prison for some legal violation – I forget exactly which – was viewed as an act of sheer demagoguery, committed by a low-ranking, upstart officer addled by his own authority. No wonder, then, that the entire foreign "establishment" and a good portion of the domestic one was against him. His base was too weak, even within the army, his following too fickle, and he himself too unresolved to stay in power. Irrefutable evidence indicates that what was later claimed a suicide was in fact a political execution, customary enough in those days. Of all those who ruled Bolivia during my six years there, Peñaranda, Quintanilla, Paz Estenssoro, Villaroel and various lesser potentates, hardly any was able to end his political career peacefully. One was forced into exile, another was thrown into prison, and a third was killed. Villaroel's fate was typical. A mere major before becoming president, he dismissed all ranking colonels and generals, on the one hand because he was proud that his relatively lower rank marked him as a man of the "people," and on the other because as chief of state he could not tolerate being outranked. During one of the abovementioned "revolutions," his opponents broke into the governmental palace and threw him out the window and fastened him to a lamppost.

And so while the country lived on in a state of constant turmoil and explosive unrest, the general living conditions never seemed to improve or really even change at all. Although the country was rich, its riches mostly lay fallow and what was skimmed off brought nothing to the general population. In Beni, for example, a tropical province in the Amazonian basin, you could find large herds of grazing cattle, while in the cities higher up, where most of the population resided, meat was impossible to find: after all, how could it be transported? One attempt at using airplanes failed, and no railway existed. At the time there was not one single paved highway in all Bolivia. Roads laboriously carved out of the mountains wound their way over dangerous passes, around hair-raising curves, past steep cliffs and deep gorges, often littered with the remains of crashed vehicles. The roads were blocked with fallen rock and often too narrow for more than one lane, so that some were designated for ascent or descent only, in shifts of several hours. If two vehicles did chance to meet high in the mountains, the drivers would have to perform very slow – and very daring – maneuvers until they finally came clear. People carried gasoline in barrels, since there were no gas stations. Resourceful drivers or their assistants repaired a damaged engine or chassis with chewing gum, thread, and spit. A major breakdown could strand a vehicle for days, until the necessary part could be fetched from far away. There were virtually no private automobiles; only pockmarked and dented cheap metal buses and trucks that had been patched together a thousand times, which chugged and clanked their way forward, loaded to the brim with people and merchandise. And over these inconceivable thoroughfares passed the business of a nation. During the rainy season earthquakes, swollen mountain streams, floods and caved-in sections of road disrupted even these precarious connections and cut off entire parts of the country. The remote eastern regions of Santa Cruz and Trinidad, abounding in sugar cane and all types of fruit, remained inaccessible for weeks.

In the mountainous reaches of a country almost ten times the size of the state of New York, but with less than one-fifth of the population, there were rich mineral deposits, where the Spaniards had already mined for silver, and where tons of tin were now being extracted. This made Bolivia one of the world's leading producers of that metal, and subject to exploitation by foreign companies, whose affairs were managed by non-Bolivians and whose profits were consumed on distant continents, while the native miners toiled away under life-threatening conditions and abject poverty. I could go on and on with such descriptions, since my curiosity, or rather my youthful indignation recorded a large supply. But my purpose is rather to account for the fate of central-European emigrants who, having barely escaped the bloody inferno Hitler was busily preparing for them, wound up in these exotic regions and now had to make a life for themselves.

I need not stress the fact that we immigrants fit in our New World like a square peg in a round hole, to use a popular expression. A great gulf separated the Indians from the Europeans, an unbridgeable abyss formed by eons of not only linguistic but also cultural separation, that precluded any commonalty except the most superficial. Virtually insurmountable obstacles also separated us from the sparse urban middle class, which was closest to the Europeans in a sociological sense. These barriers included the lifestyle and mores of the Bolivian bourgeoisie, that so clearly reflected their colonial past, their deeply rooted Catholicism and the adamantly private Spanish model of family life. In addition there were linguistic barriers never entirely conquered, and a basic mutual mistrust impossible to overcome. Naturally the Bolivian middle class was far from entirely homogeneous, neither in its psychology nor its world-view; and of course the refugees were even less so, coming as they did from so many different countries, united only in their flight from Hitler. And of course some contact did ensue between the more open-minded emigrants and the better-traveled Bolivians, so that I should be careful to avoid crude generalizations.

But let there be no mistake about it: the emigrants were bound to offend their Bolivian neighbors at every step. Coming mostly from large industrial cities, they brought with them a lifestyle that was thoroughly secular and materialistic, enterprising and industrious. Equipped with a liberal world-view that was exclusively the product of capitalist society, the central Europeans entertained aspirations that greatly exceeded their current financial situation. Their customs rankled the native bourgeoisie, particularly the sexual mores, as the European women exhibited a degree of independence unheard of among their Bolivian counterparts. By the same token, the immigrants looked down with almost undisguised disdain upon the "bumpkins," their primitive hygiene and rudimentary technology, their lack of sophistication in thought and deed, their utter seclusion and conservatism. In a word, the distance between the two groups was irreconcilable.

A single detail may suffice as illustration: in the ten years of my stay in South America, not once did I enter the home of a native. What a contrast to the United States, where the newcomer is immediately drawn into lively interaction, and where only a short time need pass before he feels himself more or less accepted as a fellow citizen! In comparison to the USA, the Andean countries, at least the ones I know best – Bolivia and Ecuador – are not immigrant societies able to absorb large numbers of foreigners. Thus it was an anomaly, one which proved to have unhappy economic and social consequences, that ten thousand immigrants, armed with the most modern expectations, suddenly found themselves in the Andean nation of Bolivia, which was wholly unprepared to receive them.

"Culture shock" is the best term to describe the disorientation we experienced. While the social sciences had yet to invent the term, the phenomenon certainly existed. Culture shock is what happens whenever a person leaves a familiar environment and arrives in an unfamiliar one, where everything is different, the faces, the clothes, the customs, the psychology and way of looking at life. This may also include a new language which can never be fully mastered and which constantly forces the newcomer to live below his own intellectual level. It can affect the idle vacationer or tourist, the traveling businessman or sales representative, scholars, diplomats or researchers. And the person affected often reacts to the new situation with discomfort, despondency, ill humor and an irascibility that can escalate to disgust and xenophobia. Everything he encounters seems to be worse than it was at home; everything is less efficient, the people are less likable, less friendly and less honest, the streets, houses and kitchens are less clean and cared-for. Even the civic institutions are less correct and humane, to the point of being ridiculous, illogical and disgraceful; the politics are wrong, corrupt, deceitful or violent. Of course some people experience the opposite reaction, whereby everything seems better and more beautiful than at home, but such cases are by far the exception. Both perspectives stem from a sense of alienation and a distortion of judgment that can lead to total loss of balance, since the average human is a creature of habit, loath to surrender his routine and generally unprepared to cope with the unfamiliar.

It's easy to understand why the émigrés suffered a particularly painful form of culture shock in South America. After all, they had been catapulted into a new environment without any immediate prospect of returning to the world they knew so well, or of regaining their positions, possessions, friendships – in short, their home. Among those of us who were fleeing Hitler, this culture shock occasionally went so far that German refugees in France received the ironic nickname "les bei-uns," or "les back-home," because they began every second sentence with the phrase, "Back home in Germany." I know from personal experience that this satiric label contained a great deal of truth. I remember clearly an absurd remark uttered by a German refugee during one of these endless conversations about the past; this particular man eagerly and earnestly launched into his tale with the words "back home in the concentration camp." Whoever and wherever we might be, we humans never feel entirely secure in the world, no matter how self-confident we may sound; at best we manage to display a superficial acceptance of what befalls us. This is why we overcompensate by claiming to come from a better city, a better country, a better family, a better school, or that we have more money and more beautiful things than other people.

For the refugees who had landed in Bolivia, the culture shock was particularly severe: differences such as those between Germany and France seemed trivial in comparison. Here one never knew what to expect; the people acted so differently: different manners, different routines – even the mealtimes were different. The stores had little to offer; if you were looking for something specific you could be sure not to find it. If you wanted to buy food at the market you could find *paltas* and *chirimoyas*, mangos and papayas, *ají* and locoto – all types of tropical fruit and vegetables. There was also an impressive array of bizarre things such as dried llama embryos which, as we discovered, the Indians used for certain rituals, or coca leaves which people chewed the way they do candy in other parts of the world. But none of this was of much use to a housewife from Vienna or Berlin.

And that's how it was with everything. The apartments were bad – dank, dark and cold; few could afford the ones new enough

88

to have toilets and bathrooms. The fact that most of us had no money made matters even worse, particularly because what we considered everyday necessities – in regard to food and drink, living arrangements and clothing – were either unaffordable or unavailable. The wealthier refugees had emigrated to "better" countries, by paying a thousand pounds for a certificate admitting them into Palestine, or by using business contacts or family connections to obtain visas to England, Australia or the USA. We belonged to one of the two or three last waves of emigration and had to content ourselves with saving our skin, even if that meant holing up in the Andes in conditions less than comfortable. After we left, the only path of escape led through Shanghai, and compared to the wretched conditions there, and the Japanese occupation later in the war, we were still well-off. But we didn't realize that at the time and besides, when has the misery endured by others ever helped anyone to overcome his own?

Actually even the visas in our passports were mostly invalid. Obliging consuls had sold them to aid organizations, either out of greed or more humanitarian motives. Thus many of the new arrivals – businessmen or office clerks who had no notion of farming; some had hardly ever even seen a farm – entered Bolivia on "agricultural" visas which required they work as farmers. Some could have received land from the government, which was interested in developing the more inaccessible regions and integrating them into the national economy, places far off in the jungle along rivers like the Mamoré and the Chaparé, both tributaries of the Amazon.

I could tell tragic stories of idealistic settlers who, for good reasons, decided to give up on western industrial civilization and embarked on such an adventurous course. Most of them failed, since no matter how well equipped they were, no group could long withstand the terrible diseases, the extreme climate and the frequent natural catastrophes. The distance alone provided a powerful obstacle; the settlers often had to travel to one of the larger towns, and because of the bad roads, each such trip involved a major expedition. More often than not, the possessors of these agricultural visas were the least suited for such daring experiments. These people no more dreamed of a pioneer life in remote and dangerous provinces of the Amazon than my family thought of ourselves as the "tourists" our visas said we were, as if we intended to sightsee around Bolivia a bit and then take the waters elsewhere.

Of course sooner or later anyone who did not satisfy the letter of the law would wind up in various government offices, at the mercy of an administrative system that alienated them even further from their new home. This Bolivian bureaucracy was rich ground for social scientists and satirists alike, although to my knowledge the country is still waiting for its own Daumier. Rampant chaos, lethargy and the arbitrary application of power characterized the "Oficinas de Gobierno." All these offices looked alike: there were more bureaucrats than bureaus, so that they tended to lounge about, in an astonishing variety of airs and poses. Bundles of yellowed, worm-eaten files stood stacked along the wall, permeating the air with the smell of dust; an occasional typewriter of seemingly pre-Columbian origin bore witness to the fact that time and work had achieved a perfect state of inertia. The same ragged *chicos*, the boys who spent their days at the market or on the streets instead of going to school, were also in evidence here, where they performed certain characteristic services. There was the traditional South American shoe shine boy who came equipped with a small bench with raised foot rest, various brushes for cleaning and applying polish, an a whole assortment of dirty rags and colored dyes. He would polish the shoes of some official until they shone, while their owner reclined smugly in his armchair. A second chico would serve coffee, while a third sold newspapers. Undoubtedly the officials themselves were terribly underpaid, bored to tears and determined to work as little as possible; at the same time they would spare no effort to remind the general public of the little power they wielded, in order to bolster their meager income or at least their self-esteem. Clients were systematically ignored: their greetings went unanswered, so that they automatically turned into supplicants. Even if you finally succeeded in attracting enough attention to present your case, it hardly meant things would be taken care of. Whatever the matter might be, it would be dragged out over an indefinite amount of time and through an infinite number of similar offices. Each case had to be written up in a very specific legal jargon, incomprehensible to the uninitiated, stamped and sealed and accompanied by photographs, supporting documents, petitions known as "solicitudes," etc. – all in the required format and form. If the papers happened to be in a foreign language – as ours were – they needed to be accompanied by notarized translations. Before you could even be heard you had to present the *prestación vial*, a document proving you had done your part to improve the very languishing state of Bolivian highway construction, either by contributing physical labor or a fixed sum of money. Concessions to collect this fee were sold to businessmen whose bailiffs were always stopping people on the streets to exact payment or proof of payment. In general, every official transaction required some specific document, for instance the receipt acknowledging payment to the *Campaña de Desanalfabetización*, a program designed to teach Indians to read and write. Here, too, one could choose, between teaching two Indians to read or else paying. I have no doubt that most of these monies went to line the pockets of private individuals, because the entire state apparatus was indescribably corrupt, from the barefoot policemen who stopped pedestrians with no reason except to exact a "penalty," up to the highest positions. I still see myself, embarrassed beyond words, crossing the polished floor of a reception room, my outstretched arms holding a cake I was to present to the head of some department because our residency permit had once again expired. No one escaped contact with the bureaucracy. Once the visa had been secured (or in the odd event it was all right to begin with), the residency permit needed to be obtained and periodically renewed. Later on you needed the *Cédula de Identidad*, a picture ID that also showed your thumbprint, which served in lieu of a signature in this illiterate society. And whenever martial law was in effect, which was often and for long periods, you needed a *Buena vista* before you could buy a train or bus ticket – not that all this paperwork allowed much time for travel.

The only way you could shake these offices from their torpor was to pass some money under the table, or else to appear in the company of some prominent Bolivian. Then the bureaucrats would bow and strut and click their heels; the asthmatic typewriters would start clacking away, the official forms would be quickly filled out with all the necessary phrasing. It turned out that things could be taken care of after all, without dozens of photos and fingerprints, just like that.

Not surprisingly, I never had either of these magical charms at my disposal. As a result, my encounters with the bureaucracy were inevitably embarrassingly difficult – something about me seemed to irritate the bureaucrats, and over the years I had to endure a number of humiliations, including several arrests. Once I spent several days in a miserable prison because some dog bit a cyclist who turned out to be the nephew of a governor. Even though I knew neither dog nor nephew, I was accused of owning the beast: after all, I was the only foreigner at the scene of the crime. Because it was Friday, I had to wait until Monday to be received by the Comisario, to whom I was graciously permitted to present the simple explanation. Another time I was pulled off a train because the man next to me was carrying that strange device known as a tape recorder, which marked us both as foreign spies and promptly landed us in jail. In hindsight these experiences are more amusing than annoying, but even uncolored by emotion, they provide insight into the fact that many emigrants lived on bad terms with the bureaucracy.

And that was the least of it. The main problem was that thousands of foreigners, displaced, dissatisfied, impoverished and impatient, were crammed together in a relatively small, in-hospitable city which was both economically and psychologically unprepared for such a flood of new arrivals. Not only did this cause friction between the immigrants and natives; it also accounted for certain troubles among the newcomers themselves. The loss of any sense of belonging, the shattering of values, the erosion of a secure moral foundation soon caused severe disturbances in the social climate. As far as the meteorological climate is concerned, I will only note that despite the many complaints – and superstitions – about the altitude, it was for the most part very healthy, especially for people with bad lungs. For those with heart problems, however, it was harmful, and many people died of infectious disease.

Healthy as I was, I experienced certain social phenomena far more acutely. For example I was painfully struck to discover anti-Semitism existed here, too, that our relief at having finally escaped the evils and abuses of fascism was in reality an illusion. I hesitate to be too free in applying the concept of anti-Semitism to a society so different, so un-European in its structure and history. Not that Spain doesn't have its own tradition of anti-Semitism, one that achieved notoriety during the Inquisition, and the word "judío" ("Jew" or "Jewish") had long been absorbed into the language as an insult meaning "usurer" or "miser." When the boys that roamed the streets of La Paz chased after blond Europeans – including very "un-Jewish" English or Germans – shouting "Judío," it was more absurdly ridiculous than insulting.

But Hitler's special poison, modern political anti-Semitism, had found its way even here, and I was deeply dismayed to hear an anti-Semitic tirade shortly after my arrival. In keeping with local custom, it was broadcast over a loudspeaker set up on the corner of the heavily populated plaza. This diatribe was so filthy, slanderous and irrational it could have been penned by Julius Streicher, editor of *Der Stürmer*. It was amazing exactly how far the Nazis' influence did reach, a fact we would discover in more ways than one during our stay in Bolivia. For example, when the war in Europe was in full force, airports were carved out of the jungle to receive the German invaders; and on Sundays I could see Germans who worked in the same mine I did performing drills, just outside town, dressed in the uniforms of the SA. The German colony, enslaved as it was to everything German, funded newspapers and radio stations, which not only broadcast pro-Axis news with a fascist spin, but the entire fascistic world-view as well. For their part, the Allies were not to be outdone and did what they could to influence press agencies, radio stations and newspapers to counteract the fascist propaganda. Thus the clash of opinions became a public debate that went on for years, especially because the governments, change though they might, always remained neutral. Not until a few days before cease-fire did some South American republics declare war on Germany. At the peak of the fighting, two loudspeakers blared away at each other from opposite ends of the plaza, so that the two hostile ideologies converged in the middle of the plaza in a grotesque tangle of unintelligible sound. But that first blast of anti-Semitism came as a hard blow, so soon after I had convinced myself that coming this far, to such an uninviting place was simply the price we had had to pay to escape such meanness. And it would be wrong to assume that the constant propaganda was completely without effect on the populace; it had to increase the hatred we often encountered.

These were the circumstances surrounding a rather chaotic process of assimilation, adaptation and further migration. Anybody could see that La Paz could not handle such a massive number of foreigners, especially since each one was looking to earn a living, and more were arriving with every passing train. Incidentally we made a point of personally examining the new arrivals; one of our many new rituals consisted in making the evening pilgrimage to the station, located high above the center of town, whenever a new train came in from Arica or Antofagasta, port cities in northern Chile. We would watch the immigrants spilling out of the cars, not merely out of curiosity but also in the hope of finding a familiar face, a friend, or a relative. There we witnessed amazing and often deeply moving scenes of recognition and greeting, which were every bit as salutary for the onlookers as for those directly concerned, and which contributed to the socialization of our group.

Another place where the emigrants met every week was the post office. We soon learned that overseas letters were distributed one day a week; which made receiving mail quite an event, whether the letters came from Europe, then ridden with misfortune, or from balmier places such as the United States or Australia (both coveted emigrant paradises). Significant passages were read aloud, addresses exchanged, and so on. Never again did mail play such an important role in my life; never again was it so essential for keeping spirits up and maintaining a psychic balance.

Along with the letters, most of us received the emigrant weekly *Der Aufbau*, and I would like to express my special gratitude for this paper, which exists to this day, though only as a shadow of its former self. The news it contained, the lead articles on the world situation, the cultural sections that reported the whereabouts of well-known artists and described their latest work helped to remind us that we were not entirely forsaken and forgotten. Above all, its dogged tracking of emigrants all over the world reassured us that we were part of a community, one which was admittedly threatened and persecuted, but by no means insignificant. The articles themselves were well-written; the journalists' diligence and craft helped many émigrés keep their mother tongue alive and well.

A slow but steady stream of departures helped relieve some of the pressure caused by the growing number of foreigners in La Paz. Before long there was a booming business in illegal border crossing, as scores of refugees were led across the far southern border into Argentina by way of secret mountain paths. A few adventurous types tried to cross on their own, simply by taking the train that connected the two countries' capital cities. Naturally this required skill as well as audacity to escape being caught; since the trip took four days, the risk was great enough to prevent many people, especially large families, from even trying. By the same token, there were just as many who couldn't resist the allure of legendary Buenos Aires, which was desired both as a center of business as well as culture. Rumor had it that it was fairly easy to disappear "underground" in the Argentine metropolis and ultimately procure "official" papers – provided you could get there in the first place. I met quite a few people whose attempts to do exactly this had gone awry, and who then had to start all over again, poorer by a few last dollars and a few lost hopes. But there's no doubt that the risk paid off for hundreds of people. Of course what later became of them, submerged as they were in the large, remote city, I cannot say.

Another trend further helped relieve the pressure in La Paz, as people looked inland, either because they were by nature enterprising or because they just wanted to escape the stiff competition and increasingly cut-throat reality of Bolivia's largest city. The lower altitude and milder climate provided another incentive for the emigrants into the interior, where they generally settled in the provincial capitals, which were even more cut off from the outside world than La Paz had been. Among these towns the favorite was Cochabamba, the second largest city in the country; its relatively low altitude (approx. 8,000 feet) insured a gentle, spring-like climate. My parents were among those who chose this route; I remained in La Paz for the time being, as we shall see.

Slowly but surely, the refugees began to find their place in their new surroundings, partly by adjusting to them and partly by adjusting the surroundings to themselves. A debate flared up as to who profited more – the refugees because they had been given asylum, or the Bolivians, because the emigrants were modernizing the country. The issue will probably never be resolved. In any case, people found homes, made friends – mostly among themselves although also with local inhabitants – and progressed with their Spanish. Many found employment; those better off, more enterprising or professionally better prepared (some had readied themselves for the future by taking "retraining" courses in Europe) opened all kinds of shops and workshops. Some had brought their machines along, and were thus able to set up shops as tailors, dry cleaners, woodworkers and stonecutters (supplying the local construction industry), grocers, innkeepers, restaurateurs and so on. The few professional scholars among the refugees, who had formerly taught at schools and universities, had a harder time finding work, as did the lawyers and doctors, whereby it's easier to understand why the former would have difficulty practicing law in a country with a completely different legal system. Exactly why doctors should have been denied the license to practice in a land so desperately in need of medical care is another matter. It was outrageous how the local medical association created every

96

conceivable obstruction to prevent their European colleagues from establishing themselves, mostly out of professional jealousy, incompetence and a feeling of inferiority. I knew more than one doctor who was forced to fritter away his life peddling small goods or doing something else of little service to anyone – and this in a country where his art was a rare and much needed commodity. In any case, those with a highly specialized profession did well to retrain as quickly as possible, and find another way to earn their living. Those less adaptable were forced to vegetate for years on end, bitterly attesting to the fact that they really were important people, while professionals with greater flexibility joined the rest of the émigrés in quickly taking up a new activity, mostly along commercial lines.

Communal life among the immigrants also progressed. The office of the aid organization itself served as the first meeting point, the place where all fates were interwoven. This office distributed information and provided some assistance. However, it gradually lost some of its importance, especially after the outbreak of the war, when the stream of refugees dried up to a trickle and then stopped completely. In its place a Jewish emigrant community center was founded. A clubhouse was set up, where you could have meals, sit together in the evening, read newspapers, exchange opinions, reminiscences, or information, or else play cards, chess or table tennis. The center also took on important religious functions as well as charitable activities. In short, the emigrants slowly turned into immigrants, whose thoughts and aspirations were focused less on the past and more on the present and future.

Of course this process was not entirely smooth; there were various negative moral and economic side effects which caused me a good deal of trouble and affected my entire outlook on life for years to come. Inflation and the black market currency exchange were twin problems intimately related to the refugees' sudden appearance on the Bolivian scene. Within a few months the exchange rate for one dollar climbed from 30 to 80 Bolivianos – generally referred to by the English expression Bobs – but the 80 bought less than the 30 had. Even worse was the fact that lying and cheating had become so commonplace that you could hardly believe or trust anyone. Various individuals popped up who claimed to have connections to the authorities, and who promised their gullible victims they would arrange to bring over loved ones left behind in Europe. In this way they conned their "clients" out of every last penny. Sure-fire business deals turned out to be scams that disappeared overnight, together with their enthusiastic backers and whatever money the duped "partners" had invested. Some legitimate enterprises couldn't get off the ground because the licenses promised by "high ranking government sponsors" never materialized. All types of shady dealings cropped up everywhere only to shatter soon after, leaving those who had invested to figure out what to do with the broken pieces.

One thing that upset me greatly was the sexual conduct I encountered. The destabilization brought about by the general uprooting was particularly evident in this area. Many of the refugees had married for the sake of convenience, just before leaving the country. Already on the ship I had observed how fragile such relationships could be, and had responded with a mixture of dismay, disgust, and prurient interest. Schiller's advice "Drum prüfe, wer sich ewig bindet,"[5] had been ignored due to lack of time, and the result was a disturbingly high impermanence of love relationships. But even older and apparently more solid marriages failed to withstand the test of the times. Small structural flaws in such marriages, which even a seasoned psychologist would scarcely notice, loomed much larger, often becoming irreparable breaks. Given the highly protected and utterly restricted role of the married Bolivian woman of the time (and perhaps even now), as well as the neurotic patronizing of girls "from a good home," it's easy to understand how the Bolivian men considered the easy-going, relatively accessible European women as free prey.

---

[5] A rather colloquial translation might be: "Check both the ends before you tie the knot."

Not only young men about town but also older, higher ranking businessmen and politicians ensnared even the most innocent in artfully spun nets that ranged from glowing glances and whispers on the open street to more concrete commercial propositions. Of course terrible misunderstandings occurred the other way around as well. A Bolivian girl might accept an invitation to see a movie without the slightest hesitation, then show up accompanied by several relatives, for whom one also had to purchase tickets. Offences or transgressions that would not have been considered such in Europe could bring the much-feared brothers onto the scene, who would often exact a bloody revenge.

The complications, disruptions and confusion that ensued, the arrangements that were made, the ménages à trois or more, the dangers, the deals, the separations, regroupings and betrayals that I witnessed showed me a force whose influence on human affairs was every bit as strong as economic circumstances. A force I would have never seen so clearly, so free of illusion, had I remained in the ordered world of my childhood. This general sexual license was epitomized by an event that took place in one of the newly founded nightclubs, an incident that reflected the general commercialization then underway, where young refugee girls were auctioned off to the highest bidder. News of this naturally fanned the fire of hatred felt towards immigrants and Jews, a fire that was already smoldering quite well, for there were plenty around who needed no additional prodding to blame all the emergent evils in the country on the European refugees who had fled from Hitler.

Related to these phenomena was the appearance of a new personality type – the roguish adventurer, the entrepreneurial fortune seeker, who turned to the forgotten and forbidden sides of life, even when these bordered on the criminal. These were intriguing characters who reacted to unusual situations in unusual ways. Of course both colorful and disreputable figures can be found everywhere living on the fringes of society. But it's easy to understand why their proportions were greater than usual at the time I am discussing and under the conditions I am attempting to describe – conditions which can scarcely be called "normal." They were so common, in fact, that they became part of the very atmosphere. And in order to better convey this atmosphere, I'd like to conjure up a few of these types, who plied their roguish trades amongst the many upright, hard-working refugees struggling against adverse circumstances. While these types were the exception rather than the rule, their doings more clearly reflect the grotesque reality of our life than the worthy activity of the majority.

For instance, there was a man named H., who must have been uniquely unconventional even back in Vienna, as he himself admitted when asked the inevitable question, posed at least a thousand times to every emigrant, namely, "What did you do 'earlier' or 'over there'?" Evidently this particular man worked in the Viennese amusement park known as the Wurstlprater, where he was a "swing thrower" – a job that consisted in providing a swing-happy public with just the right amount of push. His speech was quintessentially Viennese, a colorful suburban dialect so genuine it was music to the ears, and he could rattle it off with the certainty and flair of a cabaret emcee. Here in La Paz this same man was raking in money by scamming ambitious Ping-Pong players in one game room after the next, including the one belonging to the refugees' community center. Despite his fantastic mastery of the game, he knew how to pass as a total novice. He would graciously agree to play – provided, of course, some money had been added to spice things up a little. Thanks to his fine skills as an actor, which he undoubtedly acquired by watching the barkers at the amusement park, he was able to dupe many a new opponent into falling for his trick. Inevitably he would lose the first few games, then ask for a handicap, first five, then ten points; meanwhile the ante was being doubled and even tripled. Thus his victims would be basking in the glory of their presumed superiority, while all the time they were falling deeper into his trap. Just as he had previously lost by only a point or two, he now began to win by the slightest of margins, so that he not only recovered what he had lost, but a considerable sum besides. The handicap was taken away, and in the end he would give his opponents ten or fifteen points and still beat them roundly, since most of them simply couldn't stop playing. They didn't know what to make of their sudden, inexplicable change of fortune, especially because H. took pains to win by only two or three very hard-earned points. He really pushed the limit with one man who had been laboring away in the jungle somewhere and had come to the city for a brief vacation. It was his great misfortune that as a youth he had been a local Ping-Pong champion back in Bohemia or Moravia, and therefore simply couldn't believe that he was losing to the likes of H. – according to the usual pattern. In bitter determination the man played blindly for higher and higher stakes, and had it not been for the intervention of some people who knew H.'s *modus operandi*, he would have been burned completely and forced to return to the jungle without having any vacation at all. H., however, was so accomplished that he began to use his talents in more legitimate ways. He soon took part in official tournaments held in La Paz, where he climbed higher and higher until he finally reached the South American championship. Naturally none of us could follow him into those lofty regions, and one day he disappeared; maybe he went to Argentina, Brazil, or Chile – the distant, admired and yearned-for ABC countries – in any case he was never heard from again.

Another one of my acquaintances wanted to escape the allegedly civilized world, which treats the so-called under-developed world with such hypocritical disdain. I had met him on the boat, a setting that lent itself to forming intimate and lasting relationships. While still on the Atlantic he had refused to join the others who were bemoaning the difficult fate of exile, choosing instead to greet his new situation with enthusiasm, since it meant he could wipe his razor blades on a towel without risking his mother's wrath. Even La Paz was too modern and mechanized for this individual, and so he set off for the furthest corner of Bolivia, the tropical jungle province of Beni, located in the flat river basin east of the mountains. Only a few years before, hostile Indians had attacked the provincial capital Trinidad, plundered it and put it to the torch. What good were the military "penal expeditions" which the government sent out on such occasions, simply to save face? Trinidad was the kind of place where you had to go to prison if you needed your hair cut, since the best barber in town had been jailed for some reason or another. Incidentally this had less to do with the law than with his own comfort; the gates were wide open and the inmates could leave whenever they wanted. After all: where would they go? Anyway, it was in this idyllic place that my freedom-loving friend, only a few years older than myself, became the director of the electricity works – I have no idea how. From what he had told me his technical experience was limited to a job he had accepted earlier, claiming to be an engineer and expert on diesel motors. He had been taken to a distant mine to repair the large engine that kept everything running. Naturally he was unable to do so. But it was one of his peculiarities to be as proud of failed ventures as he was of successful ones, since for him it was the risk itself that mattered, as an even earlier job clearly showed. That time he answered an ad for a glass blower, and was told to form letters from neon tubes. To his own amazement he managed quite well, until he had to blow an "O," at which point his promising career abruptly ended. Whenever he would come into town from some distant regions, to obtain supplies and enjoy a change of pace, he would go on and on about his adventures. When I next saw him he told me about two acquisitions: a hacienda with count-less herds of cattle, and a new dark-skinned wife. Marrying a local, and especially an Indian, was a taboo observed by all the foreign colonies, as different as they might be in other respects, and breaking it was considered nothing less than high treason, the worse kind of assimilation, the dreaded loss of European identity. I myself used to listen admiringly to his seditious, Mephisto-phelean speeches against western culture, which he had so success-fully defied. It doesn't matter so much whether everything he claimed was true; the fact was that it could have been, and in this way he helped expand the horizons of the possible. He, too, disappeared in the inaccessible jungles of the Amazon. Perhaps he now owns a garage in Brooklyn. But I prefer to think of him as a gray-haired *cacique* and patriarch, lording over fertile lowlands and rubber groves, his happy moments spent rocking his dark-brown grandchildren on his knees, reciting for them the few magical words of German he still remembers.

A family I had befriended felt similarly disillusioned with western civilization. The father, a former judge in Königsberg, wanted to turn his back forever on the treacherous world of machines, racism and persecution. With his wife, children and several mules he traveled into the jungle for several days before stopping. They cleared the land, started building and finally the log cabin was ready and they could begin living the "simple life" – which turned out not to be so simple after all, judging from all the crises and diseases, accidents and attacks they had to endure. And the worst of all was the sheer amount of toil required to secure their daily bread. But they managed, at least until the children grew up and one day declared they'd had enough of the rain forest and wanted to live among people. And that was the end of their parents' playing Robinson Crusoe.

Whatever the case, the turnover in economic activity (the word "profession" doesn't quite fit), was part of the daily routine, although things didn't always happen as smoothly as they did with a man whose name I shall change only slightly if I call him Goldpiece. Although it clearly bordered on the criminal, his career seems to me an accurate illustration of the times. I first made his acquaintance from a distance, in La Paz, where he performed as a rabbi at weddings, circumcisions, bar mitzvahs and funerals. He lost this employment rather suddenly, however, when someone recognized him as a salesman from Berlin. I next encountered the man in another town as I was bicycling to the factory where I was working; a traffic policeman was stopping vehicles from our direction to allow those from the side street to pass. As I waited I realized that this policeman was none other than Goldpiece. Soon thereafter I saw him in a third incarnation. A traditional feature of the South American plaza is the Sunday concert, usually performed by a military band. People promenade around the small bandstand, women in one direction, men in the other. The younger emigrants occasionally took part in this ritual, generally oblivious to the quality of the musical talent. But one Sunday the orchestra was so bad that people noticed. It was being conducted by a lieutenant sporting the cuffs and collars of the musical corps, who, despite his dapper uniform, seemed less than qualified for the job, since long after the musicians had stopped playing, he was still beating the air with his arms and baton. This lieutenant and Goldpiece were one and the same. Later I heard rumors he had been spotted in the *oriente*, the area east of the Andes where few emigrants ventured, which was always portrayed as a land of bizarre creatures and wondrous happenings. Apparently Goldpiece had been seen there in the guise of a Catholic priest, officiating at an execution. But that claim was unsubstantiated, and I can't say whether he ended his days as a Bolivian bishop or a general, and the only reason I'm listing these occupations is because Goldpiece obviously preferred roles that enabled him to exert control over others.

All these examples show a mixture of recklessness and mystery. By way of conclusion I'd like to record one more personal history which strikes me as far less mysterious, since the stages follow one another so logically. This is the story of a friend and comrade-in-fortune, neither a charlatan nor a rogue, but a dyed-in-the-wool Viennese, who couldn't even open his mouth without giving away the district he grew up in. His entire misfortune – or perhaps his good luck (who can say which, today?) – came from having a Jewish father, and so the same political winds blew him to South America that brought the rest of us. His vagaries and professional vicissitudes demonstrate the adaptability and skill needed to survive emigration.

When I met him he was probably about nineteen. His non-Jewish mother followed him out of sheer loyalty into his South American exile, where she supported herself and her son with her skills as a seamstress and Viennese cook. My friend himself went into the furniture business, which meant he took the shipping crates that once contained the refugees' belongings and carpentered them into very rudimentary slatted tables and chairs – which served for many years as our only furnishings. But once the refugees stopped coming and all the crates had been sawed apart and nailed together, he had to find another way to make a living. More skilled and cleverer than I (who was working in a textile factory for next to nothing), he took up producing ornaments for ladies' hats – not that he earned much more, but at least he spared himself the eternal monotony and humiliation of the assembly line. As time went on, though, his bouquets became more and more exuberant and colorful, his feathers more and more fantastical, his berries – or whatever else women were putting on their heads in those days – more and more extravagant. But all these labors seemed in vain, for the feminine sex in all its nameless collectivity stubbornly refused to purchase what he had so artfully composed. And so he moved to the smaller provincial town of Tarija, accompanied only by his mother, who could always count on finding work mending and sewing – at least as long as people preferred not to go around naked. There he found a job which had just opened up – as a baker. After that I lost track of him for a while, especially because my own little ship of life was beginning to yaw and pitch a bit too dangerously.

Years later I caught up with him in a small town, where I was eking out a modest existence as a miner. One day, while climbing one of the steep alleys we knew all too well, I noticed a new store, the proprietor of which turned out to be my old friend. Now he was in the leather business, manufacturing suitcases, briefcases and other articles, a craft this dexterous person had since acquired. In turned out he had contracted malaria in low-lying, subtropical Tarija, which confined him to bed every three days, shaking him mercilessly with feverish chills and leaving him completely exhausted. Since nothing else had worked, the doctors had sent him to the mountains, to Potosí, the highest city in the world. This change in atmosphere really did cure him and allowed him to move his leather trade (for once he kept the same job) to the milder climate of the sleepy, but friendly provincial capital Sucre.

The next time we met was in Antofagasta in northern Chile. Since our last meeting my friend had unlocked the secrets of typewriters and adding machines, and had set about happily cleaning and repairing them, first in Chile, then in Quito, the capital of Ecuador, and finally in the commercial port of Guayaquil. But here his material fortune took a radical turn. I probably don't even need to mention the fact that all his industry and cheerful effort, his talent and skill, his diligence and perseverance had earned him very little. But now things were to change. Some one gave him a commission to sell religious articles – prayer books, rosaries, crucifixes, Christ figures, etc. – which sold so well that he immediately recognized the folly of his earlier, hard-working ways.

To sum up, my friend became a rich man. He moved with his family to another Latin American country, entirely independent, interested only in the stock exchange, the rate of inflation and tax loopholes. Had he relied on his skilled hands, he would have never gone so far. But the religious zeal of the South American people, whom he supplied with entire shiploads of holy things blessed by the Pope, amply bestowed upon him the rewards he had previously been denied. I suspect he might have converted to Catholicism, for the sake of his lucrative business and his good relations with the church dignitaries. Even so, considering the kaleidoscopic changes in his life, who could hold such a small thing as that against him?

All the twists and turns of these biographies reflect the conditions that brought them about, as well as the constraints imposed on individual players. But despite these constrictions there was still enough air to breathe, enough room to move, enough freedom and enough alternatives to permit me also to speak of individual will and responsibility. This shall become much clearer as I go on to describe the person whose motives I understand the best, and whose actions I can account for most exactly, namely myself. The story of my own "professions" and positions, the changes of roles, work and general activity can serve as a good lens through which to view the general emigrant environment. And although at the time I could hardly claim any authorial intent, the same story also reads like a picaresque novel, that is, the tale of a rogue, in which individual initiative and external circumstances are inextricably intertwined.

CHAPTER FIVE
The Roguish Refugee

The picaresque or rogue novel is characterized by its episodic structure, in which the cocky antihero survives one predicament after the next. This he does by adapting to the situation, by taking whatever blows and beatings come his way, by viewing his lot not as tragedy, but as a humorous grotesque. The only link between the loosely connected episodes is the ultimate picture they convey when taken together; the resulting mosaic inevitably depicts a cruel society, stupid, malicious and mendacious. There are many world-views far less insightful.

My ten years of wandering through Bolivia, Chile and Ecuador seem to fit this schema, at least superficially, since my own adventures seem likewise disconnected and present a similarly bleak view of the world. Nevertheless, from the inside things look a little different. I am by nature more melancholic than carefree, and could not help but take everything I saw very seriously. Not that it isn't tempting to recount my experiences as a series of miniature grotesques without greater significance – but that would deny the consciousness with which I reacted to every eventuality. As it was, the circumstances were such that I lived through those years with a split personality; while to all appearances I was a roaming jack-of-all-trades moving from one odd job to the next, in reality I saw myself as something more. Having arrived more or less molded by a specific culture, I felt little allegiance to whatever activity I was engaged in, and at the same time more and more drawn to the life I had been forced to abandon. Objective coercion and subjective will were at constant odds; for a long time it seemed as though the latter didn't stand a chance against the former, until one day a sudden change occurred and the previously one-sided arrangement began to balance out.

In considering the fate of the other emigrants for contrast and comparison, I am hard pressed to offer greater insight. I can recall detailed personal histories with astounding clarity, but the decisive factor, the nuanced consciousness that accompanies, resists, modifies or resigns itself to external events is not subject to observation. And without it no truth is complete, or even halfway so. To the question how, given similar circumstances, people can develop in such very different directions, the invariable answer points to diversity of temperament, vitality, intelligence, and innumerable other factors that undoubtedly do play a role.

Of course if there were no common historical moment, no shared environment, then there would be no point of comparison to begin with, and it would be impossible to speak of war, emigration, etc. as a communal experience. Even so, when several people describe the same shared experience, it often sounds like they're talking about totally unrelated events. It always depends on where, when, and how someone experienced something – not to mention who did the experiencing.

This accounts for the never-ending disagreement about National Socialism. The same regime that uprooted my whole existence appeared to other people – even fairly amicable acquaintances – in an entirely different light, as revealed by the following anecdote. My wife and I were once in northwest Germany visiting a family she had known earlier. On one of the walls in this home we noticed a square in the middle of the wallpaper which was decidedly lighter than the surrounding wallpaper. When we pointed this out to our hostess she blithely informed us: "Oh that's where we used to hang Hitler's portrait of course!" Ignorant of my own past, she put her foot even further into her mouth by adding: "Things were better in those days, weren't they?"

Of all the factors that shaped my experience in South America I shall single out one that is too often overlooked in such cases – my age. The transition to another continent was especially difficult for me because it occurred when I was only sixteen and least ready for such a totally disruptive change. No longer a child and not yet an adult, I had brought with me from Europe the expectations that had been instilled there but never given a chance to find fulfillment.

By the same token I was too fully developed as a person to adapt easily to a new environment. Had I been a little younger – even by a single year – then I might have become a Latin American, at least in the broadest sense, if not a Bolivian (which would have been culturally impossible). On the other hand, if I had been older, with a firm identity and a clear sense of my European heritage, I might have regarded this period of my life as an interlude, a passing adventure – which it actually turned out to be. In that case I would have been able to set definite goals. But as it was I didn't truly belong to either world; I couldn't give up the past and I couldn't claim the future.

To this day I have remained a person who generally feels at home everywhere and nowhere – a dual identity I should like to stress. After all, it would be a bit one-sided to dwell solely on the disadvantages, the rootlessness, the rupture of any religious, national, or philosophical ties. For all the pain of the detaching, the detachment itself offers tremendous intellectual and emotional benefits.

My point is that, while I believe I have managed to make something of my life, experience has taught me to take nothing for granted: for every gain there is a corresponding loss. As we mature we gain in stability – though we must relinquish the dizzying possibilities of youth. And to maintain this steady state we must continue to pay off the sunken costs imposed by the environment. We achieve our identity not only by claiming what is ours, but also by accepting the limits of what is not.

Enough speculation – and now to move on to the next phases of my journey. For the moment I will proceed chronologically, concentrating primarily on my material circumstances; later I will attempt to focus on my inner development, which is a far more difficult task.

In theory, my first job was that of an electrician's apprentice on a construction site. In practice I did whatever work they saw fit to assign me. This included mixing cement, hauling material from one far corner of the site to the other, and cutting long grooves into the concrete where the reinforcement bars were to be laid. It was hard physical labor and by virtue of my own ineptitude I soon won the disapproval of my superiors.

But the work was eye-opening all the same. I learned that an inherent conflict of interest divided the bosses and the workers. The first group was intent on preserving power and paying their workers as little as possible; they valued subservience, prompt and precise execution of all orders and maximum output. The workers in turn pressed for higher wages, respectful treatment and pleasant working conditions; by the same token, they cannot be said to have applied themselves with any assiduity. These differences often smoldered for long periods without anyone saying anything, but they could just as easily erupt into sudden, occasionally violent confrontations.

I also learned certain laws of probability. If your job entailed chiseling high on a ladder, then the chief electrician would invariably show up when you were so tired you could barely lift the heavy hammer. Taking the tools in his own well-rested hands, he would then pound away till the sparks flew – a reproving demonstration of how things ought to be done. Of course if you were really going at it, he wouldn't even be around to notice. Similarly, if you showed up to work on time, there wouldn't be a supervisor in sight, but if you were just two minutes late then you could be sure he'd be standing there holding out his watch, his brows knitted in obvious reproach. And everyone knows it's impossible for a young person to get up in the morning – evidently part of the same flaw in our creation which keeps old people from sleeping. I would even skip breakfast just to gain a few more moments of sleep, although I can't say it was usually worth it, since I would still arrive at work unwashed and out of breath. Then it was only a matter of time before someone would be barking at me for some careless error I had committed in my sleepy state, and the day would be off to a bad start anyway.

My rancor against the 'relations of domination' in this construction job had yet a further cause. I was given – or rather saddled with – the responsibility for the tools used by my group. Every morning I had to distribute the necessary pieces; every evening I was supposed to collect them. Saturday was payday. But before we were paid, an inventory was taken, and if any items were missing their cost was subtracted from my earnings. On occasion this meant that half my weekly pay was withheld, because the tools were expensive and my wage was low – so low in fact that if I hadn't been living with my parents, I could not possibly have sustained myself. How the peons – the menial laborers – were able to survive is a mystery to me.

Aside from these insights I learned nothing about electricity and circuitry, even though that had been the whole point of my employment. As for my future, my parents had decided that an intellectual career was now out of the question, that the famously pragmatic New World as well as our own financial straits called for a more 'practical' vocation. They went so far as to cite an old proverb glorifying manual labor as a golden opportunity – "Handwerk hat einen goldenen Boden" – unaware of the absurdity in applying a pre-industrial European experience to Bolivia. But at that time I was too inexperienced to raise any objections, and so I entered my "apprenticeship" with the electricians. But as I have noted, the tasks assigned me had nothing to do with mastering that particular trade, and I'm sure I could have worked there for decades without ever mastering anything 'electrical.' The whole experience haunts me to this very day, for whenever some electrical problem proves to be beyond my ability, my wife taunts me with the words "And I thought you were an electrician!" But here, too, I have learned to practice stoic resignation.

But none of these excuses amount to a true explanation of why I was bound to fail in these endeavors and foil my parents' efforts to prepare me for the new, pragmatic world. In actuality they were the ones who had sown the kernel of my resistance before I ever knew what a sledgehammer was, in the form of repeated threats that equated poor performance in school with the fate of manual labor. And now that fate had become the crassest reality.

Nor was that all. In addition to these verbal admonitions, my parents had from early on impressed upon me that I was too clumsy for manual labor, and had done so systematically, and unambiguously. Whenever I would reach for a hammer to drive in a nail, or a wrench to loosen a nut, my mother would immediately take it away, scoffing at my awkwardness. I'd be sure to smash my thumb or break something, I should leave these tasks to other, more able persons and kindly return to my schoolwork. This went on so long that I wound up believing in my own incompetence, and this conception of self augured poorly for an electrical or technical career of any kind. No wonder that as soon as the initial attraction of the exotic world of mortar and lime had disappeared, I began to arrive at my place of work with nothing but repugnance. How laughable it must have seemed, and yet how symptomatic of my contradictory situation, that during our breaks I tried to awaken an awareness for 'higher things' among the Indians squatting along the walls, chewing their cocaine leaves.

"What's your name?" I would ask with secret pedagogical intent, and if my interlocutor answered, "Cervantes," I would treat him to a few facts about the famous writer of this name. Or if his name were Murillo, I would talk about Spanish painting and lecture him on the responsibilities that befell anyone bearing such a glorious name. At the time, I was sorely vexed by the dopey, half-embarrassed grins with which my "pupils" greeted these noble efforts – though I ought to have admired them for putting up with such nonsense. In all probability they were far too high even to guess what the gringo boy wanted from them. Sadly, my cultural and historical disquisitions had no effect on the course of events.

Finally it became unthinkable for me to continue in the construction business: I had grown utterly disgusted with the work, and – equally to the point – my superiors were beginning to requite my feelings. So I kept my eyes open for another occupation, and as soon as something that seemed more suited to my sensibilities came along, I gladly gave up my calling as an electrician, without regretting the lost chance to make such a tangible contribution to Bolivian prosperity.

One day after work I splashed some water on my neck, threw

on a clean shirt and hurried to the other side of town in search of the *Instituto de Arqueología y Prehistoria*, because the legendary director Arturo P. needed an assistant and private secretary. The sun was setting by the time I reached the house adorned with ornaments from the Tiahuanaco Culture. An old Aymara Indian wearing a striped poncho, a cap with long earflaps and heavy sandals, answered the door and looked at me inquiringly. Hesitating because I didn't know how well the man spoke Spanish, I stated my query. He responded that he himself was the professor I was looking for, and led me into a room that immediately fell to my liking – a library filled with books up to the ceiling. Tables and floor were littered with piles of papers, some handwritten, some printed, opened newspapers, pictures and drawings, diagrams, and all types of books. Between pre-Inca bowls and vases lay a yellowed skull. And rising above all of this scientific disorder was a gigantic globe, which seemed to suggest the universality of the intellect that presided here. The old man, whose weathered brown skin had made me take him for an Indian, asked me in a laconic and, as it seemed to me, somewhat surly manner about my sadly feeble knowledge and abilities. Then he inquired where I came from, and no sooner did I answer than the interview took a sudden turn. Switching from Spanish to the purest Viennese dialect, Arturo P. asked me: "In wölche Schul' san'S denn 'gangen?" – "What school did you go to?" Evidently my gymnasium passed the test, and I was deemed fit for the job of office-boy, for he grew friendly and explained what he expected of me without further ado. Of course my monthly income would be no more than what I had been earning as a construction worker – about ten dollars – but he would provide me with meals, which I was to take together with him. In addition, he offered me a room: he wanted me to be available at all times.

I believe I would have accepted the offer even without these additional benefits, so fascinated was I by the mysterious things I had seen. In any event I started back home to my parents, drunk with the success of my petition, the promise of liberation from my penal servitude, and the colorful projections for the future opening before me. The only thing I wasn't sure about was whether my parents would allow it — after all, I had never lived under a stranger's roof.

But it turned out that my parents had encountered some new developments as well. Because of his previous experience in the textile industry, my father had found a good position in an English textile mill shortly after our arrival, and now the whole company was to move to the aspiring provincial capital, Cochabamba. My new job played into this plan perfectly. My parents would move and settle down more permanently than they had in La Paz, and I would join them later if necessary. In the meantime, I would attend to the duties assigned me by Arturo P.

The evening arrived when it was time to say good-bye to my parents, who were leaving the following morning. Instead of responding with my usual irritation, I was actually moved by my mother's advice about what to eat and wear. My father himself said little. I shook hands with both of them and started down the long road to the house where my room was already waiting. The stars spread out above me, as life seemed to stretch before me in the darkness, impenetrable. Shimmering in the clear mountain sky, they were completely untouched by exhaust fumes and unsullied by pollution, but also — so it seemed to me — cold and unaccommodating. A great anxiety gripped my heart; for the first time, I was setting out without my parents, completely on my own, responsible for myself, reliant on myself, in a strange and sinister land where I didn't know a soul. I saw my parents again soon enough; I often lived with them in subsequent years and was part of their household. But it was never again the same; on that night I had to take my inner leave of them. In the short span of half an hour, along a road lit only by the stars, and hemmed in all around by the gloomy mountains, I passed irrevocably into adulthood. I don't think I should feel ashamed that I made no effort to stop the tears from streaming down my cheeks; after all, in one hand I was carrying a suitcase, and in the other a satchel. A few days later I turned seventeen.

My time with Arturo P. proved both exciting and amazingly

enriching. My tasks were varied: I was a kind of attendant-at-large within the diverse realms that comprised his kingdom. I had to order and catalog his library, and inventory new additions. Inevitably I absorbed some of the facts contained in these works concerning the natural history of South America, as well as a general knowledge of historical and pre-historical South American cultures. I also gained a more specific familiarity with the Tiahuanaco culture at Lake Titicaca, which was the subject of a series of writings and pictorials published by Arturo P. His daring theories matched his spasmodic, choleric disposition and from what I could tell were highly contested by the guild – especially the ones concerning the age of the ruins. Using various astronomical and meteorological calculations, he estimated these to be ten thousand years old, while most scholars spoke more soberly of two thousand. I have to confess, however, that the two or three shelves of Arturo P.'s collection that interested me most were the ones labeled somewhat anachronistically as "belles lettres." Night after night, under the light of a naked electric bulb, I greedily devoured volume after motley volume, from travel books by Sven Hedin and Richard Haliburton to novels by John Knittel and Adrienne Thomas.

But I had many tasks in addition to the library work. I had to write letters, read newspapers, clip articles, and excerpt sections from Spanish, French and German treatises and translate them as needed. In addition, I had one special task which I had to perform almost daily. Don Arturo, as he was generally called, was busy writing a work with the working title *Nariz y Carácter* (Nose and Character) – no doubt in reference to Otto Weininger's notorious *Sex and Character*. Impulsive as he was, it happened not infrequently that he would roust me from my sleep at four in the morning in order to dictate some new passages. These methods did little to incline me towards the project, to which I contributed with the greatest reluctance that could be expected from a stenographer. Although I lacked any prior knowledge, I developed a deep skepticism towards this physiognomic study influenced by Cesare Lombroso and Max Nordau. Without the slightest idea of any intellectual or historical interconnections, I found myself rebelling against the basic thesis that one could discern a person's character by looking at the nose or any body part. My nascent humanism was appalled by P.'s efforts; I watched disapprovingly as he measured the bony skulls in his possession, recording their features according to information gleaned from all kinds of charts. I still shudder with repugnance whenever I hear expressions such as "dolichocephalic" or "brachycephalic" which were constantly on his lips. Most of all I disliked the vicious anti-Semitic outbursts that punctuated all his talk.

Secretly I considered the treatise he was so proudly developing as nothing more than hogwash, although now I recognize how important it was for my development. Besides acquainting me with a chapter of intellectual history, it helped shape my fundamental skepticism towards mono-causal explanations of the world, a skepticism that later served me well in my own work. This was the first experience that eventually led me to see through the entire scholarly apparatus that surrounded us and to recognize it as the pseudo-scientific charlatanism it was. Of course at that time my perception grew more by intuition than insight, although my doubts did gain an indirect confirmation, by way of an impressive counterexample. Paul Rivet, the famous director of the *Musée de l'homme* in Paris had come to La Paz to conduct some studies and give a series of lectures on the original settlement of America. As a guest of Don Arturo he stayed in the same house where I was living. As it was my job to run the slide projector, I was allowed to attend these lectures and I learned for the first time how a truly self-critical scientist pursues his research. Proceeding with great caution, Paul Rivet built on linguistic and technical correlations to expound the idea that long ago, when the continents were closer together, forbears of the South American Indians had crossed to that continent from Asia. This they had done by way of a southern chain of islands similar to the northern Aleutians. Needless to say, Arturo P. supported an opposing theory, according to which the Americans had originated on the continent and were therefore a separate and independent race. Using great tact, lest he offend his host, Paul Rivet made clear that for methodological reasons he did not think much of Don Arturo's hypotheses. That he included me in these discussions was no doubt due to my increasingly bold attempts to converse with the foreigner in his own tongue. Perhaps he also sensed how lost and lonely this young person was.

As it happened I was granted another meeting with him nearly twenty years later, just a few months before his death. In the *Musée de l'homme* at the Place Trocadero in Paris, I found out his address and went to look him up in his apartment. He had long since retired. I asked that I be announced simply as an acquaintance from South America, without any mention of my name. My appearance had changed greatly since our last meeting; not only was I then in my mid-thirties; I had also grown an ample beard. And yet he recognized me after studying me for half a minute with his penetrating gaze: "Vous êtes le jeune secrétaire Autrichien de M.P. que je connaissait en 1939 ou 40." Paul Rivet was a man to whom others mattered.

Arturo P. might not have been an important scholar, but he was a great adventurer, and these are probably much rarer. And he carried on his research with the spontaneous passion befitting the true adventurer: he took the greatest pleasure in digging up colorful tidbits and making definitive finds, he tended toward monomania in his theories, and he always drew unexpected conclusions. A better-known representative of this type was Schliemann. Such men have a drive that streams out from the unconscious scarcely checked by rational faculties, a passion that resists being channeled by professional or institutional norms. The result is that such characters often take on an aura of charlatanism that spills over into other aspects of life, until these, too, are rendered suspect in the eyes of the bourgeois. One might imagine Paracelsus as such a person. I will refrain from judging whether Don Arturo had that kind of stature, but what he had to offer in any case sufficed to make a lasting impression on his young co-worker and private secretary. The longer I lived with him, the more I discovered earlier traces of his richly variegated life, although he never took me into his confidence. One day, for example, I ran across a document attesting to the fact he had once been a captain in the Swedish fleet. How had this Viennese engineer (here too there were documents attesting to the authenticity of this title) managed to bring about this incredible transformation? Everyone in La Paz knew he had later commanded a Bolivian gunboat on the Rio Acre during the war against Brazil at the turn of the century. Other documents showed he had been decorated as a captain of science as well: I remember reading one certificate proclaiming that Kaiser William II had named him an honorary Professor of Geography, and another one declaring him member of the Royal Society. He was highly regarded in Bolivia, where he had set up a whole empire: not only was he director of the archeological institute, but also of the museum of prehistory, which he himself had founded. Adjacent to our house was a brick factory of which he was the owner, and where he occasionally intervened as a troubleshooter and managerial consultant. He further owned some porcelain clay mines in the country's interior, and an experimental farm near the Desaguadero river equipped with a new irrigation system. There he hoped to teach Bolivians modern techniques of husbandry and the cultivation of an Andean grain called quinoa. Although he was constantly fighting over financial matters with his sons, his employees and his servants, he either owned or had once owned large sums of money; it was rumored that he had often loaned the government high sums, among other things for printing the first Bolivian stamps. Ministers of state did indeed frequent the house, and – as I learned for myself from overhearing his telephone conversations – there is no doubt he was considered a man of influence. It was through him – he interrupted himself in his dictation one day to tell me – that he had learned of the imminent demise of Germán Busch. "They" had had enough of him and his nonsense and would soon be getting rid of him. When soon afterwards the country was informed of his sensational 'suicide,' I refused to believe that that had been the cause of death.

Don Arturo was said to be equally active in the erotic domain, and in spite of his age there was a lot of gossiping about his deeds. Many Indians with decidedly Caucasian features were rumored to be his children, and there was no question that one grown daughter of obvious Indian descent enjoyed complete recognition and came to the house often. To my great confusion, she was married to a heavily-accented Bavarian named Sepp; and she liked to tell of the stir that her Aymaran nanny had aroused in Munich when she wore her native garb. I was also told that one day long before my arrival, a young man calling himself Carlo had shown up claiming to be Don Arturo's son from Naples. The alleged father supposedly asked this Carlo in what year he was born, and after a quick reckoning on his fingers confessed that that might indeed be the case – he had in fact been in Naples at the time in question. Carlo was then taken into the house and given work in the tile factory; but after a while he disappeared as suddenly as he had arrived.

When I was living with him he saw only two sons, both of whom lived in the adjacent house and who behaved exactly like legitimate offspring and future heirs. They quarreled enormously with each other and with their father, always about money, as far as I could tell. But I benefited from the sons too: they took me along on all kinds of trips, and in this way I got to know some of the surrounding countryside, including Mt. Chacaltaya, where they had built a ski hut, probably the highest in the world. A ski team, the *club andino boliviano* was established and a Bolivian chauffeur who had never before been on skis won the first race. He probably owed his success to the fact that as the sole native participant, he was the only one able to withstand the enormous altitude – the mountain must be some 5,000 meters above sea level.

Given my employer's suspicious and choleric temperament, I had no small difficulty living with him, especially considering the long hours that often stretched on into the evening. I don't want to blame only him for all the irritations and quarrels. Considering my own frame of mind in those days, I must have been an impertinent co-worker, not uncooperative perhaps, but not very able either, with an awkward manner and fairly sluggish in the execution of my tasks. And underneath an apparent modesty and diligence I harbored the egocentricity that is common in unfulfilled youth. We must have made a curious twosome, sitting together at dinner, emptying our plates mostly in silence: the grumpy, irascible old bachelor and the curious boy eager to absorb everything. A quiet meal could turn suddenly into a dreadful commotion if Don Arturo didn't like the food or raised some other mysterious objection. Then he would jump up and nearly throttle to death the Indian woman who prepared our meals in a kitchen that made a mockery of even the most rudimentary hygiene. Then he would bustle loudly about the same kitchen and cook something himself, which proved equally inedible. The cook carried on her back a child swaddled into a bundle that was constantly dripping with some foul-smelling stuff. A number of squeaking guinea pigs had free run of the kitchen; they were Bolivian delicacies, and Don Arturo must have known exactly how many there were, because if just one was missing, he started boxing the cook's ears until she confessed to eating it. Whether she was telling the truth or simply bowing to the circumstances is hard to say. On occasion Don Arturo would rant and rave through the house wearing a dinner jacket from the waist up and otherwise in his underwear, fuming that someone had stolen the trousers he was intending to wear to the banquet. He was extremely suspicious and felt himself surrounded by thieves, and I can't say he was very mistaken, since everything had a habit of disappearing: clothes, cuff links, valuables and money, invariably just when he needed them most. Sometimes he even focused his paranoid rage on me. Well aware of my own passion, he constantly suspected me of filching his books. Once I caught him searching my room when he thought I was out, and just before I left his house forever, he had me open my suitcase to see what riches I was pilfering this time. If I happened to make a mistake or fail to do something he would show great resentment and curse at me or berate me with stinging remarks. On one such occasion he flung an insult at me intended to hit me particularly hard: "No wonder the world doesn't like you people." He meant the Jews, even though or perhaps precisely because – as it was rumored everywhere – he himself was of Jewish descent. By the same token, an occasional sign of kindness or concern poked through his rough manner. But I was too young to understand that kind of hidden good will.

It's hard to say how long our association would have lasted in spite of these disagreements, and what form it would have taken, had not my parents called on me one day to join them again. They wrote that they had rented a spacious apartment, and that my father was earning a little more now, so I could live more comfortably with them. They especially praised the mild, balmy climate of Cochabamba, in contrast to the higher capital La Paz, where July and August were so harsh and cold that puddles would freeze overnight. The new climate promised to be liberating in more ways than one.

Meanwhile I had begun to realize that I would neither learn a trade nor make my career at Don Arturo's, and so I left without regret. I have described him so extensively with the idea that colorful personality might help illustrate the world we inhabited. Where but Bolivia at that time could have given rise to such a willful and multitalented individuality? Where else would such adventurous unconventionality have been met with great respect? In his comical, crazy and incredibly animated household, I learned a great deal about human nature and the ways of the world. I also formed an indelible impression of how much an extraordinary individual can shape his identity. I sensed this vaguely at the time and still emphasize it today. And if the good ship *Orduña* was my first university, then it's only fair to call Don Arturo P.'s *Instituto de Arqueología y Prehistoria* my second one.

Like La Paz, Cochabamba was affected by the tropical climate of the Andes. Day and night were nearly of equal length; the nights were cool, the days warm, and there were only two seasons: a dry one and a rainy one. But the lower altitude (Cochabamba lay 1,500 meters lower than La Paz) was immediately evident by virtue of the lush vegetation, the agricultural abundance and the heavenly mildness of the air. When I arrived, the plaza was being paved for the first time. With seven or eight short streets radiating from its center, this was the commercial and topographic center of the geometrically designed city. A few taxis waited on one side of the square; there were only a handful of private cars in the entire city, which was connected with La Paz by rail, and with the rest of the country by truck. I mention all of this to illustrate how idyllic and how untouched by technology this place of asylum was to a few hundred emigrants. As in La Paz, we encountered a native population, though this time it was made up mostly of Quechuas, a different tribe with different hats and ponchos. There were also the same foreign colonies: the 'austriacos,' really Yugoslavs, who had cornered the hardware market, and the 'turcos,' Arabs from Syria, Lebanon and Palestine who generally traded in textiles. There were also the Germans who had settled there much earlier than we had and who, with some friendly exceptions, were as hostile towards us as the ones in La Paz had been. But because this latter group was for the most part hard-working and upright, and because they knew the land and in many cases had married into the Bolivian bourgeoisie, they were very well-liked. This was in contrast to the Anglo-Saxons, who were considered arrogant, who never mixed with the native population, learned no Spanish and left the country as soon as they had filled their pockets. The influence of the German expatriates did no small amount of harm to the German speaking exiles, at least for the duration of the war, although this assertion cannot easily be proven. There are stories of the uneven success with which diplomatic representatives from Germany established peace and harmony between these very divided groups in different Latin American countries after the war.

So it was that the refugees from Hitler were once again left to their own devices. A few had jobs: one repaired bicycles; two drove taxis; most of them opened sundry small shops and businesses, such as dry-cleaning services, shoe stores, clothing boutiques and tailor shops, grocery stores, and also luncheonettes, inns and restaurants whose clients were in the main the refugees themselves. They established a club with a space for gatherings, religious services and athletic activities. Overcoming the isolation I had experienced in La Paz, which had begun to reach neurotic proportions, I began to participate a little in the social life the refugees carved out for themselves. There was even a youth group: we played soccer and Ping-Pong, exchanged stamps and met in cafés bearing such glamorous European names as "Pigalle,"

"Maxim," and *"Danubio Azul"* – "The Blue Danube" – which featured musicians recruited from our own ranks playing popular movie tunes as well as excerpts from Lehár operettas. We met at the post office, the cinema, and at the plaza twice a day for news. We would go out for a glass of beer, and we romanced with the girls. In this way I was able to recover some of my youth that year in Cochabamba – entirely in the most conventional sense.

But our most important leisure activity was talking. Whenever two refugees got together, they would start up, which immediately drew in a third and a fourth, and soon another lively debate on any number of favorite topics would be underway – for the discussions always revolved around the same things. Even though many had only a modest intellectual background, each had lived through something monstrous and had in some way moved beyond himself. Everyone had something extraordinary to tell: the horrors of the concentration camps, the madness of Kristallnacht, betrayals by friends and neighbors, but also instances of uncalculated help-fulness and even heroic resistance to Hitler. Sooner or later, the talk would always turn to the question of German guilt, the different reactions of the various social classes and regions in Germany. One swore that it was the Bavarians, the other that it was the Prussians who were the main perpetrators of the evil; one thought that Hamburg, another that Berlin was the actual bastion of resistance to the regime. There were those who exonerated the bulk of the German population of any responsibility and declared their unshakable allegiance to it; and others who thoroughly condemned all Germans whether at home or abroad and the language to boot. Especially popular were debates between Austrians and Germans, for there were plenty of both, on their essential similarity or difference, on the extent of their contribution to fascism and on the role played by Hitler. Some attributed a great deal of importance to the fact that Hitler was Austrian; others felt it was significant that he had come to naught in Austria and didn't achieve prominence until he went to Germany. Many absurd claims as well as wise observations were made about German history, national character and collective guilt, and most of the arguments that preoccupied the public after 1945 were anticipated here.

Because they experienced the course of events personally, these otherwise ordinary refugees were far more aware than their contemporaries, who were still living according to their old ways, generally unawares. And even though few were politically minded, they all became profound pundits in the cafés, representing the most astounding range of ideologies.

Another inexhaustible topic concerned the emigration itself. Endless stories were told of visas secretly obtained, of great fortunes smuggled abroad, of illegal border crossings and duped guards and of adventurous escapes across Spain and Portugal, across Poland, Siberia and Japan. Even more common were the tales of worldwide bureaucratic insensitivity, of internment camps in France and England. Every conceivable individual scenario was represented; taken collectively, these stories were history in the making, as told by the living witnesses to extreme circumstances and exceptional situations.

Naturally the war loomed large as well. Various amateur strategists held competing courts, which followed every turn of fortune, no matter how insignificant. No event was too small to escape their notice, and they kept us on edge with their ongoing explanations of military and political developments, their short-term prophecies and their long-term prognoses. Naturally there were lofty-minded geopolitical experts as well, who considered themselves above such mere military reporting, and generously offered their own expansive views on how the world should be redesigned.

While the refugees had all acclaimed the outbreak of war – they saw no other way of ridding the world of their archenemy – the first years of the conflict did little to encourage or console them. One country after the other fell prey to the Nazi juggernaut, and there was no dearth of doomsayers who were predicting the imminent conquest of South America. Our own sorrow turned to despair at the news that Paris had fallen; we saw this as the subjugation of European culture, to which all of us, despite our

124

differences, felt some kind of bond. From all this unremitting talk, where emotions masqueraded as opinions and individual hopes and fears contributed more to the debate than any political analysis, I learned a great deal – most of all how not to talk about mankind and its history.

But all of this was going on in the margins of my life, while my daily work remained the central focus. I was employed in the same textile factory as my father; as an assistant in the weaving department, I had to draw up silk, cotton and synthetic threads on so-called 'trees' according to precise and predetermined patterns. The 'trees' were then in turn placed in the looms. So and so many threads, so and so many revolutions churned out by means of a hand-crank, from eight to five, from Monday to Saturday.

In the end I proved no more gifted for this work than I had for electrical construction. My threads would get crossed; I would wind up tangling them even more until I had tied the whole apparatus into a horrible matted knot, so that my coworkers constantly had to come running to my aid. But even these dreadful jams brought some excitement – as well as the fear of being discovered by the 'higher-ups' – that was far better than the dull and deadening routine when things went smoothly. I suffered unbelievably under its enforced mechanization: I couldn't tear myself away from my book after lunch; I couldn't get out of bed in the morning; and the worst thing of all was realizing the weekend was over and it was back to the same old grind. No one spoke any longer of a 'vocation' or 'career' for me; Bolivia was obviously not the place to realize these concepts, and this applied not just to me but to the majority of refugees. All of us lived from hand to mouth, work was just a question of earning money: why should I be an exception? On top of everything, my pay for this drudgery was depressingly slight: fifteen Bolivianos a day, when you paid seven for a halfway decent lunch and one for a glass of beer (the current rate was eighty to a dollar). Had I not been living with my parents, I would have sunk into poverty; and to this day I can't understand how my Bolivian coworkers kept themselves above water. The wretchedness and subservience of the workers, the exploitation of their labor and the mentally stultifying activities to which they were subjected, combined with the comfortable lifestyle of the company owners and officers, greatly radicalized my thinking and feeling. And so the split in my consciousness continued to develop in this phase as well. A novel by Ganghofer could move me to tears, despite its obsequiously false portrait of the Wilhelminian empire, simply because it offered me a glimpse of the Europe I had lost. At the same time, I pored over the writings of Marx and Bukharin, dreaming of world revolutions and just societies.

In the middle of the year my father lost his job. For a few months we were able to live off our savings, albeit very frugally. For a short time, my father considered moving on to Ecuador, where a relative of ours had ended up. But without money we couldn't get a visa. In September of 1940, after several unsuccessful attempts to find another job in Cochabamba, my father decided to move a third time, to Sucre, a town which was even smaller, more provincial and less modern than Cochabamba. He hoped to earn a living there by manufacturing shirts, a new enterprise for the isolated regions of the department of Chuquisaca.

By selling off the last valuables my mother had brought from Europe, my father was able to purchase two sewing machines, which he boxed up along with the rest of our belongings. After everything had been loaded onto the truck, we all climbed aboard – my parents up front next to the driver, myself high up between boxes and bundles – and set off on our journey. The trip was supposed to take only a few days, but it turned into a series of adventures that stretched out over weeks. I would like to include a partial log of our travels in order to impress upon the reader how civilized the 'cities' really were, no matter how modest their comforts, which the refugees so disdainfully scorned, by constantly comparing their new lot with what they had lost. In reality, these towns were veritable enclaves of civilization, islands in the otherwise untamed Andean world.

At first everything went well enough: the lovely landscape flying by, the dust settling back behind us. Our first mishap occurred after our first long stop, at a major crossroads and reloading point. Our driver explained that he was no longer going to Sucre, but to Santa Cruz – I don't remember what excuse he gave. Our pleas and entreaties were in vain: our boxes were unloaded and we were evicted, like so many orphans in the middle of nowhere. To make matters worse, not one of the many trucks stopping for gas was heading for Sucre.

We looked for a place to pass the night. Apart from the gas station with its rusty pump, however, there were only a few adobe huts perched on a cliff. We had no choice but to stay in the only *tambo* in town, a harshly primitive hostel with small holes for bedrooms and a courtyard full of horses and mules, as well as an occasional mangy dog or stray cat. Dangling from a kind of clothesline were a few scraps of meat – the so-called charqui – that had been hung to dry: each piece was covered with a thick swarm of flies. It wasn't until a few desolate days later that we found a truck willing to take us to Sucre.

In the mountains we met with only the usual delays: on one occasion a breakdown forced our driver and his assistant to make precarious repairs at the edge of an abyss; on another we spent hours waiting for a pass to open; some nights we spent in indescribable mountain eyries. And of course we had our share of near collisions with oncoming vehicles. But the main adventure began in a rough gravel riverbed that at one point became indistinguishable from the road itself. Bestrewn as it was with small boulders, such a stretch would be considered impassable in most countries. The river itself was more a stream that wound through the gorge, narrow and erratic.

Suddenly the sky darkened and it started to rain. The rainy season had not yet begun and this unexpected shower seemed to herald its approach. Apart from the fact that I was getting soaked on my high perch, I didn't think too much about it. After a while, however, I noticed that we were doubling our speed: something had obviously gotten into our driver. The riddle was soon cleared up, though; scarcely an hour after the first raindrops had fallen, we heard behind us a loud rushing and roaring. Fortunately the driver managed to maneuver the truck to safety on a high gravel mound, while muddy brown torrents went raging around us on either side.

But the rain wore on, and before long the river was foaming up the steep canyon walls, lapping at the wheels of our vehicle and threatening to wash it into the floods. We spent two days in the middle of these furious elements, with nothing to eat but a goat that had been part of the freight. Without regard for the owner, we slaughtered the animal, spitted it on a branch and roasted it. Eventually the water receded a bit and the truck made a hair-raising ford to a flatter section of bank. It turned out the deluge had caught us just as we were approaching the end of the canyon. Forging ahead was out of the question – half the road had been torn away by the flood. We made our way to a nearby village, wretched beyond words. The region was infested with malaria, and a feverish victim of the disease lay in almost every hut. We found shelter in the only concrete building, a school, and we set ourselves up between the benches. There was hardly anything to eat, and we had to wait for days until the road was repaired. Finally we were able to continue. At long last, after a harrowing drive on a road blocked at every turn by mudslides and eroded shoulders, we arrived, emaciated and exhausted, in the little town of Sucre. To us it seemed a welcome haven indeed – friendly, cultured and comfortable.

According to the constitution, Sucre was the capital not only of the department of Chuquisaca, but of the whole country. The inhabitants, with a local patriotism peculiar to them, insisted on this designation. With every broadcast, the radio announcer invariably made known that his station was located in the "capital of Bolivia." But La Paz had long ago usurped this role, slowly but surely relocating various governmental branches, and all the foreign consulates, embassies and international representatives had long since moved. Only the supreme court retained its seat there – the last remnant of an older glory. Sucre was a quiet, remote country town of colonial stamp and the tiniest, sleepiest place I have ever lived in, which I again did for about a year. But the isolation stemmed more from its remoteness; small as it was, Sucre was still the biggest shopping and cultural center within a hundred kilometers.

Even so, about twenty or twenty-five other refugees had found refuge from Hitler here as well – Jews and non-Jews, Germans, Austrians and Bohemians – where, as elsewhere, they responded to the new economic realities by setting up shops and small businesses. One even ran a hacienda an hour's walk out of town, where you could go for Sunday dinner and find yourself in a veritable microcosm of the refugees' world. Before long I had gotten to know them all so well that to this day I can still recite their life stories. And we were even more at each other's mercy than elsewhere, since the distance separating us from the Bolivian families was also greater. Deeply entrenched in the habits and mentality of an earlier age, still carrying on the spirit of Spanish colonialism, these people were inaccessible to us. The expression "time stood still" applied to Sucre better than anywhere else in the world, at least so it seemed to me, because absolutely nothing happened there and time, after all, is the experience of events.

And yet even in this simplest and most harmless of places our hitherto dire financial straits became desperate. The three of us shared one room; the communal toilet was across the hall. We rented a nearby shop (everything in Sucre was 'nearby') with a workroom in back where my father set up his sewing machines. My mother bought a few groceries, and that was it; I don't think we had enough left even to buy a newspaper. We painted the name of our new firm on an old board: "Elite" – a name that stood in glaring contradiction to our own circumstances – and hung it outside our new establishment. On the shelves we placed two bolts of poplin intended for the shirts. Then we sat back and waited, which gave the whole enterprise a strange feeling of helplessness. But rescue arrived in the form of our landlord, a cultivated man who was once the Bolivian ambassador to Belgium, and who ordered two shirts – no doubt out of neighborliness and to assure good business relations. My father cleverly secured our next meals by asking for a "down payment." In retrospect I have to admire the relaxed attitude my father displayed during all those dark days; his apparent confidence protected my mother and me from the worst

anxieties. And from then on, his business affairs began to look up
– never again did he come so close to catastrophe.

To properly fill out the store's display stands, we began to sell
other garments in addition to the shirts: underwear, shorts and
eventually anything and everything that might serve as clothing. In
this way we built up enough trade to keep my parents satisfactorily
provided for the duration of their stay in Sucre.

But the quaint charms of somnolent Sucre had little to offer
me. I was now eighteen years old, and earning my own living was
as much a psychological as an economic necessity; after all,
whether you like it or not, the world measures you according to
what you make, and like most people, my self-esteem depended on
this recognition.

Nevertheless all of my efforts were in vain. The only local
industry of any significance was a cigarette factory. But there was
no work for me there; as I might have guessed from the opera
Carmen, they only hired female workers. These were furthermore
so badly paid that they were forced to moonlight, as everyone
knew, by practicing a different vocation, which was both highly
popular and, paradoxically, not very highly esteemed. My guest
performance in our family business was equally unsuccessful.
Since I had little else to offer, I was supposed to make myself
useful as a salesman. But I either couldn't or wouldn't engage in
the sales talk and the haggling that played such an important role
in the local business world. On the contrary, I was indignant when
a potential client interrupted my perusal of Bukharin's *ABC of
Communism* or Engels' treatise on the family, which I studied with
the same rabid intensity as a religious fanatic would the Bible. The
customer would ask for some vulgar material object, let's say a
girdle, which I would toss on the counter with no attempt to hide
my genuine disgust at her and at my degrading job. I did what I
could to discourage any further transactions in the hopes – often
quickly fulfilled – of soon returning to my theory of alienation and
surplus value.

The brooding animosity I chose to show toward business led,
I fear, to tension between myself and my diligent father, who

suffered less from the contradictions of capitalism than from the contrariness of his own flesh and blood. From the workroom in the back, he began to keep a cautious eye on my actions – or should I say inaction. More and more often he would retrieve a customer who had left the store disgruntled, and conclude a new sale satisfactory to both parties – while I watched on with undisguised disdain.

Obviously this could not continue and so it was decided that I should look for a job outside of the family business. Nothing really appropriate presented itself, but as this seemed the year for me to engage in commerce, I found employment as a debt-collector. The creditor, a local merchant, armed me with the records of payment (the customers paid by installment); my job was to go from house to house calling the delinquent debtors to order. In return I was to receive a generous percentage of whatever I collected. But in all the weeks I pursued this depressing business I didn't pocket a cent. Doors would either not open or would slam in my face; I was showered with verbal abuses and given every kind of excuse – but no money.

In the light of all these failures, I finally decided to heed the advice that was being offered from all sides, which meant becoming a traveling salesman. In the more remote villages, and especially the mining towns, there were supposedly no stores at all, and even I should be able to dispose of even the most outlandish white elephant at a profit. I was commissioned with a selection of items which could hardly be said to have reflected the latest fashion: dresses, scarves, shirts, ties, pants, shoes, pajamas, hats, socks, shaving instruments, soap, toothbrushes, every kind of toiletry – in short, all the superfluous objects people generally agree are absolutely essential. All these were tossed into a crate and I took off on the train in the direction of Uyuni, in the Bolivian highlands where the lead and zinc mines are located.

The entire undertaking was a disaster from start to finish. I must confess here and now that I haven't a whit of commercial talent. What's more, I had already had ample proof of my ineptitude and was to be punished dearly for violating my intuition.

It all started with the fact that my box of goods was too heavy and too large. For the sake of convenience, I ought to have redistributed the things into several small packages; even then I would have needed five or six Indians to transport my oversized cargo. But when I arrived at daybreak there wasn't a soul in sight. An icy wind was blasting across the station and I stood next to my crate, at a loss as to what to do next. With my head lowered, I fought my way through the sandstorm and crossed a desolate area into the dismal town. The temperature was arctic; even the pond on the plaza had frozen over. The place looked abandoned: the only living thing to be seen was a duck-like bird, and even it was hiding its beak underneath its wing. But still that bird was better than nothing.

I see I have to change my approach to the story. Instead of listing detail after agonizing detail, which have lost little of their horror even after fifty years, I shall condense things – especially considering it's up to the reader's imagination to supply the most important aspect of all, namely, the sullen state of mind I was in.

In any event: I finally found a few men who loaded my crate onto a truck, and several hours later I sat holed up with my things in a miserable hotel, the only one serving the Pulacayo mine, one of the largest in the country.

Now the question was how to sell off all my wares? I tried everything. With several yards of cloth draped over my shoulder, and a suitcase hanging from my arm, I went from door to door, peddling my treasures to the wives of the men employed in the mine. I fashioned a cardboard placard, on which I announced in artful lettering the arrival of the most sensational and elegant selection of wares in room 11, Hotel Pulacayo, and encouraged everyone to spread the news by singing it to the tune of the celebrated hit "*Allá en el rancho grande.*"

I attached this placard to my back and wended my way through the streets of the sorrowful little town. Like the Pied Piper of Hamelin, I attracted a long train of village boys who ran behind me singing at the top of their lungs, "*allá en la pieza once, allá donde vivía...*" – "up there in room eleven, out where I used to live...."

I also found a box, which I filled with scarves, socks, combs and belts, arranging them as attractively as possible. Thus accoutered, I stood on the marketplace trying to lure passers-by into stopping to admire and – hopefully – purchase my things. But all my efforts proved in vain. No one wanted anything I had to offer, except contraceptives, for which there was no lack of clientele. I wished I'd had more of them! But people so shunned all my other treasures I began to suspect I was the victim of some police order or other conspiracy.

I was despondent. I was cold. One morning as I was washing up I lost a tooth. I developed a bladder infection and a lingering cough. The only warm spot in town was a movie theater, a miserable shack which I frequented every evening, staying for both showings of Disney's *Snow White and the Seven Dwarfs*. I must have seen that movie over two dozen times and to this day I continue to baffle people with my prodigious knowledge of this film's most minute details.

But I still couldn't get rid of my merchandise, and I no longer had the strength to lug the crate, intact as it was, halfway across the Altiplano back to Sucre. Even so, my survival depended on my leaving – so I reasoned – and my leaving depended on my getting rid of my wares. So I had some flyers printed up, which I personally distributed, in the hopes of enticing the inhabitants of Pulacayo to my hotel room with the promise of immense bargains and unheard-of discounts. This time it worked. The first buyers walked away deeply satisfied, and the news about a crazy benefactor of humanity and his bargain prices soon spread through the town like wildfire. I began selling at a marginal profit, then for the price of purchase, at half price and, finally, I was giving things away. Seeing so many happy faces, I became more cheerful and relaxed myself. Finally a carpenter acquired the crate itself for next to nothing, and as to a small, absolutely unmarketable remainder, I sewed it up in a burlap sack light enough for me to lift onto the truck all by myself. In a fit of gallows humor on the train home, I treated myself to a last meal in the dining car. Once returned, I promptly had to lay up in bed sick with a fever. It took me a long time to pay off the commissioned things which were supposed to have established my prosperity and which in fact did nothing more than bring a little joy to a few impoverished miners and their pitiable wives. And thus ended my first and last attempt to make my way through the world as a free-lance merchant.

It became obvious to me that a world that displayed so little understanding for my needs, that so snidely refused to honor my talents, was a world that needed change. And so I became a Trotskyite. This step was hardly haphazard. In spite of Hitler and his Operation Barbarossa, in spite of the Allies' new dependency on the Soviet Union, and in spite of my tender age, I was disturbed and disgusted by the Stalinist "purges." In this respect I was ahead of hundreds of thousands of shrewder and better informed intellectuals. (I have an allergic reaction to any abstract or euphemistic phrases designed to veil inhumane actions, such as the Nazis' "final solution," the Americans' "pacification" of Vietnam, or the recent "ethnic cleansing" practiced by the Serbian nationalists. I was an implacable opponent of the tyrant that had orchestrated these purges, and I already regarded the socialist experiment in Soviet Russia as a failure. Given my own leftist sympathies, however, Trotsky, pining away in exile like ourselves, represented a very passable alternative.

Actually Trotsky himself hardly figured into the scheme; we were merely borrowing his name. As for the program, we were a Bolivian group intent on devising Bolivian solutions for Bolivian problems, which were vast indeed. Another important aspect of my involvement was the bond I felt with my new party friends: all were unsparing enemies of Hitler and sympathetic toward the Allies.

If as a member of a Trotskyite cell I had been implicated in some violent coup d'état or reckless act of terrorism, I would happily admit them here and now. After all, the statute of limitations would have expired long ago, and the United States government would be unlikely to extradite me to Bolivia. Moreover, I swore on my fiftieth birthday that from then on I would tell the truth, the whole truth and nothing but the truth. Yet there is nothing to confess.

Concerned as they were with the plight of the have-nots, my Trotskyite comrades were generally peace-loving, and so instead of fomenting violence, we focused on spreading enlightenment. We published a newspaper by the name of *La Chispa*, "The Spark," which reflected our small size as much as our commitment to illumination. Endowed with the superior understanding of its creators, this organ offered insightful commentary on the state of the world, the country and the province of Chuquisaca. I was in charge of the joke section, and in this capacity I saw to it that Hitler and his consorts were constantly exposed to the derision of the local inhabitants. On May Day, the international day of labor, I provokingly donned a red tie, much to the irritation of conservative businessmen, and accompanied by a few daring sympathizers I went out at night to paint prophecies on the most important walls of the town. In incendiary red lettering, these slogans proclaimed as indisputable fact that the Allies would win the war and Hitler would perish: "Los aliados vencerán" and "Hitler perecerá."

While these actions undoubtedly contributed a great deal to the demise of fascism, they hardly earned me a living, not even the proverbial "red" cent. Yet my circumstances were constantly focusing my consciousness on precisely that issue. My suit was in tatters, and I desperately needed a new one. My shoes were worn. I was allowed to eat with my parents, and I am grateful to say they were always ready to help and to make sacrifices for me. But we didn't have any extra money, and I could sense their worrying and disapproving looks. In the middle of all the confusion, one thing was clear to me: I had to find a job that brought in money. But that was not to be found in Sucre, where I had already exhausted the few possibilities.

I was now familiar enough with Bolivia to know that since I had so dismally failed in my career as salesman, the only option still open was in the mines, the industry which dominated the entire Bolivian economy. And so I made my way to Potosí, the mining town where the Spanish had once found so much silver that it was said they could have built a bridge to Madrid with it. And in the Potosí mint, where the same metal was stamped into coins, you could still see where the laboring shoulders of thousands of slaves had worn deep indentations into the wooden machinery. Although the silver had long since been depleted, tin was being extracted from the local mines in great quantities.

All my previous experiences were only a mere overture to what awaited me in the tin mines of the Compañia Minera Unificada del Cerro de Potosí. The years I spent there form the crux of my experience as an exile: they were the most instructive years of my life, profoundly marking my consciousness and shaping my view of the world.

Potosí lies four thousand meters above sea level, the highest city in the world, which stretches along steep slopes in a landscape of cold, almost sublime sterility. Rising a few hundred meters above the town is the Cerro Rico, a famous landmark and the source of all the fabled wealth. It is a red sugar-loaf mountain from whose interior men have extracted ore for hundreds of years, leaving it burrowed with tunnels, shafts and passageways. To arrive in Potosí is to enter an alien world, where the air is so thin and the pressure so low that it's impossible to cook eggs properly – the water boils so quickly. Moving there requires both physical and psychological acclimatization: one must get used to the cold, to the bare mountains devoid of vegetation, to the shabby ugliness of the town itself. I had no difficulty making the climatic adjustment – after a few days of a dry throat I was able to move and breathe as easily at 4,500 meters as I had at 2,000. But I was never able to adapt to the utter desolation of the life itself.

I found a job immediately. The Compañia's business manager, a meticulous Swede – the "international" character of the mine is a subject to which I will return – sent me to the mill superintendent. He was the manager of the enormous empire where the ore was refined. The machines could be heard pounding away from quite some distance, and in the mill itself the noise was deafening; it not only numbed the ears, but echoed in the brain and set the entire body vibrating. The ore came by cable car from high up the mountain; it thundered into immense wooden bins, while mammoth crushers and grinding machines cracked and crunched away with nerve-shattering intensity. The drive belt screeched, the motors revved, the conveyor belts turned, the jigs shook, the sieves rattled, the water thrashed, centrifuges hissed, and hundreds of iron tables washed off tons of gravel and sand in a great rhythmic tremble, each in a different pitch. The whole thing was an uninterrupted pandemonium. Only the shrill siren announcing the change of shifts periodically penetrated the din. And this inferno was to be my home.

The lord who ruled over this kingdom, a pale-eyed North American of slight build, looked me over and said hesitantly: "You're very young."

"Age is merely a number," I countered.

"Are you willing to work through the night? To wade around in mud and cold water up to your ankles? To give up Sundays and holidays?"

After I had listened to these questions amid the general roar and assented to everything, I was hired as night watchman – or rather, as the nightwatch supervisor. My job would be to monitor the exits, search anyone who passed through them, and patrol the walls that enclosed the vast mill: in short, to prevent anyone from stealing the refined tin that was being produced. Some large quantities of the precious product had recently disappeared, so the company decided to hire a reliable, that is to say, Anglo or European overseer in order to plug the leak and to put an end to the losses.

For the first time in my life, I was earning more than I needed to spend – an evident reflection of my inhuman assignment. At first I rented a room in town, and night after night I would descend into this Hades where you could not hear your own speech. Unremittingly I made my rounds, surprising the watchmen who worked under me, observing the workers in their activity, and writing my nightly report. I soon got to know every machine, every operator; I could even rank each site according to the refinement of the tin produced. I knew every place where tools were kept, every platform where the mineral dust was dried and bagged, every storage room where these bags were housed. Before long I was onto all the tricks the workers used to filch a bit of metal. The concentrate took the form of dust, mud or fine gravel which one could smear into one's hair or pour into one's shoes. The Banco Minero didn't much care about the provenance; a given amount was weighed and tested for tin, and its value paid out in cash – no questions asked.

At the same time I realized this pilfering could hardly account for the huge sums that were missing. Month after exhausting month I was exposed to every hardship predicted by the supervisor, as well as other ones, such as the icy night air and a permanent lack of sleep. In a sense I was even worse off than the workers, for they at least changed their shift every two weeks. And in the end it turned out that the whole phenomenal loss was due to an error in arithmetic.

When that finally came to light, I would have been out of work if I hadn't gotten to know a metallurgist from the US. This man saved me from rejoining the ranks of the unemployed by hiring me on as his helper. From then on I became a kind of permanent employee-at-large, moving from job to job, moving from metallurgical workshop to the chemistry laboratory, from the mill to the mine. In this way I served the same company for several years, in one capacity or the other according to its needs.

In the metallurgical workshop we experimented with the preparation of the ore, with the separation and grading of the various minerals according to value. Our results then found large-scale application in the mill. For the most part, these methods derived from the higher specific gravity of the nobler metals: the lighter impurities were simply washed away with water. In the case of the tungsten ores, which were encountered more frequently as one penetrated deeper into the mountain, the separation was achieved electromagnetically, or else by a chemical refinement called flotation. This latter method used various oils and essences to turn the dross into a glistening foam which could then be siphoned off. Both legal and economic considerations played a part as well: one had to know which concentrations were the most lucrative, and which impurities were inadmissible by law.

One day, while engaged in this interesting activity, I had an accident. My hand got caught in an iron propeller and, though the machinery was stopped immediately, in response to my shouts, what I retrieved was nothing but a clump of flesh, tendons and skin. I was then sent to the company hospital.

This institution could easily comprise its own chapter in Dante's *Inferno*. During the time I spent there, there was no end to the stream of injured and maimed victims being admitted. As I learned, the safety measures in the mines defied description. Doctors and orderlies ran around in bloody coats, hacking and sawing as though they were in a butcher shop. Their first instinct was also to amputate my hand, but I resisted, and as my supervisor voiced his own objections, they simply shrugged their shoulders and complied.

Here was another decision that influenced my life. My wound was washed, the bones set, and a bandage was applied. Had I been an Indian without a family, they wouldn't have made such a fuss – that much was clear: for such cases they had neither the time, nor the personnel, nor the inclination. As it was, I developed an infection, my arm swelled up to my shoulder, and for days I lay in bed with a high fever. The doctors were almost vindicated, for now it was no longer just a matter of my hand. But at long last the swelling and the fever abated. Today you can still see a scar arcing from my palm to the back of my hand; but it is nonetheless the same hand with which I am writing down these recollections.

In the chemistry laboratory, where I was transferred a little later, I learned techniques of analysis: I filtered, titrated and used a pipette; I learned to handle micro-scales and test tubes, to make calculations with atomic weights and concentrations. Every day twenty thousand samples of rock were brought in from various parts of the mountain in order to be tested for their tin content. The results pointed the company towards the richest veins.

The laboratory resembled a factory, with sixty people working in two shifts. In the evening after work, I studied chemistry. After a while, I became so well versed in the subject that I was entrusted with newly found substances to identify. By now, of course, I've forgotten everything, but there was a time when I could have passed for an analytical chemist.

This praiseworthy example of professionalism was interrupted when the company's directors decided they needed me elsewhere. A managerial post for the *Relaves y Veneros* had become vacant, and I suddenly found myself supervising hundreds of people, a responsibility that still frightens me in retrospect, probably even more now than it did then. The *Veneros* were alluvial tin sediments where the metal was gleaned from a fairly shallow source, by open-pit mining. The measures of support and safety available to us were thoroughly inadequate; cave-ins occurred weekly, often with fatal consequences. It depressed me to see how the poor bemoaned their dead and yet accepted the violent death itself with resignation, as an expected everyday event, a necessity of nature that had been imposed upon them.

Relaves was the name given to sites all over the region where the Spaniards had washed the earth for silver, unmindful of the tin they were leaving in the earth. I was provided with a mule, a stubborn beast that gave me much grief but nevertheless carried me many a kilometer. I rode wherever old maps led me to suspect the presence of the Spanish placer mines. I would take samples, have them tested for tin content, and if it proved worth the effort, I would negotiate private contracts to obtain mineral rights. The long and somewhat hazardous rides into the isolated mountain world, the interaction with contractors and mine technologists, the legal and business knowledge I had to acquire – all these things made this job, which was the equivalent of a mining engineer's, one of the most interesting ones I held.

Absorbing as it may have been, however, this employment, too, ultimately came to an end. In paradoxical contrast with my previous adventures, it was my very success that lost me this particular job. A few lucky finds, a few ambitious and greedy coworkers, my own diligence in uncovering the old sites, and a strict watch over the milling machinery increased production considerably. It was a feature of this half free-lance position of *Relaves y Veneros* that the person in charge was to receive a percentage of whatever profit his department earned. For months my earnings were paid out to me without further ado, but finally the bookkeepers took note of the leaps and bounds in my income. As a reward for my services, I received a punitive transferal, to the dreaded highest mine, where I was to become a "weigher." The company obviously didn't place much stock in humanitarian considerations. At my new employment I had to get up at dawn to be taken by truck up to places so high they were vertiginous, and blasted by icy winds. Regardless of the weather, I was to man my outside station, recording the weight of the ores coming out of the quarry – a task so simple that even a grade school pupil could have mastered it. All the company cared about was that the weigher be honest and precise.

This last change in my fortunes was too much. Angered by the company's questionable motives, indignant at the impersonal and inconsiderate treatment I was subjected to, and crushed in body and soul by the hardships and privations of three years, I gave notice overnight. I was fed up with everything: the company, the mine, Potosí, the whole country – I longed for a change. And so with a definite plan in mind, I turned my back on that inhospitable land.

Two factors in particular made my life in Potosí especially difficult. The first was a subjective one; my own oversensitive disposition exaggerated the desolate surroundings, the melancholy solitude, not only of the physical but also of the cultural and psychological landscape. This was an immense, inhuman world of stone unbroken by a single grove or meadow. Furthermore, it was devoid of any cultural offerings; there was no music, no theater, no artistic endeavor that might otherwise have consoled the heart and reconciled me to my fate. The American films seemed so incongruent with the grotesque setting that they only increased my longing for something better.

The local mores also disturbed me. If a European woman happened to end up here, she created such a tremendous stir that she nearly drove the men out of their senses. The extreme sexual privation led to aberrations and abuses I am loath to describe. Suffice it to say that a crude sexuality, card games and alcohol provided the only escape from the drudgery, and whoever refused to participate excluded himself from the only existing social life in Potosí.

The other factor which made my life miserable were the sheer conditions, which would have touched any but the most thick-skinned person. Social determinists would have found ample evidence for their theories.

To begin with, there was an immutable hierarchy, at the top of which stood the powerful engineers, the mine and mill super-intendents, and the general manager, all of whom lived in luxurious houses. They were North Americans. A little lower came the Northern Europeans – Germans, Englishmen and Scandinavi-ans – who held intermediate positions and ran the stores, the workshops and the administrative offices. Next were the Bolivians from middle-class families who tried to 'pass' as white. They found more or less respectable jobs in accounting and admini-stration, in the export branch and especially in the company's law offices. After them came the category to which we belonged, which consisted mostly of Jewish emigrants who, as I have already indicated, often received low-level supervisory positions. Just below us were the *mestizos* and the *cholos*, Bolivians of mixed origin from the lower middle class who could speak, read and write Spanish. They were given minor jobs such as assistant office clerk or crew foremen. On the very lowest level were the masses of Indian mine workers in their unthinkable misery.

Today the structure that underlay this hierarchy would be called racist and colonialist. The few exceptions to this arrange-ment only confirmed the rule, since the very fact that they were possible showed that the inequalities were not the result of some kind of tyrannical will imposing itself on everything, but rather reflected the reigning system of values. In order to explain why these conditions made me feel so indignant, I must take a moment to talk about the Indian peons and mine workers. I don't know what the miner's life is like now, given all the changes that have taken place. In those days, however, the miner's life was truly miserable. The wages were entirely inadequate. Nothing in the least was done to provide clean living quarters or healthy nourishment, or to maintain even the most rudimentary safety measures at work. They were starving, worn down and dirty figures everyone was only too happy to avoid. The *pulpería*, a company-owned store where food and clothing were obtainable at reasonable prices, tempered the harshness of the situation somewhat. You could also buy cocaine there, in the form of dried leaves, at a fraction of the market price. This was consistent with both Bolivian tradition and the company's own policy. Early in the morning before work, the workers squatted there chewing their 'coca' with the obligatory balls of potash which were needed to produce the desired chemical reaction. During the day, when the effects began to wear off, fresh leaves replaced the old, so that one cheek was always full of the foul-smelling, black-green pulp. If you asked an Indian why he did this, he would smile slyly and say: "Me da fuerza, señor" – "it gives me strength, sir." Its effect was such that a man under the influence of the drug could carry a sack of *barrilla* or tin dust up steep slopes, while I would have had trouble simply lifting it off the ground. Cocaine not only makes people strong, though; it makes them docile. The intoxication it induced clouded the mind and helped them bear the pain of their existence. Acts of insubordination or resistance were extremely rare. Only once in three years was there a strike. Informed of it by the company's general director, the governor of Potosí sent in the military to drive the recalcitrant peons back to work like slaves.

I never saw a miner who could be called old. I imagine that the alkaloid poison must eventually prove fatal. But the mine contributed its share, so that you could actually predict with great probability the course of a man's life by virtue of what he did. At fifteen, he would come to the mine as an *alarife*, an apprentice who might for example carry around the engineer's tools. He earned the best money of his life at around twenty, as an actual *minero*. Enshrouded in a dense cloud of dust, he would stand in front of a wall of rock and carve tunnels with his pneumatic drill. Although he was supposed to wear a mask, for the sake of comfort he often didn't, and sooner or later he contracted the *mal de minas* or "black lung" as it is known in English, within a few years. At that point he had to be transferred to a surface job, in the open air, where he continued to do lighter work until he died, usually between the age of thirty and forty.

Nominally, the Indios were "Christians," which mostly meant that the church covered them with a little cloak of superstition embroidered with Catholic notions, and otherwise left them to their own devices. I attended a number of their festivals, and these seemed to me to be pagan through and through. True, at first they would carry some holy image to church in a procession; but that was that as far as the newfangled Christian rite was concerned. The actual ceremony took place high on the mountain. Llamas would be bound and thrown to the ground, and anesthetized with pisco, the Bolivian brandy, and coca. Then their throats would be slit with a knife, the blood collected and sprayed on all the entrances to the mines, to secure a year's protection from accidents. Finally, a lot of brandy would be poured all over the ground as an offering, and the celebration would conclude with a banquet.

The Indians are still oppressed, exploited people, having been robbed of their cultural identity. However, I have often met with the argument that they are satisfied with their lot, as they don't know a better one, or that they're basically happy with their life, as that's what they're used to. This reasoning has always struck me as fallacious, part of a malicious ideology that violates the basic principle of doing unto others what you would have them do unto you. It also contradicted another principle, which I formulated myself: "he who profits from a given circumstance should refrain from praising it," or if humans are too fallible for that, then at least such praises should not be believed.

Difficult as things were, my reckoning would be incomplete if I failed to list the positive aspects of my years in Potosí. After all, we seldom reject our past no matter how harsh it has been. Adverse circumstances often bring compensation in the form of

144

enriching experience. In my case other more concrete advantages came from Potosí as well, such as my fluency in English, of which I had had only a rudimentary, classroom knowledge. With the help of the metallurgist Norman Anderson, who in his friendly way had taken me under his wing, I achieved a degree of competence that was to be of great help to me both intellectually and professionally in later years. With no better primer than *Life Magazine*, I meandered into the treacherous labyrinth of a language that begins so innocently and becomes more and more impenetrable the further one strays. Norman would read an article aloud; I would repeat the words, learn it by heart, translate it with the help of a dictionary while he would explain idiomatic expressions and difficult passages and help me with the pronunciation. A few such lessons were enough to enable us to make English the language of our daily interaction.

My reading provided another useful pleasure – following the Horatian *utile cum dulci* – for which I was very grateful. The books I read belonged to my boss in the chemistry lab – a Viennese who, incredibly enough, had managed to bring his library into this wilderness. I must have read three hundred volumes in my three years in Potosí; even if I had done nothing else, that would have been enough to justify my time there. I became familiar with the literary canon of the European educated class – from Flaubert to Dostoyevsky, from Dickens to Ibsen, from Thomas Mann to Gide, Proust to Rilke, the Koran to Gobineau. This list nicely complemented my wide reading in sociology and contemporary affairs, which (although I hadn't the faintest idea of it then) was to provide a good foundation for my later profession. So I can't say that in all those years I never managed to escape the Andes. I did so almost every day and night, transported by poetic fantasy into all the geographical, historical and psychological regions of human experience.

Another benefit of Potosí was the rough and somewhat superficial camaraderie I found in the *"Rancho Judío"* – the Jewish Rancho, as they called the house where a number of the employees from central Europe kept house.

This was a notably motley bunch. One man from Berlin had worked as a taxi driver in that city and could dish out stories for hours on end in his thick accent. Another fellow, a tall blond man, literally stumbled in one day from the wilderness; he had been shot and was looking for help. He hardly spoke German anymore and had taken on native ways. In a half dazed state, he told us how a swindler had tricked him out of the money he had intended to use to bring his parents over from Europe, whereupon he withdrew in his grief to one of the many small mines scattered in the mountains. There he had been wounded as the result of a quarrel, after which he had found his way here. A third was a boy of seventeen whom we teased for his naiveté but whom we also spoiled. Every one had his positive sides as well as his odd quirks. We ate, drank and argued; we played cards and chess; we told each other jokes and anecdotes and recounted our adventures. Sometimes we sat around the smoky fire and someone played familiar German and Austrian melodies on an accordion. And even if it was only some popular ballad or a tune from a movie, it still reminded us of what we had lost; it created a common bond between us and made the present moment a little easier.

But the most cherished experiences were the trips to Sucre, which you could reach by *autocarril*, a kind of streetcar, in a six hours' ride to the valley. You first had to travel to the station called *Cumbre* or "summit," at the height of the mountain pass, where the winds were howling in every direction. Then you slowly descended into the river valley to the first green haciendas, and to the vendors offering you cheap bananas at the trolley stops, and to the tropical winds that wafted their warmth into your heart.

Having given notice, I made this same journey to Sucre for the last time, feeling doubly liberated, as I knew I would not be returning to the mine. It was late in 1944; we were no longer afraid that Hitler might win the war, which was then nearing its end. On the contrary, my parents and I could now entertain earlier desires to move on to another country. However, since we lacked the means for any longer journey, we almost automatically fixed on Chile as our goal – Chile, that advanced, enlightened land with its scintillating capital, Santiago.

We were now able to obtain the visas that had been earlier denied – even if they were only temporary ones for tourists. After all, we'd been through that before, and we thought we'd be able to 'make arrangements.' It remained for my parents to liquidate the shop and put their affairs in order. Since I had neither things to pack nor business to arrange, I had no reason to wait, and so I went on ahead to look things over.

I stood for the last time at the train station in Sucre, where I had been so many times – my first arrival, seeing off people who were leaving, waiting and watching to see who the world would send our way, and as a sad passenger headed back to Potosí. Nearly six years had passed – flown by – since I first set foot in Bolivia, six richly varied years in a land that was colorful as a kaleidoscope, as difficult as it was fascinating, a land which had given me many bitter experiences but where I had also grown into manhood. Precisely at this moment of departure Bolivia took on a new meaning for me because it was here that I left so much of the substance of my youth.

On the platform there was also a young woman who had come to bid me farewell. After all, this sphere of my life existed as well, even if I have chosen not to dwell on it, on the grounds that it hardly seems "historical." But I mention my companion at this point because her presence underscored the permanence of my departure, and imbued it with a sense that what I was leaving behind was irretrievable.

CHAPTER SIX
In Which Our Hero Undergoes Further Adventures
Passing Belief but Nevertheless True

After six years of isolation, a new emigration reminded me that a world did exist beyond the borders of Bolivia, though I had nearly forgotten it. And while this move scarcely brought about the fundamental changes I was eagerly awaiting – as I hope my readers are as well – it does seem distinct enough to warrant a separate chapter. For the time being, however, my picaresque life continued as before.

Nevertheless, when the train descended the Western slopes of the Andes and the air grew thicker and heavier as it streamed into my lungs, when I once again saw the ocean after so many years high in the mountains, I thought that perhaps a new, freer life was beginning. Nor was I entirely disappointed in my hopes, for Chile was so wholly different from the insular, almost suffocating world from which I had just descended.

Just arriving at Antofagasta was enough to cheer me on; backwoodsman that I was, I felt blinded by the nighttime sea of lights, deafened by the hustle and bustle of the port. Santiago, the international metropolis, city of millions! Of course I can't say how Londoners or New Yorkers might react to its splendors. I recall an experience I had much later, in Iceland. Upon our arrival, Reykjavik struck me as a dreary little fishing village. But after two weeks of hiking through the barren region in the northwest of the island, where there were no traces of people, not even a trail, we returned to the capital. This time I found the city a magnificent metropolis of admirable sophistication. So after living in a world where Sucre and Potosí counted as centers of culture, I was overwhelmed by Santiago, by the crowds of people, the elegant streets, the boulevards, the parks, the skyscrapers, the traffic, the display windows, the shops, the food. For two days I plunged into the fray, strolling along the Alameda, sipping espressos in the

Brazilian cafés, drinking my first milkshake in a glittering malt shop. I paused to enjoy the Chilean *once*, a kind of snack; I attended a concert; I even obtained a library card – the height of civilized luxury – at a lending library.

But I wasn't destined to reap these cosmopolitan pleasures for long; my stay in Santiago proved to be brief and difficult. The old issue of money immediately intruded, and I soon came to know a far less glamorous side of the radiant city.

Many thousands of people had found refuge from the Nazis here, too, and although there was of course no lack of political anti-Semitism (which resurfaced rather viciously under Pinochet), these two phenomena neutralized each other in the international atmosphere. This was after all a Spanish-speaking country with a national hero named O'Higgins, whose soccer team boasted a goalie by the name of Livingstone and where German counted as an official language in a few Southern cities, especially in Valdivia.

Even we weren't entirely without connections in this new, complicated environment. While still in Bolivia, we had resumed contact with some acquaintances from Pressburg who had once lived in my grandfather's house and had long been close to our family. These people now tried to talk me into becoming a salesman, by peddling merchandise in the suburbs, on installment. They insisted this was the best and only way to get a start in Santiago; one could do it without ready money and yet still 'live like a king.' To initiate me into the secrets of the trade, they took me along on a 'grand tour.'

The road to royal riches began rather inauspiciously in the proletarian quarter across the Mapocho River, where the workers lived in miserable shacks crudely constructed from earth, cardboard and sheet metal. This district was a precursor of today's Barriadas, the slums that have since become the horror and shame of the larger South American cities. What I saw there awakened many unpleasant memories.

My instructor went from door to door pushing a handcart that contained all manner of household items: dishes, aprons, cloths. A mere two or three pesos was enough to gain possession of the desired article: name, address, price and date were all noted down in a ledger. The buyer committed himself to minimal weekly payments, the sum of which was well in excess of what one would have paid for the same item in one of the department stores. As soon as the agreement had been concluded, we hurried on to the next potential customer.

The following day we went out with an account book instead of the handcart, for this was collection day. The Chilean workers were touchingly honest and failed to pay only when they had been set back by illness or unemployment and were absolutely without money. In cases where the customers had gone out we would invariably find what money they owed us lying on a table, weighted down by a glass or an ashtray.

Given these circumstances, the job seemed easy enough. My companion generously offered to start me off by ceding me some of his territory, which was of course strictly divided up so that no one solicitor could impinge on another man's work. But I declined, wiser from my earlier experiences in Bolivia. I shuddered at the thought of 'living like a king' off these poor people, who could have bought whatever they needed in a store, for a third of the price. This glance behind the scenes had a powerfully sobering effect on me.

So I had to find something else, and I had already been warned it wouldn't be easy. I ended up having to work literally morning, noon and night at three different jobs. From eight until two, I was a factotum for an ill-tempered, miserly importer who was impossible to please. He prophesied regularly and with relish that I would one day starve to death. And I probably would have if I had stayed in his employment. One of my tasks involved delivering merchandise, which meant I had to haul motors, perfume essences, household appliances and other "imports" from one end of the city to the other. My tyrannical boss calculated in advance how long it would take me, and I couldn't be gone one minute too many. When I returned I had to take dictation in Spanish and English, after which I typed letters and price estimates and took them to the post office.

At two o'clock I rushed off to my next place of work, a furrier's where in a last effort to learn a trade I had wangled myself an apprenticeship. I stood there till twelve at night pounding and nailing skins, cutting white stripes out of black pelts, sewing together pieces of fur. I was supposed to learn many other skills besides, but being too clumsy with my hands, I hardly made any progress.

I was thus a double victim, of a brutal tyranny in the morning and my own inadequacy in the afternoon – and still I didn't have enough money to live on. So to supplement my income I spent my weekends tutoring lethargic high school students in English and other subjects, although I didn't even have my own diploma.

As a result of all this most of my time was consumed by unrewarding work, racing from one place to the next, never getting anything right. I had too little sleep, too little money, and too little time to take advantage of what Santiago could offer. Like so many millions of others in similar circumstances, I probably would have gone under in the big city if the Chilean authorities hadn't come to our aid – albeit involuntarily and without humanitarian intentions – by refusing us a residency permit (my parents had long since joined me in Santiago). I have already castigated the Bolivian bureaucracy, but the Chilean one with its pedantic exactitude wasn't any kinder to us. On the contrary, it even proved impossible to make an 'arrangement' (although this was more due to the amount offered than any incorruptibility). Our tourist visas expired after we had renewed them twice and finally we received an order of expulsion.

What were we to do? Where should we turn? We didn't want to go back to Bolivia. We had no connections in the United States, the great magnet for refugees. Meantime, the war came to an end, and there was a little dancing in the streets of Santiago, but we were as removed from the cease-fire as we had been from the fighting, so this had little effect on our daily lives. The thought of a return to Europe didn't occur to any of us. Perhaps there were a few who fit the image of a banished writer sitting for years on an unpacked trunk while fervently awaiting a signal to call him home, but that wasn't us. We had no one and nothing in Europe to return to. We felt more driven out than banished, more immigrants than emigrants. The only problem was there was no place we could immigrate to.

In our desperation, we reactivated an old scheme. A relative in Ecuador had long been sending us letters urging us to try our luck in that country. The end of the war made this plan possible, we obtained our documents with surprising speed, and what's more, this time they weren't mere tourist visas but bona fide residency permits.

Our stay in Santiago had lasted half a year. One evening, without further regret, we boarded a boat in the charming city of Valparaiso and watched the famous half-circle of lights disappear over the horizon as our coastal steamer slowly plowed northwards. I love to travel on the ocean and I thoroughly enjoyed this trip, freed at last from all furs, imports and grammar books. The ship was a freighter carrying saltpeter and it stopped at all the small Chilean ports: Coquimbo, Antofagasta, Iquique, Arica and Mollendo, Peru. You could disembark and look around as you pleased. We had to stop at Callao for several days to unload. From there you could take a streetcar to Lima, so I was able to acquaint myself thoroughly with the Peruvian capital. On board I learned a great deal about collecting saltpeter. I also found out why the Chilean and Peruvian coasts are so dry: the cold Humboldt current flowing north along the continent so abruptly cools the overhead clouds traveling inland from the sea that they empty their contents into the ocean. Meanwhile, the Andes intercept any precipitation coming from the east, so that it never really rains west of the mountains. If once in fifty years a few drops do chance to fall from the sky, the strange phenomenon so frightens the children that they have to be comforted by their parents. At the northern end of Peru, the Humboldt stream suddenly takes a sharp turn to the west, past the Galapagos Islands, so that the coast of Ecuador receives ample moisture and is covered with abundant tropical vegetation.

My fellow travelers also contributed a great deal to my

edification and amusement, including the members of a traveling circus who displayed a lot of clever tricks and who also brought us food from first class. An amusingly blasé South American diplomat told us ironic anecdotes about his government as well as his own career. A high-ranking Salesian on an inspection trip reported on the moral conduct of the Catholic clergy and on the accomplishments and setbacks of the Catholic missions in the countries he had visited. Almost all of the travelers had unusual experiences to relate, which made my own appear less exceptional.

But the most interesting personality on board was a Peruvian patrician named Juan Seoane, who thanks to a turn of political events was now able to go back to his homeland after a long period of exile in Argentina. He described his ten years spent languishing in Peruvian jails with hair-raising detail. He has even written an exciting book, *Hombres y Rejas* (Men and Bars), about his experiences, and critics have called him "the Dostoyevsky of Latin America."

It's amazing how much effort and energy historians devote to the political confusions, terrors, oppressions and persecutions in Europe, while the history of almost every Latin American country is so little known and even less researched. And yet that history is just as "colorful": certainly as far as grotesque savagery is concerned, South America has in some respects left Europe far behind.

The three weeks of the journey flew by in an instant, and even though our boat sailed at a snail's pace, it was still too fast for me. When we landed in the Ecuadorian port of Guayaquil on my twenty-third birthday, I felt once again a mixture of regret and anticipation.

But even these feeling were muted by mournful tidings transmitted to us through the International Red Cross, the first news we had received in years about our Pressburg relatives. They were sent by my mother's oldest brother and consisted of two French words: "Resté seul" – of the whole, huge extended family, he was the sole survivor. As a Catholic convert, he had enjoyed certain privileges under the Tiso regime, and later, when the Nazis put an end to such preferential treatment, he was hidden in a dry well by a farmer in

the Slovakian mountains, where he waited until the end of the war.
Eventually we learned more of how our relatives had been
murdered. One uncle was beaten to death in the concentration
camp with a rifle butt for "insubordination"; his wife and his two
small daughters had been sent to the gas chambers in Auschwitz.
Another uncle had also been interned in one of the eastern camps.
One day he answered a call for precision toolmakers, was separated from the other prisoners, and was never heard from again.
We have no idea what became of him. My grandmother, aged
seventy-five, and my grandfather, over eighty, were taken away.
Eyewitnesses told us that my grandmother had been shot on the
highway and thrown into a ditch because she couldn't keep pace
with the others. I learned of my grandfather's last days from a
Pressburg survivor whom I ferreted out in Montreal. As a young
man, he had been apprenticed to my grandfather as a watchmaker,
and so when he worked in the kitchens at Auschwitz, he gave the
terribly emaciated old man a potato in gratitude, for which my
grandfather kissed him on the hand. The next day he again hurried
out of the kitchen to bring my grandfather something to eat, but he
had disappeared; my acquaintance never saw him again. Most of
the members of the family died in the death camps, so that I was
unable to find out when and under what circumstances each of
them met their violent death. It is enough to know, of course, that
an entire large clan, men and women of every age as well as a
number of children, were wiped off the face of the earth. In
essence, I no longer had any relatives left in this world.

My parents and I separated the moment we reached Ecuador.
They went to Ambato, a small town in the provinces, where my
father, thanks to his tailoring skills, was able to become a partner
in a joint venture. I knew from bitter experience that tiny Indian
marketplaces held little in store for me, and so I chose to travel
directly to the capital.

By this time I had adapted a routine for arriving in unfamiliar
cities. No sooner would I leave the scrap metal on wheels that
usually passed for a bus, than I would begin my quest for a place
to live. I had a good idea of what quarters might fit my limited bill

154

– extravagant leaps were out of the question – and soon enough I had found a room.

Next I explored the marketplace, where for little money I acquired a bed frame and a bag of straw, both of which I carried home on my back. There was no room for any other furniture. Three nails in the wall served as a closet; I stowed my suitcase underneath the bed. For private needs I had access to the land-lady's toilet on the next floor up. There was no place to wash up, but around the corner the chauffeurs' syndicate had a center with some private stalls that the public could use for a small fee. My move to Quito was complete.

After Chile, which had appeared so different, Ecuador seemed like a mirror image of Bolivia. The ethnic composition was a similar mix of indigenous people, whites, and *mestizos*, with more or less self-contained islands of foreigners. The political structure and social hierarchy also resembled Bolivia's. Even the climate and topography seemed familiar: the high Andean peaks such as the Chimborazo, the Tunguragua and the Cotopaxi, the practically unexplored eastern slopes, and the adjacent tropical valleys. Except instead of the Chaparé and the Mamoré, the rivers that flowed here were called the Napo and the Pastaza.

But the differences were equally important. Ecuador is a smaller country with a much denser population. It is also less isolated than Bolivia. Most of the cities are situated at a lower altitude and therefore enjoy a milder climate, which is also enhanced by its latitude. Just a few kilometers south of Quito there is a monument to the eponymous equator, erected by a French geodesic expedition.

By far the most important geographical advantage over Bolivia is the coast, although at that time the largest ocean steamers had to lay anchor at a distant bay and transfer both freight and passengers onto smaller vessels capable of navigating the Guayas river all the way into Guayaquil. But even that access was enough to stimulate a lively trade, and let in enough of the world beyond to influence the intellectual atmosphere. Ecuador was a softer, tamer, more comprehensible version of an Andean state.

My story is either becoming repetitive or else a pattern seems to be emerging, from which I was unable to escape. Once again in need of a job, I scoured the newspaper ads for openings and applied to Shell Oil as well as various import-export firms, because it was there that I suspected the money was. I also applied for a position as translator at the newly installed American military mission, which meant taking an exam together with dozens of competitors. By that time my English was solid; evidently they didn't find anyone better, and I was hired.

After all I've written thus far, my views on military missions will hardly come as a surprise. Uniforms in general give me the willies and military missions strike me as the last thing this world needs. And although my antipathy was less pronounced at the time, I was still quite skeptical regarding this particular military, with its lack of diplomatic experience, stumbling along the slippery paths of a South American republic.

But were they any worse than their Italian predecessors? The fact that the fates of war had replaced one with the other seemed to me a rare case of just desserts. But the more I saw of the new order, the more I began to have doubts about it as well. Were the presumptuous, semiliterate people I encountered really supposed to be the new wielders of power? Was the world now going to revolve around these scheming adventurers, with their mix of arrogance and audacity? And why did Ecuador need all these complicated weapons with these poorly written manuals of operation that I now had to translate into Spanish? What was the purpose of this 'lend-lease,' that was stockpiling tanks and jeeps, machine-guns and ammunition in a country that needed streets and bridges, tractors and hospitals? Did these things serve any other function than to help prepare the next putsch? What I observed day-to-day, the little details, local and concrete – taught me to ask questions of global proportion.

Often it seemed like a poorly staged farce. I watched how highly coveted American goods – canned food, cigarettes, rubber boots, and parkas – traveled from the PX straight onto the black market. I saw how the officers of the allied armies gaped and gawked at each other without love or respect, I heard their badmouthing and backbiting, and witnessed how each group tried to profit off the other. Not that any of this was any of my business: I went on translating so that I could take off Wednesday afternoons as well as weekends and so I could collect my hundred dollars per month – a fraction of what a corporal earned at the same mission. Evidently if you refused to do one dirty job you wound up with another; either you conned Chilean workers out of their hard-earned pennies, or else you ended up being a lackey to the imperialists and the military in Ecuador. The system was the same everywhere – it seemed impossible to escape.

Happily for me, human sympathies can overcome institutional incompatibility, and I myself was always treated well in the mission – something I couldn't say about my other employers, and least of all the European ones. It even proved possible for me to develop a friendship with one of the officers, and the fact that this friendship continued later in the States shows how an individual can act independently of systems and hierarchies – at least to some extent.

Apart from that, I spent my time in Quito with younger and older people in all kinds of activities. I climbed mountains; I played chess with the masters (I still have newspaper articles describing my matches); I even acted in a refugee theater where we performed anything from German drama that struck our fancy, from Curt Goetz to Schiller. I ate one meal every day and with the money I could have spent on the second one I bought books; I bought a notebook in which I jotted down aphorisms and well-turned phrases from my readings, and even began to write short essays, sketches and poems on my own. I felt an urgent need for self-expression, and I suffered because the world had little use for the result. Nevertheless I managed to hold out in Quito for two years before my discontent and inner restlessness won the upper hand. After that I was so thoroughly fed up with the military of both nations, with the city and its people, that I dropped everything and left.

For a change of air, and no doubt with the secret hopes of

finding fulfillment that are harbored in every such move, I traveled to Guayaquil, the bustling, tropical port that was rival to the more lethargic mountain town of Quito. Here it was so hot and humid your boots would mildew overnight, and your socks would dissolve into little woolly flakes. The streets were crawling with beetles, a brown carpet furrowed by the wheels of cars. Anxious young mothers dangled their babies under the tap just to cool them off a little. All this was just fine with me, for it seemed to promise the renewal I desired. Of course I still needed a job, as well as no small measure of good luck: it was as if the tropical heat makes people even more cold-hearted than usual.

At this point a character we have already met reenters our story – the Viennese disguise artist whom we last encountered as a mender of typewriters and adding machines. There was something about the two of us that always brought us together. We not only chanced on each other in various cities of Bolivia, Chile, and Ecuador, but years later, after all contact had been lost, we met by complete coincidence in Lima. Still more time elapsed, and we bumped into each other at the Houston airport – but that was to be our last encounter before he passed away.

Our rendezvous in Guayaquil was far less miraculous, since I always looked him up whenever I came to the coast. Now I visited him in his workshop every day, to report on my efforts at finding a job, and discuss the various setbacks and prospects. It was he who encouraged me to take a step that was to have no small effect on the course of my life.

One of the contracts my friend had taken on involved maintaining all the office machines of the Compañía Bananera del Ecuador, a branch of the United Fruit Company. During the time I was in Guayaquil he had to leave on his monthly tour of inspection, and when he came back he told me excitedly that he had overhead talk of a possible opening for a bookkeeper. At first I couldn't quite understand why he was so excited; after all, how did that concern me? But he refused to let me off so easily. Without pulling any punches, he proceeded to lambaste me as a fearful, lazy coward; all my existential discontent was my own fault. In this way he cudgeled me until I finally agreed to try my luck where fortune beckoned.

At the offices of the Compañía, the chief of personnel met me with the usual whys and wherefores. I could actually see his ears prick when I deftly wove the word bookkeeping into the discourse of my knowledge and abilities. The fact that I was fluent in both English and Spanish – the languages of employers and employees – must have helped, and I returned to my friend both delighted and ashamed to confess I had been hired at favorable terms. My new position was as a bookkeeper in the Contaduría, the accounting office of the Compañía Bananera del Ecuador.

On the Monday morning I was supposed to start, however, I woke up feeling a little uneasy, and not without cause. How long would it be, I asked myself, before they discovered that I knew nothing about bookkeeping and turned me out in disgrace? But no sooner had I arrived at my place of employment than I was sent home in a rush to pack an overnight bag: a boat was just leaving for the plantation and I was to come along. Evidently it was company policy to acquaint new employees with all aspects of the vast enterprise. Having been granted this stay, I collected my things and boarded the company boat. We floated down the lethargic river to the open sea and then followed a jungle river upstream.

The plantation produced a number of tropical fruits and coffee, but its most important product by far was bananas, which were cultivated in endless groves. My first order of business was dinner with the farm's Australian manager, who had many tales to tell and many things to explain to me. The next day I was given a horse and told to ride straight through the banana groves to the plantation outposts, where I was to take inventory of all the structures, vehicles, machines and tools. Even with my total lack of training that seemed simple enough; after all, all I had to do was check things off a list and record what was missing. So I rode off feeling chipper enough.

In the several days I was gone I got to know the people and their work; the hardest part was getting used to the horse, who, despite his friendly nature, managed to keep my buttocks constantly sore. Up to then my equestrian experience had been limited to riding a mule – which involved a completely different technique.

Before returning to Guayaquil, I had an opportunity to watch bananas being loaded at sea. Near the mouth of the river, a freighter belonging to the Grace Line had dropped anchor, and the plantation's barges, laden with freshly harvested bananas, pulled alongside a platform, where brown figures were tossing lurid green stalks onto waiting pans, which an elevator moved up and down the black side of the ship. It made me shudder to watch while one worker clipped the banana stems with his machete, swinging his blade a hairsbreadth away from the neck and shoulders of the man who had brought the clusters of fruit. Once the elevator reached the top, it went back down the other side and deposited its load in the ship's refrigerated hull. I thus became acquainted with virtually every phase of the banana business.

Finally the day arrived when I had to begin the duties I was hired to do. But fortune smiled on me once again, sparing me from a shameful exposure. All the bookkeeping operations expected of me were so clearly spelled out and whatever I didn't understand was so thoroughly explained that I soon felt comfortable. Before long I felt so much at home it was as though I had been working in the office for years.

So despite my initial fears I was able to keep my job with the Compañía. For quite a while I lived in Guayaquil as well as anyone in that town could – as always deeply absorbed in my books and writing poetry. At the same time, however, I was not impervious to the noisy, gaudy life around me, especially since the hustle and bustle of a tropical city was still new to me.

The United Fruit Company is decried as a cutthroat enterprise that exploits its labor and intervenes in the worst manner possible in the politics of those countries where it has branches, much to the detriment of the working population. It has even become a kind of symbol for the excesses of US monopoly capitalism in South America.

While there are probably good reasons for this reputation, I never had an opportunity to thoroughly investigate these accusations. However, on the basis of my personal experience with the firm, I cannot confirm their veracity. The reader will recall that I have nowhere refrained from criticizing social ills wherever I encountered them. But I must say that in the Compañía Bananera del Ecuador, neither the field laborers nor the office clerks were treated badly, and the pay was no better or worse than the going rate in Guayaquil. The company also did more for its workers in matters of housing, health and hygiene than was the norm, and the overall atmosphere and morale, always palpable in firms that size, was not at all bad. And so I could have stayed on indefinitely, for even though I never became an ace accountant, I was not entirely incompetent, and in any case I was not sent home packing.

But things happened differently; my life took a new turn: new circumstances ensued which spelled the end of my days as a picaro. It was precisely these developments which led to my present perspective, and which are ultimately responsible for my writing this account – although naturally none of this occurred as seamlessly as it may sound in the retelling.

No matter how frivolously the chronicle of my adventures may have hitherto unfolded, I hope I have also managed to convey at least some of the bitterness and profound dissatisfaction I felt with myself and the circumstances of my life. These feelings had nothing to do with Ecuador, a friendly country I would recommend to every traveler who would appreciate its mix of otherness and beauty. But as I wandered from place to place, job to job, and country to country, the roguish carefree guise I showed the world was actually a mask. As the turmoil of war began to settle across the globe, a storm was brewing inside me that finally broke and changed my life.

CHAPTER SEVEN
The Turning Point

What does a literary historian do? He teaches: he gives lectures and offers seminars, he advises students, criticizes papers, suggests dissertation topics, examines candidates and writes recommendations. He also researches: he reads old and new works as well as critical studies of these works; he ruminates, consults archives, attends conferences and publishes the results in the form of lectures, books and essays. It's a career like any other.

But there are many intellectual and professional barriers that separate this particular career from that of an electrician, secretary, textile laborer or tin prospector: in other words, there was a substantial gulf between what I had been and what I would eventually become. My next task is to show how I bridged these disparate spheres, and I would be remiss if in doing so I failed to account for my own intellectual progress, which is what ultimately enabled me to cross from one domain into the other. Of course by now I have described – albeit sporadically – several important influences on my thinking, so that this development will hardly come as a complete surprise, even though I have up to now focused primarily on the external circumstances of my wanderings.

In any event, no matter how inadequate it may have seemed to me at the time, my *Gymnasium* – and perhaps the entire intellectual climate in Vienna – did induce me to read. With my parents' encouragement and my own predilection, this habit became a passion, and ultimately an indispensable form of sustenance. Wherever I was and whatever role I had assumed, I was constantly reading. No matter where I was or what I was doing, the books always had something to offer: distraction or escape, education or edification, philosophical enlightenment or emotional nourishment. They also served on occasion as a surrogate for worldly success and a consolation for my general dissatisfaction.

I have already mentioned my use of various libraries, such as

Arturo P.'s collection in La Paz or that of my chemist friend in Potosí. But I have yet to describe the lengths I would go to procure reading material, anywhere and at any time, even under the most unlikely circumstances. No person – and certainly no institution – was safe from my insatiable longing. When a new refugee arrived in whatever town happened to be my temporary home, I would immediately seek him out. After only the barest of preliminaries I would get straight to the point and ask if he happened to have any books.

No one was able to withstand the insistence and persistence of my entreaties. Even the pedants and eccentrics who principally refused to lend their holdings (if only I were strong enough to adopt such a stance!) were no match for my avidity; I would simply read the books on the spot – (stealing it from beneath their Argus-eyes was never something I considered). In fact I read more at that time, when I didn't have to, than at any other point in my life. Nowadays I often long for that lost ability to lose myself so completely in a novella by Storm or Keller or Thomas Mann's *Magic Mountain*. I would walk around in a kind of trance, deeply and painfully affected as I took part in the destinies of the various characters.

Of course this haphazard method of acquiring books meant that my reading was entirely unselective, but I didn't really care whether the texts I read were easy or abstruse, deep or trivial, momentarily popular or something more venerable, technical information or belles-lettres – I read anything and everything. Later on this indiscriminate eclecticism led me to feel a little unsure of myself, but now it strikes me as a very good way of developing a true appreciation of literature in all its tremendous variety, unfettered by any dogmatic approach.

As undirected as my reading was, though, two main tendencies emerged spontaneously out of my own circumstances and needs. On the one hand, since most of my 'suppliers' were middle-class Europeans, the books they owned generally reflected the taste and interests of that social group. My own political bias, on the other hand, caused me to seek out 'leftist' literature of various countries.

I have already mentioned my affinity for language, which proved very felicitous, not only because it enabled me to attain a relatively high degree of competence in various foreign languages – particularly Spanish and English – but also because it inclined me to sustain my German. Had I not had this natural inclination, my native language would have surely suffered at such a distance from the soil that nurtured it.

As it happened, though, I have always appreciated language not only for its practical advantages but also for the sheer joy it can bring. From early on I have reveled in puns and witticisms, rhyme and assonance, and any kind of verbal play. When I came across Freud's writings on jokes and slips of the tongue, I was well prepared – as I was for other studies on the history of language and linguistics. Naturally my sensitivity to language did not develop all at once: it evolved over time through many stages, and I frequently let myself be taken in by some seemingly profound rhetoric or other brilliant nonsense. But there's no question that my whole life has been animated by a palpable love of words. And whether that affinity was inborn or whether it grew from my early environment in Vienna, it did predestine me for a career in philology.

A number of experiences contributed to my ongoing education; I have already claimed that a job and a voyage were my first universities and I meant that only halfway jokingly. Among the other influences I will mention a few here which I recognized early on as seminal.

I owe a great many thanks to an Argentine I met in a small inn in Bolivia, where he was traveling to further his own education. The green star on his lapel alerted me to the fact that he was an advocate of Esperanto, and I won him over by addressing him in that language (though I wasn't exactly on firm ground here and we soon had to continue the conversation in Spanish). It turned out that this man was a doctor who had become convinced that modern medicine had reached a dead end. With its chemical and surgical obsessions, so he opined, contemporary practice focused exclusively on treating symptoms rather than the illness as a whole or its underlying cause. This he viewed as a violation of nature.

164

He himself had turned to the art of natural healing, which was attuned to the inner rhythms of the body, and in general recommended 'natural' means both as a curative regimen and a way of life. He also followed a strict vegetarian diet.

His thinking was constructive insofar as he didn't stop with medicine but applied his therapeutic principles to the world at large. His respect for things natural led to a respect for Nature itself, and in all spheres. This point of view made a profound impression on me: it was critical of the status quo and yet this was no artificial program, no tacked-on agenda. He was the embodiment of his own philosophy; this was what he lived and breathed.

I only spent a few days in his company; then he traveled on and I never saw him again. But for years afterwards he provided me with writings, including his own, concerning both the Esperanto movement and natural medicine, so that I ultimately became thoroughly acquainted with his philosophy – which of course entailed more than the commonplace ideas I have mentioned. But there's no need for me to go into his teachings in more detail, since these are not what had such a lasting effect on me. For my part I neither believe that the world's sorrows stem from its linguistic chaos, nor that Esperanto or any other invented language can end this Babel. Even so, I honor the universalism that is the aim of this movement, the attempt to bridge the chasms that divide whole peoples; and just because Esperanto is ultimately inadequate in no way means it is contemptible. Similarly, while I do not believe that mud baths, cold water cures and a strict diet of plants are enough to heal the sick, I appreciate the philosophical core at the root of this natural medicine, the awe of nature that is so sorely lacking in society today. And my acquaintance's fervent beliefs inspired in me a respect and appreciation of the natural world that has remained an important part of my own thinking to this day.

Another friend influenced me more by simple example than by extolling any systematic philosophy. This man was an Eastern European Jew who wrote marvelous poems and stories in his native Yiddish. From him I learned how powerful and at the same time how subtle this language can be, despite the fact that many people foolishly regard it as a kind of jargon or pidgin dialect – whereas in actuality it has a significant body of literature. My friend had been a Zionist and moved to Palestine, where the British had imprisoned him for being a social revolutionary. While incarcerated, his Arab cellmates converted him to a worldview that was incompatible with the current definitions of Zionism. Upon his release he first went to Paris and later to South America, when the political situation in Europe worsened. What I came to admire in him was his commitment to creative nonconformity – here was a man who dared to be a political poet unfettered by religion or nationalism, who dared to be a rebellious Jew at a time when being Jewish at all was fraught with peril. He could dispel the contempt, the misguided notions about the inferiority of Eastern Jews that were both felt and fostered by so many Germans – Jews as well as Gentiles – like a fresh gust of wind can disperse a breath of foul air.

For the most part, the refugees in Quito were no more and no less interested in questions of philosophy and literature than people are in general. Luckily for me, there were two philosophically minded individuals living there at a time when I needed them most. Both of these men attracted the more intelligent refugee youth like magnets, so that a kind of seminar began to cluster around each of them. They themselves were fundamentally different and the few young people who like myself frequented both were introduced to two completely distinct intellectual perspectives.

One of these mentors was essentially a historian, who once a week would deliver a carefully prepared lecture on the cultural history of the seventeenth and eighteenth centuries. His small group of devotees would gather around their patriarch – a sharp contrast to the lives they lived outside the four walls of his house. He also let us have access to his vast library – which I later acquired in its entirety, although that is a different story altogether – even outside our designated meeting times, and on occasion would honor some of us by allowing us to accompany him on his

Sunday walk.

Our other guru was the author of a speculative treatise on the philosophy of history, and he was inclined to favor the why over the what, by emphasizing philosophy and dialectics over pure knowledge. Whenever he was confronted with the question that was posed every day to each refugee, namely "what are you doing" – he would answer simply: "I'm thinking." That laconic assertion both expressed his disdain for the external hardships he was forced to endure as well as cut off any further inquiry.

He also hosted occasional informal seminars, which usually began with someone reading a short thesis that set the tone of the ensuing discussion, in which the paper was subjected to all forms of irony, logic and criticism. As long as he felt the debate was productive, the master would listen, but the moment it became too confused or too petty, he would intervene, and guide the discourse back on track with a few pithy remarks. In this way I made substantial progress in my understanding of Rilke and Spengler, depth psychology and Marxism.

It is easy to categorize these two teachers according to a common dichotomy that pits the positivist historian against the man of ideas. But more important for us was the high standard they both set, and the selfless enthusiasm they both exhibited. After all, neither man was paid; their teaching was truly a labor of love, for the sake of learning – perhaps tinged with pity they felt for us neglected youths.

These and other contacts kept the spirit of intellectual inquiry alive within despite the numbing aspects of the outside world, and over time my reading, my enjoyment of language and my immediate personal experiences all merged to shape my intellectual personality. At the same time these same three things set me apart from the majority of refugees, and they were the only group able to provide me with a frame of reference. My alienation thus came to a peak, and for a long time this increasing sense of isolation dictated my entire worldview. Of course even then I did find some outlet in poetic and literary activities, and ultimately a radical change of circumstances would enable my sensibilities to find their full expression.

Superficially it was a physical illness that brought about this crisis, but there is undeniable evidence that my inner self, in its instinctive search for an escape from my conflict with the world, was actively involved. When the physical symptoms were most acute, I hovered for a long time between life and death. When they subsided, I learned that in the many years I had spent eating food prepared without the most scrupulous hygiene, certain parasites had attacked my body. I also learned that these tropical irritants could not be treated in the tropics: I would have to go to New York, to one of the acknowledged centers for tropical medicine – or at least that's what I told myself. In those days this necessity seemed to be logical and ineluctable, but today I suspect that these travel plans concealed the clever workings of my subconscious desires. I had saved up enough of my salary as an employee of the Compañia Bananera to pay for the trip there and to get along for the first few days: somehow I'd have to scrape together everything else.

Obtaining an American visa was no problem, since at that time they were always issued for reasons of health. The only embarrassing question the consul asked me was where to stamp it, as my German passport had long since expired, its garishly red "J" faded with the Reich itself. In fact, Ecuador no longer had any German or Austrian diplomatic representation – in other words, no one who could issue me a new passport. As I had not acquired a new citizenship in the interim, only one possibility was open to me, the *salvoconducto*, an Ecuadorian travel document for persons without nationality, which I finally acquired after a tedious navigation of a very labyrinthine bureaucracy.

The suspenseful moment arrived when I found myself at Pennsylvania Railroad Station, a half-savage backwoodsman engulfed by the rush of taxis, buses and private cars, all of which seemed to be racing towards one single insignificant point, namely me. I felt radically displaced and practically crushed by the skyscrapers that formed the vertical landscape, for it is one thing to read and hear of such monsters, and another to be actually exposed to them. I would have felt much safer atop Chimborazo than in Manhattan, and it's easy to imagine how the city first suffocated me and then animated my entire being. But I won't dwell on the impressions of a shy, awkward stranger in the big city, since I have other matters to attend.

Suffice it to say that I did not get lost, that I found tolerable lodging, and that a charitable organization intervened just at that moment when my consumptive pocketbook had coughed up what little it had left. I checked in at one of those huge, impersonal clinics equipped with all the requisite medical paraphernalia and was treated at virtually no cost. After undergoing some fairly complicated procedures, I was finally rid of my parasites. After nearly three months, I was almost a regular tourist making his way through the megalopolis, in which the slums and the derelicts of the Bowery fascinated me as much as the art treasures of the Metropolitan Museum and the elegant Frick Gallery.

One experience of that visit is worth special mention. One of my schoolmates from the Viennese *Gymnasium* and I had kept in correspondence during all these long years, and he was now working as a physicist in Boston. He invited me to come up for a visit and I accepted. Proudly he showed me the magnificent buildings and the well-tended, shaded lawns of his alma mater, Harvard University.

The American campuses with their many facilities and spacious settings are enough to impress any unbiased visitor, but I, poor wretch that I was, nearly fainted with awe at the very idea of a university, the inaccessible Mecca of my dreams.

I let myself be led around as in a trance, barely able to contain myself at the sight of the lecture halls, the art collections, the laboratories and even the obligatory glass flowers in the Agassiz building. I saw the students crossing the enclosed center of campus known as the Yard, carrying books on their way to class or else to the world-famous Widener Library, or toting tennis rackets on their way to the gym. These well-kempt boys and girls were for the most part younger than I, and I watched them with that mixture of burning envy and selfless hero-worship so characteristic of people who have been left behind or shorted or deprived. If someone had suggested that within a few years I might be teaching as a bona fide academic on that same campus, I would have immediately summoned psychiatric assistance.

It goes without saying that I was traveling very lightly; by far the most important thing I had taken to the United States were my report cards from Vienna. I had miraculously been able to save them despite all the chaos of emigration. Today I suspect that my sole motivation in undertaking this elaborate and difficult trip was to convey these documents to New York. Necessary though they may have been, the medical treatments were more to appease the rest of the world, which is always demanding a plausible explanation for this action or that. But to explain why this is so I'll have to backtrack a bit.

In retrospect, my various occupations appear quite entertaining, either because of their inherent triviality or their harsh conditions or else because they were so unusual. But at the time I was more embittered than amused. I longed for nothing more than to be a student, instead of taking all those hateful jobs. When I turned twenty, then twenty-two and finally twenty-four, this yearning began to be accompanied by a terrible, growing panic that life was passing me by, while I was just making do and getting along. I worried that it was getting too late to do anything with myself that I would consider meaningful and right. My vast readings began to be a burden, as their eclecticism only stressed my inability to evaluate their relative worth; my autodidactic knowledge seemed a hodgepodge of random ideas rather than an ordered body of learning. And I realized that what was lacking was a regulated course of study under competent guidance.

This wish became so strong that one day I decided to take a first practical step, without knowing how in this unfriendly world things would turn out. I gathered all my surviving school reports, and handed them in to the Ecuadorian ministry of education along with translations into Spanish and an official petition, printed on official paper with the appropriately official language. My request was to be given a chance to earn the South American equivalent of a high school diploma by taking the necessary exams.

The response was negative: my request would be given consideration only if my documents were accredited by an authorized institution. It was shortly after the end of the war; as I have mentioned there were neither Austrian nor German representatives in Ecuador, and in the Spanish consulate, which supposedly represented those states, I was dismissed with a wave of the hand. Trivial as it was, my petition proved beyond the realm of the bureaucratically possible.

Everything thus remained as it had been. Meanwhile, I had discovered that an Austrian consulate had been opened in New York, and as I prepared for my trip, it was with every intention of having my papers officially stamped and approved.

Indeed, I was obligingly received at the New York consulate of the reestablished Republic of Austria – which considering the record of treatment I had received in other contacts with bureaucrats, was a refreshing departure from the norm. They immediately issued me a new Austrian passport, even waiving the fees because of my penury, and officially confirmed that my report cards came from a Viennese gymnasium that was still in existence. The Ecuadorian consul in turn attested to the authenticity of the Austrian consul's signature, and then I had all these documents, certificates and declarations notarized. It was a complicated exercise that cost me a number of days and dollars, but finally I had collected an impressive package of papers, translations, signatures and stamps.

My United States visa had nearly expired. One day I stuffed all my belongings into a duffel bag someone had given me, bought a bus ticket to Miami and took off in the middle of the night, more than a little anxious as to how I would manage the long trek back with so little money. I was en route for several weeks; it was a taxing, even risky journey but it led me to my goal – and more than in just one sense.

At first everything was pleasant enough. I slept aboard the bus during the night, while by day I would go sightseeing wherever we happened to stop. Limited as this exposure was, I did spend a day in Washington and managed to acquaint myself with the most important sights. I also saw Charleston, South Carolina, with its former plantation homes and stately gardens, as well as St. Augustine, a resort town whose fortifications were very present reminders of the former Spanish rule. There I even earned myself a bus tour of town by acting as a Spanish-English interpreter. Finally I made it to Miami in decent condition, although I no longer had my bed on wheels. Even though I had eaten very little along the way, I had to economize as much as possible, so I decided to spend the warm nights in the parks. This, however, led to unexpected difficulties, such as being chased away by the police, who never left you alone no matter whether you were on the benches or on the grass. In addition, the other vagabonds and bums kept harassing me with all kinds of demands and impossible proposals. And all the time I had no idea how I was ever going to escape.

On the second day I decided to avail myself of an address I had of a Jewish women's charity association, whose offices I looked up and then entered with great embarrassment, worried that the good ladies might shrink back in horror at a bum like me. But whatever inner shrinking they may have done they didn't let it show, and confined their scrutiny to their files to make sure I wasn't some notorious, recidivistic mendicant who presents himself for a handout every two months. And when my slate came up clean they took me into their able, motherly, American hands, assigned me a hotel room and saw to it that I was given a sorely needed meal. But the greatest service these humane ladies rendered was arranging for my passage on an air freighter that transported me from Miami to Barranquilla on the north coast of Colombia. How else I would ever have crossed the Caribbean and where I would be today without the help I received I do not know – but I'm sure it wouldn't be in the Schiller National Library in Marbach, West Germany, where I wrote these memoirs.

For Barranquilla I had another address of a Jewish aid service, which I finally located after a long search through the suburbs, lugging my bag on my shoulder. Unfortunately, the contact proved to be a dead end. The head of the organization turned out to be a baker; when I first encountered him he was bending over a trough kneading bread. During our short conversation he kept rolling up his cuffs, and the man cooperated no more with me than his sleeves did with him. Despite my repeated declarations that I had not come for financial assistance but for advice on how to get to Ecuador cheaply by road, all the man would say was that Ecuador was a long way off, that all of Colombia lay in-between (which I of course well knew). Besides, his job was a difficult one as I could see and he didn't have time to get involved in issues of geography. Finally he mentioned a café in the center of town where the wealthier Jews imbibed their afternoon coffee – I could ask them – and with that I was dismissed.

As I had no brilliant alternative I actually went there, but the coffeehouse was full of people and I had no way of knowing who was a wealthy Jew and who wasn't. Not to mention the fact that it seemed preposterous to enter a restaurant and ask total strangers, regardless of their religion, what was the best road to take to Ecuador. Unsure of my next step, I wandered on.

My eyes happened to light on a store sign with a well-known Sephardic-Jewish name. Grasping for straws, I went into the shop and recited my piece, which by now had become quite routine. The owner did indeed belong to the Sephardic community, although it turned out that group was at odds with the Ashkenazi one to which I evidently belonged by birth. He therefore agreed to see me to the right place but would then have to leave me to my fate. I was grateful not to have to go on by foot; we climbed into his car and drove to a corner, from which he pointed some distance away to a store belonging to the leader of the Ashkenazi community.

Once again I repeated my story, and when I was through I was happy to see my interlocutor pensively scratching his head, rather than sending me on my way. On the other hand, he didn't really know how to reach Ecuador overland: as far as he knew everyone heading to Cali or other places south took the plane. In any event he promised to make some inquiries. Meanwhile, since it was already getting late, he suggested I spend the night at a cheap hostel he described to me; tomorrow we'd see. I had no choice but to follow his advice, and headed for the door quite discouraged. On the threshold I was hit by a sudden inspiration: somewhere in the depths of my subconscious I remembered an older friend in Vienna named Paul, who supposedly had emigrated to Colombia at the critical time. My parents were friends of his family; he himself had been studying medicine. For some time my parents hired him as a tutor for me, not so much for my sake but more to provide the man with a little extra income.

In my distress, then, I turned back to the shopkeeper and asked – without expectations or hopes – whether he happened to know a Paul Rosenzweig. Much to my delighted amazement he answered that he did indeed know a Paul Rosenzweig from Vienna. He now went by the name of Pablo Rode, and ran a hotel in Cartagena – hopefully it was same person I had in mind.

A ray of light in the darkness! Especially the word "hotel" had an understandably electrifying effect on me. Abandoning all other options I left the place with a quick thank-you and at the nearest station took the next bus to Cartagena, which was only a few hours away. I was placing all my bets on one card.

During the ride I was in a better mood than I'd been in a long time and entertained the incredulous passengers – local country folk – with accounts of New York and all the wonders that I claimed to have seen with my own eyes only one week previously. Not until we arrived in Cartagena at midnight did my courage begin to flag as I imagined the embarrassment of presenting myself and the possible difficulties of recognition. The initial reception seemed to justify my fears. From a distance the night porter was already giving me unmistakable signals that there were no vacancies; I should go elsewhere. But I had come too far to be turned away now. I asked for Don Pablo. He was in the hospital! My heart sank two flights more. What to do? One last, final chance: Paul had had a sister, Francisca. What about Doña Francisca, was she there? Yes, the sister was there. (I breathed a sigh of relief – at least I was dealing with the right people, and thank God that even in these turbulent times some families managed to stay together!) I asked whether we might call the sister, but she was upstairs in her room asleep – after all it was one o'clock at night!

In moments like this customary courtesy loses its validity. I insisted that she be awakened. The porter hesitated, but finally, confronted with my determined manner, he disappeared up the stairs. The next moments were anxious ones for me. I hadn't seen Paul's sister Francisca since I was fifteen years old, when I had admired her from afar with an infatuation typical of that age group. She was eighteen or nineteen at the time and seemed ethereal and unapproachable. Had she ever even noticed me; did she even know of my existence? What should I say to her now, when both of us were ten years older, and after so much had happened? How should I explain myself so that she would recognize me? Word for word I rehearsed my speech, so it would be as rhetorically effective as possible, so that I could prevail upon her to excuse my nocturnal invasion. Suddenly there they were, coming down the stairs – a somewhat sleepy young woman in a kimono looking me over without the slightest enthusiasm, and behind her the night porter, who was awaiting the ensuing scene with undisguised curiosity. I took a deep breath and began as soon as she had reached the lowest stair, with the utterly unremarkable words: "I'm Egon Schwarz . . . "

I got no further. She clasped both of my hands – she knew exactly who I was and remembered everything. The hardships of my journey were over. I was immediately put up in the hotel and commanded to stay, which I did for a whole week. Paul came home from the hospital; we celebrated our reunion; I had to tell about my parents, our circumstances and experiences.

During my stay they showed me around Cartagena, a Spanish town of colonial stamp. I swam in the ocean. With one stroke of fortune I was changed from a vagabond into a tourist. It happened that my twenty-sixth birthday fell during this time and when I came to breakfast that day the table had been decorated and on it lay a present wrapped in a brightly colored ribbon: a two-volume Spanish translation of Aldous Huxley's novel *Point Counter Point*.

How had they known? I had given Francisca my precious new Austrian passport to hold in the hotel's fireproof cash box and she had leafed through it.

Finally, when I took my leave the two insisted on changing my precious few dollars into Colombian currency and returned to me a whole pile of bills. Astonished, I began to protest, but they assured me that everything was all right, that it was the going rate of exchange, at least in this hotel, and that was that. I was thus freed from my financial worries; my trip could continue; they were even able to instruct me as to how to continue.

Nevertheless I was still a long time getting home, but at least now the pace was no longer slowed by my financial situation; that painful uncertainty was gone; all I needed was patience. Day after day I traveled, by bus, by train and by truck, covering only short distances on bad roads and stopping for the night in miserable lodgings. I passed Cali, Popayán and finally Pasto, after which I crossed the border, and rolled southward over the Ecuadorian highlands: Tulcán, Ibarra, Otavalo, Quito. The validation of my school reports had cost me something, but I had arrived.

This was my last adventure as a pícaro, a turning point on my life's path, which from now on would be 'the road back.' I resubmitted my petition with better documentation; it was accepted and I moved to Cuenca, where my parents were living. This town resembled Sucre and Cochabamba: the kind of isolated, colonial provincial capital I knew so well. It housed the Colegio Benigno Malo, where I planned to get my diploma, and one of the four or five Ecuadorian universities, where I hoped to begin my studies after passing the exams. I had a whole summer to prepare the subjects that the Ministry of Education had determined would be tested: Spanish language and literature, Ecuadorian literature, the history of South America with special attention to that of Ecuador, as well as Ecuadorian geography and the political organization. The normal course of study in the Colegio covers six years, from age twelve to eighteen, but I was like the servant in the Grimm tale who, freed from the weights on his legs, suddenly rushes forward without stopping. It had been a long time since I had studied something systematically; I enjoyed the task and submitted to it with great eagerness. I passed the written and oral exams without difficulty and was given a certification that conferred upon me the title of *Bachiller en Humanidades Modernas*. I now had my diploma: the tear rent by 1938 had been patched. With my new diploma in hand I enrolled in the University of Cuenca as a student in the "School of Law and the Social Sciences." At this point I knew pretty well what I wanted, even if I had little idea how to achieve it. The advantage of beginning my studies well beyond the usual age was that I had had enough time to probe my talents and to define my interests. Clearly I was inclined in the direction of philology and literature. I would have wished more than anything to be matriculated in a "Facultad de Filosofía y Letras," but in Cuenca, where I had to be on account of my parents and our finances, the only three fields of study available were engineering, medicine and of course law. The students themselves didn't think much of their university: they called the law students *ladrones*, or thieves; the medical students *carniceros*, or butchers, and the engineers *albañiles*, or masons. I chose what I considered the least of the three evils. But I didn't agonize over this necessity; after all, I had no intention of becoming a lawyer. Besides, even if I had wanted to I would have faced other obstacles; to practice law in Ecuador at that time you had to have the right social and political contacts. But even without these impediments, the mere thought of being a lawyer filled me with dread. I only wanted to use my study of law as a springboard to find a more appropriate means of fulfilling my desires elsewhere.

As a result I was not overly disappointed when the teaching at the University of Cuenca proved to be a farce, or perhaps a tragicomedy, considering the cheated students. All courses were prescribed – the student could not choose one topic, one teacher himself. Our teachers were practicing lawyers of the city: they viewed their teaching as meagerly paid moonlighting, on which they wanted to waste as little time and energy as possible. They read their lectures from yellowed pages so old they were falling apart. Most likely these were the notebooks they themselves had kept as students, and in this way The Law became timeless and immutable, a subject to be transcribed from one generation to the next, without passing through the brains of the participants. Textbooks were not used; most students never even entered a library during their term at the university and few read any other books on the side. After the lectures (which preserved much of their etymological root of 'readings'), I rushed home and copied over my notes neatly, so that I could 'assimilate' everything I needed to pass the examination on family law, Ecuadorian criminal law, economics, and so on.

Two courses alone departed from this norm, both under the cover of an innocuous or obscure title. One of these, entitled "territorial law," had the express purpose of familiarizing the students with the numerous transgressions that Peru had committed against Ecuador in the course of their common history. Naturally the Peruvian state was soundly condemned; its territorial conquests were exposed as brutal or scheming robberies, its concessions and rapprochements unmasked as hypocrisy. Ecuador, on the other hand, was only a poor, pious sacrificial lamb. Our professor scarcely taught us; he was more inclined to drink than teach, and cancelled four out of five sessions. As a result I can neither confirm nor deny the validity of the Ecuadorian claims. I myself had no emotional stake in the matter; as far as I could tell, the few people that inhabited the regions in dispute – particularly the Amazon basin region – couldn't care less which government was neglecting them. If anything I suspect there may be some truth to the Ecuadorian side, since it is the smaller and weaker of the two countries, and Peru did in fact appropriate much Ecuadorian land. In any event it was curious that this particular subject formed part of the obligatory curriculum.

The other atypical course, "International Law," was taught by a fiery, rhetorically powerful teacher, the youngest and most gifted of the law faculty. This title also concealed a political motive. While the introductory lectures focused on the emergence of international organizations and especially of the recently established UNO, the rest of the year was devoted to the

178

scandalous US exploitation of Central and South America. The course covered various forms of intervention – from the Monroe Doctrine to the incitement of the Panamanian rebellion against Colombia (as preparation for building the Panama Canal); the manipulation of Cuba after the Spanish-American war, and repeated interference in the Central American States and Mexico. The combination of meticulous documentation, sparkling irony and righteous indignation that the speaker brought into play had an explosive effect. The students flew into a rage; their deep-seated resentment against the overly powerful, profit-hungry and arrogant colossus in the North erupted wildly and swept up the listeners. In this way I saw with my own eyes the radicalization of South American academics about which one so often reads. In spite of the demagogic strain and the tendency to redefine domestic socioeconomic problems in terms of international conflict, this course was the only one I took in Cuenca that had any intellectual value.

This latent radicalism, which had much to do with the country's inability to provide educated academics with appropriate occupations, was expressed by the students in several other ways. At one of the larger universities, in Guayaquil if I remember correctly, the students were striking to protest some real or imagined injustices, and the students of the other universities declared their solidarity. What had a moment before been a lethargic, indifferent herd, plagued by nothing greater than an abysmal boredom, was suddenly transformed into an excited crowd. Leaders appeared as though we had sent for them; the students gathered for heated debates and fired off incendiary speeches denouncing the shortcomings of the faculty, the curriculum, the administration and the system as a whole – goodness knows there were plenty of faults. It's just that previously they had either not been noticed or else not considered worth the trouble. But this time the chancellor was presented with a long list of non-negotiable demands, which he could not and would not satisfy. In retaliation, a few students took over the university – there was only one building – locking out the chancellor and the deans, the professors and the rest of the student body, the curators, librarians, secretaries and janitors, and so we had our own strike which lasted for weeks. Every day a basket of food was hoisted up by rope to the students under siege. During this time we gathered to discuss the evils of the world; to send friendly messages to the students at the other schools in Quito, Guayaquil and Loja, and to deliver provocative pamphlets to the Secretary of Education or explanatory ones to the public. Gradually our enthusiasm began to wane and finally it evaporated altogether because our efforts had absolutely no effect.

Among the hundreds of incidents, I would like to single out one grotesque episode, which was entirely without significance except for me. As one of our strike activities, we planned a trip to the neighboring university in Loja. We 'organized' an old truck and started off. To minimize our dependence on the extremely rare and unreliable gas pumps, we carried our own gasoline in an open barrel, which blended in quite harmoniously with the raucous crowd standing on the bed of the truck, singing and smoking away. All of a sudden one of these fellow students carelessly tossed the burning match with which he had just lit his cigarette into the gasoline. I watched in horror as the matchstick hit the liquid splashing around in the barrel – and was inexplicably extinguished. It was obvious to me that the whole vehicle – together with all its passengers – could equally well have been blown sky high. I furiously called the negligent student to account for his action, but all he did was put his arm around me good-naturedly, and attempt to soothe me with feigned astonishment: "What's the matter, *gringuito* – you're not superstitious, are you?" Trivial as this incident was, it struck me as characteristic and even became a kind of symbol for an entire dimension of Latin America.

Somehow the strike was finally settled and the building restored to general use, with no change to the system whatsoever. Even so, I don't think the strike caused any sufferings or setbacks; the teachers and employees of the university enjoyed a vacation from tasks they clearly did not cherish, while the leaders of the movement had a chance to direct and control the masses. The students themselves felt released from their routine, excited by the unusual events, and at certain highpoints inebriated with a sense of common experience. The media had something to report; everyone was talking about the Secretary of Education and the members of the government, who in turn had to travel around and negotiate and who in the end could take credit for having ended the conflict.

Despite this somewhat frivolous analysis I do think the uproar might in the long run have contributed to a change in consciousness and to an amelioration of conditions in the Ecuadorian universities. And I do not believe that protests are necessarily without dignity if they bear no fruit: all I am saying is that I, as a non-Ecuadorian and outsider, experienced the university more from the comic side, and it didn't matter whether the performance was entitled "strike" or "semester." Unlike many others, however, I really wanted to study, so I had to concentrate on getting to a better university where I could pursue my interests on a more advanced level.

To this end I spent a great deal of effort and care in making hand-written copies of my diploma and report cards, as well as lists of all the lecture courses I had taken. I compiled my poems, essays and translations (for example, I had translated Rilke into Spanish) that had been published in various places, and drew up a long cover letter of application. Then I culled a number of addresses from a library reference work and sent the whole package to dozens of institutions around the globe, to a number of European universities but mainly to American ones, where I stood the best chances of getting in, so soon after the war. Considering photocopying machines had not yet made their appearance, one can well imagine how many hours I spent every day, typing and retyping every document, over and over, how many private lessons I had to give to earn enough money to pay for all the mailings.

In light of all my exertions, the payback was discouraging. Some of the addressees never answered. My application and the personal history that it indirectly bespoke must have struck the average admissions counselor as peculiar or even incomprehensible. As I later learned, applicants from South America were considered suspect – another instance of my being punished for the fate that had been thrust upon me. Moreover, although I would have never guessed it, the poems I naively thought qualified me more than anything else for the study of literature actually branded me as an unreliable applicant. As it turns out, there's nothing that the official academy of philologists and literary scholars fear more than creativity and poetic expression. But how was I to know that, given my complete lack of experience? After all, it was just the opposite in South America: there anybody with a smidgen of self-respect had to be a *poeta*, and the more extravagant and grandiose his rhetoric, the better.

A few universities expressed their willingness to let me take a shot at an entrance exam. But admittance wouldn't do me much good without some means of support. Any kind of financial aid would do, whether it was a teaching assistantship or a scholarship, but I was a mere beginner and a foreigner to boot, with nothing to show for myself, and so these were beyond my reach – something that is obvious to me in retrospect. Knowing what I know today about academic bureaucracy, when I think back on my high hopes, I shudder to think what little prospects I actually had.

Weeks became months and my applications became ever more pleading, while the rejections, tacit or explicit, continued to follow. The year at the University of Cuenca drew to a close. I had feared that the strike might prevent me from getting a transcript, but the final exams were administered according to schedule and I passed them easily. Later on, after I had already left the country, I was even sent a prize for having been the best student in my class. But in the meantime, there I sat, stricken by a brooding melancholy because I could no longer believe in the fulfillment of my wishes, in the release from what by now had become an impossible existence.

Among all the negative answers I received, only one letter had been encouraging. It came from a Professor Bernhard Blume, head of the German Department at Ohio State University. My application interested him, he wrote, although he also confessed that my unorthodox education raised certain bureaucratic obstacles.

However, he assured me that he was attempting to overcome them and to find a source of financial aid for me. Naturally I greeted this news with great enthusiasm, but more months passed with no news, and my further inquiries elicited nothing more than concisely worded, conciliatory replies. I once again lapsed into a general despondency.

But all that changed in one solitary instant, one I have often relived while ruminating over my fate. One day I opened my mailbox as usual, completely unsuspectingly – and there in the metal receptacle lay – I still see it clearly before me – a single letter from the USA. The name Otterbein College on the return address meant absolutely nothing to me. Agitated by a presentiment, I took a long time in opening the envelope, and inside . . . was a letter offering me a position! For a yearly salary of two thousand dollars – an enormous sum for me in those days – I was supposed to teach German so and so many hours daily in the foreign language department. Since they were informed that I planned to continue my academic training, the letter went on, all my teaching duties had been scheduled in the morning. Otterbein College, located in Westerville, Ohio, was only eighteen miles from Columbus, where Ohio State University could be reached conveniently by Greyhound.

I owe this sudden turn of fortune to Bernhard Blume. Only later was I able to fully grasp under what unusual conditions he paved the way for me. Something about my unsophisticated application must have touched him, for he had requested a teaching assistantship on my behalf, but that had been denied due to my insufficient training. Nevertheless, he continued to keep me in mind, and when Otterbein College turned to him, the chairman of the largest German Department in the area, asking him to recommend a part-time German teacher, he suggested me, a complete stranger sitting thousands of miles away among the Indians. This he did instead of choosing one of his own doctoral students, who were experiencing bad times and anxiously waiting for job openings. With no offense to my professional colleagues, I suspect he acted as he did because he was not originally an academic, but an artist who loved what was unusual and risky. Bernhard Blume began his career as a writer in Germany: he was a successful playwright and novelist who turned his back on Germany because he was disgusted, not only by Hitler but also by the reaction of his compatriots to National Socialism. Later he told me it was the little word "eigentlich," or "actually" that drove him from his homeland. For when his friends were asked what they thought of Hitler, and whether they were going to put up with his regime, they would answer by saying that the situation was actually intolerable . . . But of course they had to consider their careers, their positions, their incomes, their families and could hardly be expected to leave the country or do much in the way of protest. In America, Blume had to change professions – what was a German playwright to do in an English-speaking country? Although he occasionally remarked in sardonic-wistful tones that he had merely been switched from the artists' *Who's Who* to the scholarly one, the many honors bestowed on him by the profession attest to his outstanding achievements in his redefined capacity as teacher and researcher. While I don't deny my own bias towards him, I believe I have enough circumspection, experience and objectivity not to attribute good qualities to someone simply because of the generous favors for which I am grateful to him. On the contrary, it is a psychological truism that one is especially critical towards people to whom one is indebted. In this case, however, in the decades I was associated with Bernard Blume, I came to admire him as man of superlative qualities: intellectually incorruptible, superbly kind and modest to a fault.

The two biggest obstacles – my further education and a means of support – were now taken care of; now all I needed was to finance my trip. But this matter was settled too in the most benevolent way. Through the intervention of my friend at Harvard, a Viennese physicist sent me the necessary sum, provided that I pay it back "whenever I was better off than he," a condition that I amended to "whenever I could without too great a sacrifice."

We fastened our seatbelts; the stewardess made her little speech; the machine rolled onto the runway and rose into the air.

Powerful contradictory feelings once again took hold of me. After all, how could I be indifferent to this fantastic continent where I had spent the ten most important years of my youth in a whirlwind of adventure? Sorrow and joy, pain and anticipation all merged in a jumble of emotion. In order to soothe the conflict within me, I closed my eyes and said, thinking of Rilke: "You have changed your life." Even from my present vantage point I think I had a right to this view: the whole thing had required enormous self-motivation, I had tenaciously stuck to my plan year after year and had spared myself no exertion or effort to bring it closer to fruition.

This ought then to settle the question of free will, of a person's participation in his own fate. Yet I hesitate to assert as much. True enough, without these efforts success would have been unthinkable. But I have also indicated how everything hung by a thread, how little promise circumstances showed until simple good luck made its sudden, unexpected appearance. And much of my drive was a deep-seated, unconscious striving, which had been inside me since early childhood, and which never abandoned me through all the turns and pitfalls of fate – so can I take credit for that? Anyone who claims such a thing as his own doing reduces these complex forces into an overdetermining idea of "life" as the prime mover and motivator – but such a "life" is too vague, too vast a notion for analytical investigation. For my part, I am certain that all my desire, all my effort and all my will would have changed nothing if the circumstances hadn't worked in my favor. And above all if there hadn't been that one person among the hundreds I had contacted who retrieved my message from its bottle and believed enough in the castaway who sent it.

CHAPTER EIGHT
The Road Back

For all intents and purposes, I have pretty much finished with what I set out to do in stirring so many past events and recalling times that would appear to be lost. And even if I compress several decades into one chapter this is not to imply that nothing of note transpired after I moved to the United States. On the contrary, the years I have spent here have been rich and varied. But my life was no longer so driven by history, no longer so dangerously close to the destructive power it can unleash: I no longer felt like a cork on a storm-tossed sea.

My subsequent development may be seen in terms of inclusion, integration, and return. Soon after my arrival in the States, I met a woman who would be my life's companion, a German who had experienced the war in Nazi Germany – in other words, from the other side. Nevertheless, she had been caught in the same whirlwinds as I, and so we both spoke the same language figuratively as well as literally. By bonding on a personal level we achieved the reconciliation and understanding that had so tragically eluded the two groups throughout their common history.

North America readily accommodates newcomers, and so together we experienced our social reintegration. In adapting to the new circumstances we made a conscious attempt to become middle-class citizens, at least insofar as that was possible; after all, certain differences can never be shed. But gradually we succeeded in mitigating our extreme individualism, our raw nonconformism and the crass alienation we felt from our surroundings. And though we live in our own house, drive a car, have a social life and raised our children like our neighbors, we know that some people, more settled and at one with themselves and the world, find us unconventional and even think there is something "gypsy-like" about us. Even so, our desire to become assimilated ultimately gained the upper hand, and while we have continued to have many adventures, our normalization cannot command the same interest as the social disintegration to which I as an individual was subject during the tumult of the fascist epoch. In the words of Walter Benjamin: "When the hero has helped himself his existence no longer helps us." For this reason I will now sketch what has happened since in broad strokes without too much detail.

In one sense I was almost immediately successful in the United States, and that was academically. This was a very welcome change from my previous occupations, which displayed a depressingly regular pattern of my own inadequacies and my employers' dissatisfaction. Naturally these were mutually reinforcing and had a very disruptive effect on my work.

My new activity, however, was happily free from this dynamic. As intellectually starved as I was, I threw myself into my studies with fiery enthusiasm. I compensated for the many hours that I had to devote to teaching by especially applying myself in my academic work, and as a result I attracted the attention of my teachers. Even though I was twenty-seven years old, I was enrolled as a freshman just like all the eighteen-year-olds fresh out of high school. However, the university advanced credits for my studies in South America, for my languages, and for the placement exams I passed in several subjects, so that I was able to earn my B.A. after one year instead of four. Here, too I received a prize for being the best student of the graduating class.

As a graduate student I could finally turn my attention to more advanced literary studies, which I did at first by including the Romance literatures but then restricting myself more and more to German – a movement that might be perceived as a kind of return.

I was also very content with my teaching job. Initially I must have cut a fairly comic figure, as so often happens when new circumstances force one to recall or imitate a past activity. Unwittingly I found myself emulating my teachers from the Gymnasium, which in this new environment must have seemed absurd indeed. But despite all my earlier reservations, it was the only method of teaching I knew. Not until I became more aware of what I was doing, either intuitively or by virtue of self-observation, did I develop a more appropriate, more democratic approach.

I must now resist the desire to reflect on the American university system, although I have a wide range of experience on which to draw: it is such a complicated subject that it requires a whole science of its own to understand it. I will only mention that Otterbein College was run by a strict religious sect and that neither teachers nor students were allowed to smoke or drink alcohol. In other words, I fit into the surroundings like a square peg in a round hole; both my lifestyle as well as my worldview must have been quite disconcerting. Nevertheless, students and colleagues alike not only tolerated me – they treated me as an equal whom they received with respect and amiable hospitality. Many people invited me into their homes and within a few months I had established closer connections with the residents than I ever had during a whole decade in South America. Both the large public Ohio State University with its twenty-seven thousand students as well the small Christian college with its enrollment of six hundred demonstrated such tolerance and flexibility in their attitude towards me that I was able to feel at home in the shortest period of time.

To this day I have maintained a similarly good relationship with academe, although I have switched institutions a number of times. Ultimately the American university became a kind of second home to me. This is by no means to imply that I failed to take note of its many weaknesses; it's just that I succeeded in finding an institution which accepted me with all my shortcomings and virtues, where I could put my talents to use and continue to develop them. I don't recall ever considering the study of literature as a possible career or even as a means of supporting myself, although in pursuing this profession I was fulfilling my most ardent desires. I viewed it as a privilege and committed myself to it as best I could without concern for whatever material gain could be extracted. I had to work hard: I got up early, taught for hours on end, and took the long bus rides every day. In the evening I prepared my classes, corrected my students' papers and wrote my own – as well as completed whatever other work was required. My income did not allow for any extravagance, but I was so used to poverty that this seemed almost natural – at least I didn't waste any time thinking about it.

As it happened, my worries about future employment resolved themselves in the most natural way. Since it never occurred to anybody at the university that someone might be studying without prospects for a job, I was automatically treated like a future academic, and as a result I began to grow into this role. But this came about very gradually; I don't remember any particular experience or moment of epiphany. When the time came, I was given a topic for my master's thesis, and upon finishing my degree I became a teaching assistant. As it turned out, I had to look for a new position anyway, since the number of returned veterans studying in the wake of World War II began to dwindle, and it was for their sake I had been hired at Otterbein. So I switched over to the university.

Finally, scarcely five years after my arrival in the States, I received my doctorate, and soon after that I was offered my first full-time teaching job. From there on, I stepped up the academic ladder in the usual manner, starting as an instructor, proceeding from assistant professor to associate and finally to full professor. Neither I nor anyone around me questioned the propriety or necessity of this process, and in this way the very thing that had always eluded my grasp in South America – namely a profession – causing me no end of anguish, just fell into my lap. And this with scarcely any effort on my part other than that to which I joyfully submitted, not out of duty, but from inner necessity.

There was only one major obstacle to overcome, and that was more internal than institutional. When I began, American literary studies were dominated by New Criticism – a methodological approach based on close readings of texts – and the best, most intelligent teachers subscribed to it. For a variety of reasons, perhaps mostly as a reaction against earlier treatments of poetry that were pedantically dry and philistine, criticism had become a hagiography of the great metaphysical poets whose writings were interpreted like Scripture. The new fashion regarded the author as an inviolable oracle whose every utterance was subjected to shrewd interpretation, and whose writings contained meanings so lofty they could only be intuited by listening, as it were, with one's inner ear. The inner correspondences, the euphony of the rhymes and syllables, the melodic line of the verses, the sentence cadences, the deep meaning of the metaphors: all these were hearkened to with great reverence. The hidden consonance of the parts, the structural elements that merged into a unified whole were eagerly sought and found, so that the main object of investigation ultimately became the self-referentiality of the poetic work itself. Naturally this orientation privileged particular writers, since not every text makes this almost sacerdotal claim to being Art; not every author addresses himself exclusively to a highly educated, refined public with a taste for decoding complex linguistic constellations.

Anything that failed to satisfy these standards was branded as popular, trivial literature, even pulp. And any attempt to connect a given work and writer to life in its more material aspects, any social or historical investigation, was treated with disdain and intolerant disavowal. After all, the whole purpose of Art was to rise above the workaday banality of the profane, commercial world and to transport the initiated to a higher, hermetically sealed sphere.

But it was such forces that had shaped my own ineradicable experiences. To concern oneself with art without accounting for history seemed to me to be hopelessly removed from reality. Not that I didn't find any pleasure in the New Criticism or that I totally rejected the techniques developed by its disciples. I even proved myself quite an able acolyte, and developed considerable skill in applying New Critical methods. To this day I believe that close reading of the text, respect for authorial intention, comprehension of craft, and insight into generic paradigms and the suggestive powers of language are indispensable tools for the literary scholar. But the worldview that emerged by such exclusive focus on the text per se did not appeal to me. The idea that humans are determined by historical circumstances was too deeply ingrained, too much part of my own life experience to allow anyone to persuade me to repudiate it, and why should my historical outlook suddenly cease when it came to art? I could not or would not make exception for a method or cult that deemed itself free of such dependencies. In short, a gap inserted itself between my cultural perspective and my literary training, and in my mind I began to design a bridge to span the two spheres. This project was as much existential as it was professional; it was as if I were made up of two separate halves, one that lived in the world and one that analyzed literature, and the split between my biographical and professional self caused me considerable discomfort. I felt I couldn't rest until I had joined the two.

The effort to close this gap kept me preoccupied for two whole decades. My first attempts to join these two 'halves' drew on comparative literary histories. I felt that any legitimate comparison between literary works from different societies had to take into account the particular conditions of their genesis. My own familiarity with two different languages and cultures helped me greatly in this endeavor. I focused on the study of German-Spanish relations, which I pursued not merely from a literary standpoint but from a general, 'cultural' perspective. In the context of these studies I wrote a book about Hofmannsthal and Calderón, which included a historical dimension. Much to my satisfaction, a Belgian reviewer remarked that mine was the first work that helped the reader place Hofmannsthal in the context of European social history.

But I was ambitious enough to seek an even more tightly knit connection between literature and the soil that nourished it. And so began my in-depth study of German history and politics, which of course was also a reflection on my past and myself. My two books *Nation in Conflict* and *Banishment* are the results of these efforts, although they by no means exhausted the subject. In the first work I explored the confrontation of two distinctly German traditions, one humanistic, one pathological. My second book purported to be a phenomenology of exile under Hitler.

Since then I have gained greater confidence in my methodological approach. Because in both my research as well as my teaching I have concentrated on modern literature, the attendant economic and social forces are especially complex and therefore require particular attention. It is not difficult to perceive that the fundamental forces that have determined our era have been secularization, democratization and modernization. The history of modern culture can be viewed as a multiplicity of reactions to the gradual spread of industrialization.

While I didn't ascribe anything and everything to this historical process, I did attempt to understand what forces helped give literature its shape. Lectures on fascism and German literature, a book on poetry and politics in the work of Rainer Maria Rilke, an essay on the different receptions of Hermann Hesse in America and Germany, an anthology on inner emigration from Hitler and exile – these works clearly reflect my intellectual concerns.

One good thing about my chosen profession is it affords time – at least on occasion – to take a favorite subject and pursue it in more depth. And so at last I was able to fulfill an old wish and to write a book on an especially cherished poet, Joseph von Eichendorff. By this time it was almost out of habit that I emphasized aspects of the writing that were socially relevant.

Obviously the times were not very conducive to the Romantic attitude of the poet, with his introspective cheerfulness and inner tranquility – nor could they be: history had determined an entirely different Zeitgeist. And hence the title of these recollections.

Even so, among the many possible lines of work available, that of the literary historian is hardly the most objectionable. In my definition, it is a field devoted to prolonging the life of past literary works, in order to have them illuminate present-day concerns. As it happened, I broke with tradition by relating (but not relegating!) the poetic realm to the sociopolitical one – but this does not exactly weigh on my conscience. After all, German literary scholarship has always borrowed from fields ranging from anthropology to zoology. To express it more chemically: German studies is a highly volatile substance, seldom found in a pure state, and as such has an unmistakable tendency to bond with other matter. Not that these other substances are any more solid; after all, the same people who threw their hands up in despair when we looked for inspiration to the social sciences sat by perfectly content when we drew on aesthetics or theology.

But before we continue with my own approach to the 'study' of German literature, it is worth pausing to examine what it was that was actually being approached. To say this consisted solely of an analysis of German literature is inadequate, in part because of the difficulty in defining either 'German' or 'literature'. The study of German literature is not always and everywhere the same. There was a time when it meant being concerned with anything that fit within a range of categories from 'Gothic' to 'Goebbels', from the sword-brandishing Teutons to the most esoteric problems arising from contemporary poetry. In those days German studies was the knowledge of all things German and had to be understood as a reflection of Germany's role as a world power. For ideological reasons the German state eagerly supported any and all interest in such disparate subjects. These dreams have long since disappeared and given way to a new reality.

When the second World War came to an end, Germany was nothing more than a heap of smoking rubble. (I speak here of the developments in West Germany, which I know better, having followed them through my many professional contacts.) Nothing seemed to have remained of the old order except for one single institution: the university, which continued to enjoy high public esteem as it conducted its usual business with undiminished conservatism. But this astonishing robustness, this apparent indestructibility proved to be illusory. Beneath the venerable ivy its walls showed the same cracks as other institutions, and in the sixties they caved in with proverbial German thoroughness. What was happening before the very eyes of fascinated observers was the transformation of an elite academy into the educational instrument for modern mass society. These upheavals naturally also destroyed the old ideology. The last remnants of aristocratic Romanticism which had dominated Germany longer than other countries were swept away, making room for a pluralistic perspective, one more suited to the democratic system that, while late in coming, now seems to have become firmly established. This was not without repercussions for German Studies, and this highly inclusive and respected area of specialization began to adapt to the new circumstances. Gradually it shifted its orientation away from Romanticism towards the Enlightenment, acquiring in the process a more pragmatic and less nationalistic focus. The literary canon changed; more progressive authors gained recognition; popular literature was deemed worthy of study; writers who had been banned in the Third Reich received particular attention. Entire movements discredited by the Nazis, such as modernism and expressionism, celebrated their reinstatement, and authors once vilified in the Third Reich – such as Heine – were rehabilitated in seminars, conferences and monumental editions. The critical tradition of the intellectual left, represented not only by Marx and his followers, but perhaps even more by the members of the Frankfurt school, such as Walter Benjamin, Theodor Adorno and their disciples, wielded enormous influence. In this atmosphere people had little patience with the metaphors, word plays and rhythms so crucial for the New Critics.

In particular, the German school of close reading fell into disfavor, as the professors who taught immediately after the National Socialist era had used it as a shield against the contamination of historical thinking. In reality they were defending themselves against a growing conviction among Germans who came of age after the war that the past could not be overcome unless it was confronted, and it was precisely this past which the old professors had loyally supported – or at least compromised themselves into accepting.

All this had had profound effects on American German departments, which had followed in the wake of the Reich well into the war and were thus in dire need of a thoroughly new orientation. Precisely because it is the mission of German departments to familiarize succeeding generations of students with developments in the German-speaking countries, it is hardly surprising that they are quick to pick up trends coming from those same places. This sudden about-face, however, had an additional personal significance for me; after all, like the young German students I had rejected the fascist ideology and the reactionary traditions on which it drew. Like them I was exposed – albeit in reverse order – to the ebb and flow of historical experience and an aestheticizing conception of literature. I soon found myself serving as a mediator between the German and American scene, between those who viewed literature as Art, and those who saw it mostly as a historical mirror – and ultimately I reached the conclusion that one does not exclude the other.

While the New Critics' narrow focus on the text has been called into question – not without good reason – one should distinguish between the method and the ideology of its practitioners. Just because Hitler ate with a knife and fork doesn't mean we have to stop doing so. A method that has been applied to achieve specific ends in specific circumstances can, when the circumstances change, be used for different purposes altogether. And those who reject 'close reading,' the art of empathetic attention to the text's details, are essentially committing the same mistake with which they reproach the New Critics: they are ignoring the historical context that gives the isolated element its meaning.

Let me use an analogy to illustrate the importance of meti-culous textual study. For the sake of comparison let us turn to something that has even more "play" than literature, namely, the game of chess. I choose this example because, like literature, chess has a long history, enjoys great popularity and possesses obvious aesthetic qualities.

Clearly one could analyze the game in all its socio-historical dimensions, by studying its development from its adaptation in Europe to the modern embattled world championships with their mass audiences, the intervention of television, the press, the judges, lawyers and gaming officials, with all the political and economic trappings. Equally fruitful would be an investigation of the changes within the game itself, for these, too, provide substantial insight into Western intellectual history. One could for example point to the unmistakably feudal origins of the game, as revealed in the figures themselves, starting with the king and his all-powerful grand vizier (this figure was transformed into a "queen" only in chivalric Europe, with its latent women's liberation). These are followed by the lower aristocratic orders of castles, bishops and knights, and finally the pawns, or peons, the major instruments or victims of slaughter.

Along with these considerations, we should examine the shift in playing philosophy, from the 'romantic' gambits, where victory is achieved through the sacrifice of figures (illustrating the power of the 'mind' over 'matter'), to a more 'technical' strategic positioning which, as we know from computerized partners, can be calculated mathematically. Isn't it possible to discern a global human tendency in all this?

A comprehensive study of all these aspects could no doubt lead to a better understanding of a popular game, through which we could no doubt glean a whole series of insights into human beings and their world. But anyone who really wants to understand the game has to get down to the nitty-gritty, which in this case means analyzing individual matches between masters. The essence of chess was and remains what Bogolyubov's twentieth move was and how Tartakower responded to it.

I will not go further into the application of my little parable. As it happens, chess does contain quite a number of parallels to literature; perhaps it can even be regarded as an "art" – the commentators on the game certainly imply as much, by describing certain solutions as "beautiful" or "elegant." But there are also considerable differences. And the thing that separates literature from chess more than anything else is language, which is so essential to any literary work, which carries meaning beyond a narrowly circumscribed world, a medium with its own richly substantial life. In other words, the language of literature is the language of society itself. Written for and absorbed by a broad public, its dissemination is shaped by the dominant economic system; as a result it is bound to historical reality by thousands of threads, and the magnitude of this dependency is much greater than the game of chess. And although my analogy has shown that it is indeed necessary to examine the inner workings of a literary text, such a study alone remains insufficient.

To explain a phenomenon in and through itself is a logical absurdity comparable to the idea of pulling oneself out of the swamp by one's bootstraps. To understand something fully it's not enough to become mired in it; you have to look at it from the outside as well, to confront it from different points of view, to explain it from a perspective that is outside the thing itself. Scientists have long been aware of this basic principle. A biologist will not rest until he has explained a living thing in terms of its chemistry; a chemist is only satisfied when he has succeeded in describing a problem in the language of physics.

Once again I would like to resort to a parable to illustrate the fact that a segment of text will not reveal its true sense until its connection with a historical context has been accounted for. After the Second World War, a letter was found in a Nazi archive; in it a young officer was being praised by his superior for his unshakable loyalty to National Socialism. On the basis of this dubious letter of recommendation, the officials in charge of deNazification – eager to pursue their duty – were ready to pull the young man in, when at the last minute a whole new perspective was revealed. As it happened, the officer had been under considerable suspicion for statements he had made criticizing the regime, and the long arm of the secret police was already making motions to nab him. The incriminating letter had been written by his commanding officer to protect him from political persecution. This action in turn could be explained by the fact that small pockets of independence, indeed, of resistance against the regime had been preserved in the army. As an isolated text, the letter presented an inadequate or even thoroughly misleading picture of reality. Only knowledge of the historical background that produced this verbal document could disclose its true meaning; judging by appearances alone can be downright dangerous. The lesson afforded by this example can be applied, mutatis mutandis, to every literary text.

Far from being a closed subject, this complex problem strikes me as an increasingly urgent present concern. Certainly I have devoted years of my professional life to better understanding these relations, and continue to direct my research in this direction – which is why I have chosen to dwell on these reflections at such length here in this autobiography. In an effort to understand why I held the views I did in my professional life, I am merely tracing a path that from the earliest moment on links individuality with historical circumstance. Anyone undertaking a similar exploration into the source of his opinions will find that there is no such thing as objectivity independent of historical origins; our most personal perspectives are a function of our station in life. To go even further, they are the sum total of the experiences that have formed us. My work as a literary historian had first to integrate the experience of the times before it could become an expression of my personality. And so in order to emphasize the interdependence of my professional activity and my own life history, I could say – perhaps with some exaggeration – that in my search for authentic self-realization I have had to develop an autobiographical method of literary analysis.

Curiously enough, another potential conflict between my profession and my existential experiences proved less a source of suffering than a spark for reflection and discussion with colleagues. Historically, the relationship of German studies to Judaism has been a strained one, to put it mildly. I needed to explain or even justify the fact that I, a German-speaking Jew, had chosen to make a career of it, especially so soon after the Second World War and the massacres of so many Jews at the hands of Germans.

While the history of German culture reveals countless examples of anti-Semitic, "völkisch" aggression – as well as other objectionable ideologies – my thinking has never been nationalistic. From my point of view, it was never "the" Germans who said and did these things, but rather individuals who represented themselves as well as certain groups and tendencies. There were enough thinkers or writers who opposed them more ably and articulately than I could have done. Other cultures were by no means free of similar faults: neither Russia nor Spain, France nor England. Anyone intent on avoiding such base behavior had best stay away from history altogether. Besides, the anthropologist doesn't necessarily identify himself with the tribes he studies; no matter how attached he becomes to a culture surely he cannot approve of everything he sees.

For my part, I was interested in literature; in how it comes about, how it mirrors the world and in what it can accomplish in society. It also happens that I know German better than any other language, and am familiar with its subtleties and idiosyncrasies, although I've read as much non-German literature, and with equal pleasure. The German language has been the medium for humanistic visions worthy of anyone's respect.

All too many refugees made the mistake of venting their wrath, justified as it was, on anything and everything German, including the language and the culture from which they had been expelled. For my part, I was more inclined towards focusing my skepticism on a field of study that had grown overly specialized and utterly obsolescent. It seemed that so much of German studies had become a kind of arcane rummaging through the literary dustbin, with little or no concern for the outside world and the forces that had so recently torn it asunder.

But even this skepticism hardly affected me on an emotional level, and while I clearly recognized the legitimacy of my doubts, I wasn't about to abandon the whole endeavor because of this intellectual disapproval. I had struggled too hard to achieve what I had, and besides, there was nothing I could do to change the way things were anyway. A far more useful challenge, so it seemed to me, would be to provide a counterexample, to offer an alternative examination of the given topics in a way that would shed light on the underlying social conditions. But perhaps my highly critical approach, my undisguised irreverence and my reluctance to play the yea-sayer both as a journalist and literary historian – attitudes that have disturbed some of my colleagues – are directly related to my special situation within my field, and the detours I had to take to reach it.

Nevertheless, as these various intellectual and emotional tensions were seeking resolution, external developments continued on their merry course. After it became clear we would not stay on in Ohio, we boldly planned our future by sitting in front of a map and applying for jobs wherever the brown highlight indicated a particularly scenic area. Before long we were happy to hear we could continue our studies, as teaching assistants at the University of Washington in Seattle, which was idyllically located between the mountains and the sea. In a second act of derring-do we decided to purchase a ten-year-old Chevrolet which was still running despite the hundred thousand miles on the odometer. The only problem was that I didn't know how to drive, so that it was a little frustrating having to walk by my car every morning on my way to the bus that ate up so much of my time. But finally I was able to find a few spare hours and passed the driving test.

Here I took advantage of that vaunted American virtue, individual freedom. This basic principle has very tangible manifestations – for example, unlike in Germany, you don't have to notify the police every time you move. (Of course, given the enormous mobility of the population, a rule like that would soon lead to anarchy anyway.) Similarly, in most European countries anyone who wants to acquire a license must first attend an official course, at officially high prices. In the US, the authorities aren't concerned with how you learned to drive, they're only interested in whether you are able to. Moreover, despite the relative ease of obtaining a license, driving in the US is sheer joy compared with driving in Europe, with its culture of motorized aggression – but that's subject enough for another entire book.

Enough said: the big moment arrived when we loaded up all our earthly possessions and bade adieu to our friends and acquaintances. Then we set out in our "new" car, whose more recent dents testified to my newfound mastery, and headed west – a little anxious but mostly in good spirits. By that time I had been in the country two years; I had gotten to know many areas – New

York, Boston and northern New England, as well as Chicago and the Great Lakes. But this was the beginning of my real "American" experience. Ohio is a very good state for the new arrival, since its own rich diversity reflects that of the country at large. Its economy is half agricultural and half industrial; it officially belongs to the Midwest, but enjoys close contact with the East Coast as well, with only Pennsylvania between it and the ocean; its northern border is the Great Lake Erie, while on the south it verges on Kentucky and Appalachia. But the state's continental climate, with its icy winters and searing summers running one into the other with hardly any transition, as well as the general flatness of the landscape (at least around Columbus) – make it hardly the most appealing place in the world.

No, no one can claim to "know" the US unless he's explored the endless expanses of the American West, camping out in the wild, and surrendered himself without prejudice to its incomparable displays of beauty. Whenever people ask what, in my fifty years of living here, I consider the best thing about this country, I answer without a moment's hesitation: the huge national parks and wilderness areas that offer people a chance to experience nature in its pure state. Of course, part of this is the spirit itself that was bent on preserving these lands, untouched, for future generations, a spirit already active in the nineteenth century and still alive today, although recent policies unfortunately tend to favor exploitation over preservation.

But rather than go on raving I merely wish to report that my young wife and I spent six weeks on the road; we traveled to Rocky Mountain National Park in Colorado, then on through the isolated areas of Utah, New Mexico and Arizona. We followed the Grand Canyon on our way to Los Angeles, then moved up the coast through California, Oregon and Washington, where we finally settled in Seattle. The entire time we avoided both hotels and restaurants, sleeping and cooking out in the open, in part due to our meager financial resources, but also because we so preferred: this was our way of taking possession, so to speak, of our new home. Since that time we have crisscrossed the continent

201

many times in a similar manner, although in later years we have made increasing concessions to creature comforts. We have been in forty-nine of the fifty states, and have made similar treks across Canada, Mexico and Central America. During the 1960s, when Woody Guthrie's "This land is your land" became a popular retort to the hawkish slogan "America – love it or leave it," I felt both very familiar with the landscapes being evoked, and very included by the refrain "this land was made for you and me."

In Seattle we spent three wonderful years teaching German language and literature, and studying even more for the challenging Ph.D. exams known as the "comprehensives." After passing those I wrote my dissertation on the free thinker Georg Christoph Lichtenberg, the eighteenth-century physicist and popular philosopher from Göttingen, whose Enlightenment views bore a clear affinity with my own.

Whenever we had a few free days, however, we packed our camping equipment into the old Chevy and disappeared into the mountains. At that time you could wander around for weeks without meeting a single soul – except perhaps the bear who trotted over to sniff at our sleeping bags one night (do bears have souls?).

Of all the states, Washington is one of the most enchanting, or perhaps two of the most enchanting, since the state is divided into very distinct halves by the Cascades, whose peaks like Mt. Baker, Mt. St. Helens, Mt. Adams and the majestic Mt. Rainier rise over 4,000 meters above sea level. The western half is damp, and blessed with a mild climate throughout the year; its forests, streams and lakes extend downward to a richly variegated coast dotted with islands. The desert-like eastern side, which is transected by the Columbia River, offers a similar wealth of natural splendors.

The birth of our son, and later our first daughter, interrupted our insatiable explorations only temporarily. Once the infant was a few weeks old, we would wrap him in a crocheted tablecloth that had holes for breathing, and drape him, papoose-like, over my back. In this way he could accompany us even on our most

202

difficult climbs.

The early fifties were not easy times for academics. I will pass over the many vain attempts I made to secure a position, even with my Ph.D. in hand. The fact that I landed a job at Harvard may have been thanks to my first publications, which had by then appeared, but more likely it was simple undeserved good luck. In those days it was so unusual for someone from the University of Washington to go to Harvard, that I became the talk of the campus, to the point where someone once asked me whether I'd heard the news about a fellow in the humanities going to Harvard!

Once again we had to cross the continent. The Chevrolet, older by three strenuous years and many thousands of miles, was now in such bad shape that practically the entire bottom had rusted away, so that the person sitting up front had to be careful where he rested his feet. Furthermore, the car's electrical system gave up the ghost just a few days before our departure, so that neither headlights nor horn, or even windshield wipers were working. A kind-hearted mechanic who felt that the problem was beyond repair donated a handful of fuses and showed me where to insert them in case we were stopped by the police: supposedly that would make the lights go on for a few seconds. Another person took pity on us, seeing that we had no spare wheel, and gave us an old tire to use in case of emergency.

At last we set out east, just as we had set out in the opposite direction three years earlier, similarly laden with all our bags and baggage – although this time we had two energetic children as well. Our progress was extremely slow: the old wreck couldn't go more than forty miles an hour. Through the holes under our feet we watched the American highway whiz by, while out the window there was always a drying diaper, waving in the wind like a flag of truce. If on the way we happened to find a rabbit that had fallen prey to a passing car but was still fairly intact, we would throw it into the trunk, to be skinned and roasted over a fire at our next stop.

We also experienced an occasional crisis, as for example when we had a flat tire in the middle of a godforsaken stretch in

Wyoming. We replaced the tire with the spare we had been given, but after two minutes back on the road that one burst into a thousand pieces. So we stood there stranded by the road, where we couldn't stay because of the rattlesnakes but neither could we leave with only three good tires. On top of that it was getting dark and we didn't have any lights. In desperation I put the flat tire back on the wheel and rolled at a snail's pace through the dark, until several hours and a few miles later we reached the next town, which consisted of three tiny shacks. There we set up our tent by the side of the road. The following day we spent half of our cash on a new tire, which we had to mount ourselves because the storekeeper who had sold it to us had his arm in a cast.

It would be flouting all sense of proportion – even more than I have already – if I were to recount all the details of our trip. As a last thing, though, I would like to describe an episode when fate almost caught up with us after all. We had made it to the state of New York, just two days' drive from our destination. A wailing siren signaled the sudden appearance of a police car, and the uniformed guardian of order asked to see my papers. I doubt very much that he suspected our car of having been stolen, but it was after all his task to protect the haves from any disagreeable contact with the have-nots, and our unkempt appearance must have made him apprehensive. The officer wanted to check my lights. The long awaited moment had finally arrived; I sprang into action and quickly plugged one of my fuses in the designated spot. For an instant the lights did their duty, at least enough to satisfy the policeman, who studied me thoughtfully as he returned my license. A light must have gone off in him as well, since he glanced at the backseat piled high with junk and asked: "I guess you're coming East to start a new life?" Apparently this was an acceptable idea, for when I answered yes we were allowed to drive on unhindered, all the way to Cambridge.

The man was not all that far from the mark, since ours had been a journey towards respectability. I was now a teacher at one of the most famous universities in the country, and our financial situation was improving steadily. Even so, I should add that, in those days, teaching at a university was one of the worst paid and least regarded of the professions. Any doctor or lawyer earned far more than a college professor and enjoyed higher public esteem. But changes were beginning to take place. The United States was undergoing a period of great expansion in terms of politics and trade, and professors in particular fields, such as economics, sociology, political science, chemistry and physics were increasingly being asked to serve as advisers, both to the government as well as to large corporations. The prestige that these consultants earned in the public arena even began to rub off on those of us whose fields were thoroughly useless. Finally, when the Russians launched Sputnik, the patriotic Americans saw themselves surpassed precisely in a field where they had thought to be invincible, namely the technical mastery over nature, and that by rivals whom they did not exactly hold dear. Billions of dollars began pouring into schools and universities, and somehow public opinion adopted the naive hope that a rapid rise in the knowledge of mathematics and foreign languages would help restore the nation to its former supreme position. As a result, job openings started to proliferate; even salaries showed a general increase. And when the newly elected President Kennedy began to appoint professors from Harvard and other universities to key positions, we professors began to matter a little to other people, and were so able to extract all kinds of advantages from this shift.

The constant growth began to level off about ten years later, and remained at that plateau for some time afterward. Since the early 1980s, however, a steady decrease in government support has brought the American university to a point of crisis. Slowly but surely we are being reduced once again to our original insignificance, both because of the drastic cuts being implemented at the institutional level, as well as the inflation which has tended to outrun any increments in salary. Nowadays many young Ph.D.'s are unable to find permanent positions, so they drift from one part-time job to the next, with the result that we now have an academic proletariat. Meanwhile those of who do have jobs are still living well. But, other than Spanish, the languages are suffering a decline, especially German, which might as well be listed as an endangered species.

The seven years I spent with my family teaching at Harvard were happy and fruitful. A lively intellectual atmosphere, an extensive social life, the arrival of a second daughter, the acquisition of a modest but pleasant home, practically in the country, a number of trips to Europe, which we traversed from Lapland to Andalusia and the Peloponnesus – all this hardly left us time to breathe. Exploring the mountains of New Hampshire and Vermont, or the solitary coastal crags of Maine easily assuaged our constant longing for the great American landscape. One day we looked up to catch our breath, and found that we were forty!

In the early sixties, we moved to St. Louis, where I had accepted the job I held until my retirement, which isn't to say that we've settled down completely. Research trips and lecture tours have brought us to various countries; I have been a guest professor in Hamburg, at Berkeley and other universities.

On a number of occasions I have even gone back to Vienna, where at first, in the 1950s, I felt very strange indeed, standing in front of our old house in the Geologengasse – it was half destroyed by bombs – or else in front of the Gymnasium, where I had once struggled so hard with questionable success. But with each return trip, these bittersweet feelings are less powerful, and I have become more like the other tourists who travel there for the sake of the sights. One difference will no doubt always remain: unlike most of the strangers, I know my way around fairly well; in some parts of town the buildings are so familiar that I could name the next cross street and describe the neighboring house with my eyes closed. And I still understand every word and every nuance of even the broadest Viennese dialect. This will never change.

I've gone back to Pressburg, too, where I stared, stunned, at the deep ditch that was once my grandmother's house, as though it were the abyss of time itself: it could have been thirty or three hundred years since I last stood at that very spot. Below me lay the ruins of a wall; a few children were playing in the rubble over-grown with bushes and weeds. The Judengasse had been razed to the ground, into one long pile of debris out of which a single house, dating from the Middle Ages, rose like a ghost: it had no doubt been spared for the sake of the Gothic style.

St. Louis, where we spend most of our time, is hardly the eighth wonder of the world, but two hundred years make it an old city by American standards. It has everything you need and more: museums and galleries, an excellent symphony orchestra, out-standing chamber music, theaters, and several universities that are active cultural centers. It even has something like a literary tradition: T.S. Eliot was born here; Tennessee Williams wrote his best plays here. His *Glass Menagerie* is full of allusions to the city and even to Washington University, which he briefly attended. The Missouri and the Mississippi rivers – at least in the parts that have remained untouched – resemble the riverscape that Mark Twain eternalized in his books (he lived in nearby Hannibal); watching the languid current, it's easy to picture Tom Sawyer, Huckleberry Finn or Jim gliding by on their rafts. This is even the spot where the German writer Karl May set the first scenes of his novel *Winnetou*, where the German Greenhorn, later to become the invincible Old Shatterhand, tamed his first horse and acquired his legendary "Bearkiller" rifle, and a gun which could fire twenty-five shots without reloading. This and other "Western" novels by the same author used to be rejected as low-brow trash, despite (or perhaps because of) the fact that millions of boys read them assiduously. Now academic critics treat them quite seriously as mythological tales.

In the nineteenth century, St. Louis was an important cross-roads, the last outpost of western civilization, where the expedi-tions like Lewis and Clark's supplied themselves with all the necessities before setting out on their daring treks into the West. Heavy river traffic connected the city with the South; a steamboat could take you all the way to New Orleans and back. In 1904 the city celebrated a symbolic triumph when it hosted the World's Fair and the Olympic Games in grand style. For that occasion, the German Professor August Sauer came from the University of Prague to lecture on the influence of American literature abroad.

Max Weber visited here and the observations he made with his sharp sociological eye were among the first to help him understand the connection between Protestantism and the spirit of capitalism. Since then Chicago has taken the lead over this city, but St. Louis is nevertheless worth a visit, as are the Ozarks, which abound in caves and springs and primordial rivers. In some places the farmers speak an archaic dialect and even live as they did in the olden days, at least to some extent. Here there is still genuine America.

Of course I don't live in St. Louis for the sake of any of these attractions, but rather because it is the home of Washington University, an old private university whose humane spirit has kept me here for over three decades despite many opportunities for change.

Time flew, and one day I noticed to my astonishment that I was the oldest member of the German Department. Like an old desk, I belonged to the university's furnishings, perhaps not a "venerable old man," (as Immanuel Kant had been addressed in the auditorium of the University of Königsberg on the occasion of his fiftieth birthday!), but a kind of "elder statesman" of the university. And so I thought the time had come to write my autobiography and to depict how everything had come to be the way it was. That is now done and I am ready to break off my story, for my life has settled irrevocably into a single track, one among many – I lead a university life which can hardly be distinguished any more from any other.

But before I turn off my word processor (I have to put it like this, although it would sound a lot better to say "Before I lay down my pen"), I would like to describe my relationship to the Unites States. I began my account by describing Vienna, which had at one point been my home but which lost that meaning for me in the wake of historical developments, so it's only right that I conclude it with a focus on where these same events ultimately led me. Perhaps that will shed some light on where I stand in the world at large, after so many adventures and experiences, and what has become of my ideals and my commitments to them, as well as my present hopes.

To start with, I should stress that I am far from blind to the terrible social problems this country faces. As it happens, many of my German students in particular are surprised how sympathetic I am to their own indignation at finding so much inequity in so wealthy a land; in fact, I am generally able to support their own critical stance with more facts than they can.

There can be no doubt that this society is a hierarchical one, where the upper classes appropriate the available goods for themselves, leaving very little over for the lower ones. Moreover, the easy ascension to the top, the opportunity once so proudly extolled as "unlimited" has become quite restricted. On the other hand, no society is classless, at least I have never encountered such a place, so such an observation doesn't say anything specific about the United States. To limit the critique of this problem to one nation would be to divert attention from the underlying causes, a reductionism easily conducive to reactionary points of view.

In order not to avoid losing myself in generalities, I had best proceed chronologically. When I arrived here thirty-five years ago, my image of America was determined by three factors. A good part of it was shaped by my very mixed reactions to individual Americans. While I can't say that everyone I met in the mine or at the military mission won me over, it's true that I consistently met people who impressed me or helped me in some way. As a result I was prepared for a wide range of possibilities.

My expectations were further shaped by American literature, mainly by the sharp satires of Sinclair Lewis and the anti-capitalist novels of Jack London and Upton Sinclair. Although in many ways they could be considered dated, the knowledge on which they were based provided a healthy counterweight to the deceivingly rosy notions that I – as well as most refugees from Hitler – had gotten from FDR. For us he was not only Hitler's leading antagonist during the war, but the personification of political reason and good will in the world. The American image he projected had reached the farthest corners of the earth, and they continued to carry weight long past his death. I distinctly remember the nervous interest my fellow students in Cuenca took in the Dewey-Truman election and the relief they felt when Truman won, contrary to all expectation.

At first I found this Rooseveltian friendliness confirmed wherever I went. I was warmly received; people helped me or did things on my behalf without my asking, they guessed my needs and persistently overlooked the shortcomings that I, as a stranger in unfamiliar territory, necessarily exhibited. My opinions, which differed from theirs in so many ways were considered original; even my accent elicited approval. In short, I was considered interesting. Nor did my meager finances affect their relationship toward me in the least. Never in my life had I been treated so well.

For the first time, I had come into contact with a population deeply suffused with a democratic spirit; to this day I think this personal interaction is one of the greatest assets of the United States. And this is evident whether at home or at work, on the street or in the store. If this assertion seems puzzling in the light of the country's glaring social inequities, one must remember that there is an immense gap between individual and group behavior. In the spheres of everyday life, at any rate, a helpful, friendly relationship between individuals is generally the rule. Naturally this has something to do with the country's sheer expanse: the farther you travel away from the overpopulated regions in the east, the more you can detect the old pioneer spirit, according to which a neighbor is more a helper than a competitor. By the same token, the comparative aggressiveness and mean-spiritedness often found in Europe are undoubtedly linked to the relative lack of available living space.

I was also impressed by people's honesty. Having come from a milieu in which everything that wasn't nailed to the floor was filched from right under one's nose, I couldn't believe my eyes when I saw a mailman leave oversized packages on top of a mailbox. Even more amazing was the fact that they were still there an hour later. We have often experienced concrete examples of this respect for other people's property. After our wedding, we cashed a check at the bank for a sum large enough to last us the whole summer. Just after that, my wife chose to forget her purse somewhere, along with all the money. When we discovered that the bag was gone, we had no idea where we had left it: we retraced our steps, until we had excluded every place except a large department store, where we thought we had the least chance of recovering our loss. Nevertheless, the improbable occurred: in response to our inquiry, a saleslady – not the one who had been there before – produced the purse from under the counter without a word. A customer had found it and given it to her, and they had kept it for us without even looking inside.

That's the way it was everywhere: if you were on foot somewhere, on a walk for example, a passing car would invariably offer you a ride. If your own car broke down on the road, within minutes someone would stop to help. If you were on a bus and found to your embarrassment that you had left your money at home, another passenger would jump up and pay the fare. Everywhere you went, you were taken along, invited to dinner, helped with your shopping, assisted in your work and encouraged with all kinds of intervention and advice. I had never experienced anything comparable, neither in fascist Austria nor in socially conservative South America. True, some of these countries had 'democratic' governments, but here I learned the political lesson that democracy and parliamentarianism were by no means the same thing.

Unfortunately all this has changed for the worse since I arrived. Economic crises, unemployment and the vast increase in crime have dealt a heavy blow to American openness and trust. People are much more suspicious of each other and close each other off to an unprecedented extent. But some of the old openness still remains.

Naturally my euphoria did not continue unabated, and my exaggeratedly one-sided view of the good things in America ultimately gave way to more realistic insights. While in this unbelievably huge land you could travel for the longest time in spheres that seemed thoroughly unscathed by modern social afflictions, there were others rent by chaos, discrimination and crime. This was the first traumatic discovery about the US that I had to confront.

A second, more political one soon followed, with the arrival of Senator McCarthy and his movement. In the nascent Cold War climate, a rabid anti-Communism began to terrorize public opinion, so much that openly critical remarks by independent thinkers became acts of bravery that could result in the loss of job and reputation merely on the basis of suspicion and hearsay. It was only too obvious that this enslavement of conscience was being organized for specific purposes. Because of the funds that McCarthy received from the multimillion-dollar oil companies, McCarthy was often called in bitter irony the "Senator from Texas," though everyone of course knew he hailed from Wisconsin. Officially this movement sought to address matters of foreign policy having to do with military preparedness, the competition with the Soviet Union, and relations with communist China – but behind these issues there were other agendas, economic and nationalistic. Most discouraging of all was the credulousness with which such a large part of the population let itself be duped by these machinations, the fear and hatred that had evidently been slumbering beneath the humane and congenial surface, and had so easily been roused.

Naturally the universities soon came under fire, as centers of liberal thought and intellectual analysis, and we passionately joined in the fray, even though we were technically foreigners who could be deported at any time. Soon inquisition-style committees were meeting all through the land, and the infamous "witch hunts" began. Given my previous experiences I couldn't help but think that fascism, which I thought had been defeated, was once again on the march. At first I refused to believe my American friends and acquaintances who brushed this off as a European prejudice and predicted that this nuisance, this McCarthyite state within a state, could not last. They were right of course, but it took years before a counter-movement finally asserted itself. Blinded by his many successes, McCarthy had set his sights on the army, but this turned out to be more than even he could swallow. Television, which brought his intolerant, hysterical behavior into every American home, did its share to dispel the McCarthy myth. Resistance grew; Congress had to take cognizance of the change in public opinion and one day, McCarthy received a mild reproof from his fellow senators in an open ballot. That rare event seemed to suffice; the waves subsided; the abuse came to an end; McCarthy's power eroded and he vanished from the limelight. When he died a few years later, nobody paid any attention.

But the damage had been done. The injustices that had been perpetrated could not be reversed, even though for years the courts were blocked with lawsuits from the period. Moreover, the country's integrity had been compromised; its moral fiber had deteriorated. For my part, I emerged from these events strongly disillusioned. I now understood that there were at least two Americas, Enlightenment America with its quest for independence and its eighteenth-century constitution, and its praiseworthy principles such as "due process," or "innocent until proven guilty." Then there was the covert America, with its anti-intellectual obscurantism, its chauvinist and racist elitism, a mob only half held in check, ready to burst forth at the slightest provocation.

The next several years saw the rise of militarism, and the increasing power and prestige of the army. While Eisenhower benignly putted away his presidency on the golf course, his more sinister foreign secretary was busy engaging in international power plays that would go down in history under the apt name of "brinkmanship."

It was in this atmosphere that Kennedy assumed the presidency. Now bona fide citizens, we cast our votes for him, since his opponent Richard Nixon was already then one of the most notorious figures in American politics, who in the course of his career had supported practically every cause we ourselves deemed detrimental to the world. But in contrast to most Europeans, we didn't trust Kennedy either; we merely considered him the lesser of two evils. Our suspicions were soon borne out; among his first acts as president were an enormous increase in the military budget, the invasion of Cuba, and the escalation of American intervention in Vietnam. Significantly, while measures like these were protested, held open discussions, staged one of the first teach-ins and published one of the earliest anti-Vietnam books, *The Politics of Escalation*. But the protests of a few professors were not enough to turn the tide without more mass support; it wasn't until the students joined in and created the American youth movement that the anti-war movement began to take on political significance, dividing the country into two camps. From then on, we redoubled our efforts: my wife and my adolescent children participated in boycotts and other anti-war activities. In St. Louis, they stood with placards in front of the draft centers and the companies implicated in the war economy; in Washington, they demonstrated to prod the government and the entire world to stop the carnage.

As the student movement began to spill over into other areas, challenging the status quo, many universities were rent with violence. However, in contrast to their peers in other countries, the American students did not turn against the professors *per se*. And because I had sympathized with the protestors from the very start, I was able, together with a few like-minded colleagues, to play a mediating role between the students and the administration. These efforts ultimately helped prevent excesses on both sides and contributed to the reform of the university.

Those first years of opposition were lonely and difficult; almost everyone turned away, uncomprehendingly. But in the end the movement grew to such proportions as to bring about a veritable paradox of history: Nixon, the most zealous of cold warriors, was forced to end the intervention. When one analyzes the country's state of mind at that time, it should be remembered that a third of eligible voters did vote for McGovern despite his extraordinarily inept campaign. Furthermore, the entire, protracted movement – in many ways reminiscent of a mass uprising – against a government embroiled in a war of enormous proportions took place without mass assassinations, emergency measures or the bloody suppression of the insurgents. Where was the German resistance to the First World War when Hindenburg and Ludendorff forged the dictatorship that drove the country deeper and deeper into a hopeless war? How many Russians took to the streets immediately approved and put into effect, the social measures Kennedy had proposed were effectively blocked in Congress. Perhaps it is true, as some have suggested, that Kennedy's true and better nature would have become evident had he been given more time. But he was assassinated, and his regime was succeeded by the catastrophic Johnson administration, later to be confirmed in office by a landslide victory over Barry Goldwater. Of course, what choice was there, considering that the latter, an Air Force general, seemed bent on playing hardball with atomic weapons? And as it turned out, it was Johnson who pushed the Kennedy social program through a Congress ostensibly wracked by contrition and in the throes of hero worship. But it was also Johnson who escalated the conflict in Vietnam into a full-fledged war, betraying his holiest vows to do the opposite, and so negated whatever good he had done, for as we now know, the Vietnam War became one of the most shameful chapters in American history.

I opposed that war from its earliest and relatively inconspicuous beginnings, and I spent almost a whole decade protesting this irresponsible undertaking, allowing myself to become distracted from doing what I enjoyed most – teaching and studying literature. At first the groups that openly opposed the American intervention and the lies being propagated to justify it were small. "Lies" is of course much too simple a word for the manipulation of language and sense, for the suppression and invention of news, for the whole repulsive network of euphemisms and hypocritical assertions in which the official propaganda machinery enveloped the public. As so often happens, a single utterance has come to express symbolically this macabre twisting of words, which even Orwell could not have foreseen in his worst nightmares. I am thinking of the statement made by an otherwise insignificant officer, a statement that underscored the nefariousness of the entire undertaking, as well as revealed his own total acceptance of the ruthless killing it entailed: we had to destroy this village, the man declared, in order to liberate it.

I can proudly say that Washington University was one of the first in the country to organize an effective counter-movement. We to protest the violation of Hungary and Czechoslovakia? And how would they have been treated had they dared to do so?

Nothing ever happened to me personally at the demonstrations I took part in, except that I was constantly being photographed, but that is a pleasure I am willing to concede to the keepers of law and order. I was not arrested or given a hearing; I did not lose my job; and I was not pressured from any side. The FBI probably has a thick file on me, to which, incidentally, I would have access under the Freedom of Information Act – if I wanted to, but I'm not all that curious. Of course: unlawful arrests did take place; tear gas was used in ample amounts; more than one protestor was beaten by the police, and the victims of Kent State remain unforgotten. But I shall leave it to the reader to imagine how these acts of protest would have been received in other countries.

This is another aspect of the United States that should not be disregarded. The postponements and machinations with which Nixon and his Secretary of State sought to draw out the end of the war, the so-called "Christmas bombing" – these are inexcusable tactics which in my view can compare to some of the acts perpetrated by the Nazis. And of the many political aberrations I have witnessed in my lifetime, conferring the Nobel peace prize on Kissinger was one of the most ludicrous. But in the long run all this was of no use. The American troops had to be withdrawn from Vietnam, where they never belonged in the first place.

I learned a great deal from the war in Vietnam – not only did it cost me any last illusions about America: it made me a confirmed pessimist with regard to world history. The final triumph of reason had been too ambiguous, the sufferings too great, the losses too irrevocable to impart any sense of victory.

Strange as this may sound, the war in Vietnam also deepened my understanding of National Socialism. This phenomenon, which had so altered the direction of my own life and about which I thought I knew everything worth knowing, suddenly became more transparent to me than ever, in intimate, psychological and therefore human terms. As the US government embarked on this adventure, my good neighbors and democratic acquaintances simply stood by and watched. At least at first they seemed utterly incapable of questioning the values and giving up the illusions that had been handed down to them, of forswearing their almost innate belief in the rationality and constitutionality of their country. I realized then that many German patriots must have witnessed the rise of National Socialism in much the same way – helpless, unbelieving, uncomprehending – although they were perhaps more shielded from the truth, while in the US the news flowed freely through the media. As a result I have a much more tolerant attitude towards Hitler's fellow travelers – insofar as they have shown signs of moral regeneration after the war – than I did before the war in Vietnam.

For its part, the Watergate crisis offered little in the way of new insight. I had been convinced of the deep-seated corruption and bottomless immorality of the clique in power long before the scandal broke out. The only thing that surprised me about Nixon's exposure was the public reaction, the fact that so many people had been taken in for so long, while I hadn't had any illusions about the man for the past twenty-five years.

In the end the American system of checks and balances once again proved itself, as it had in the case of McCarthyism and the Vietnam War. Naturally the institutions moved at a snail's pace; years passed before the public took a clear stand, but at last Nixon was swept aside. The circumstances of his resignation were not exactly cause for much cheer, but at least they permitted a glimmer of hope that not all was lost. And even though I voted for Carter without great enthusiasm, I did stay up on election night, glued to the television, in order to savor Ford's downfall along with that of the rest of the Nixon crew. I felt as if my whole physical well-being depended on this form of detoxification.

The next swing of the political pendulum was more painful for me, when Reagan replaced Carter, who after his defeat began to appear in a new light, transfigured. And although my mood was hardly jovial, I did joke that Reagan's election was part of an overall scheme to rehabilitate the institution of the presidency. After all, compared with Reagan, Eisenhower was a model of diligence, Kennedy an advocate of detente, Johnson an apostle of peace, Nixon a fanatic for truth, Ford an intellectual and Carter a paragon of competence.

Carter's foreign policy, for example, sought not only to establish stability; it also attempted to introduce morality as a political guideline. And although critics both at home and abroad condescendingly pronounced his human rights doctrine utopian, it did succeed – albeit despite the resistance of Congress – in helping achieve a bloodless transfer of power in Rhodesia as well as – at least for the moment – in Nicaragua. The latter was freed from the yoke of the Somoza dynasty, which the United States itself had earlier installed; ultimately, however, Reagan's policy of supporting the Contras brought renewed violence to that country.

Carter's more open foreign policy, the willingness to support fledgling independent governments and the corresponding disinclination to fight them helped keep these new states from following the Cuban model and joining the Soviet camp. Nor should it be forgotten that it was Carter who set into motion the peace negotiations between Israel and Egypt, and for all his crude mistakes, his behavior toward Iran on the whole remained quite moderate.

But that was precisely what led to his ruin. For as little as Americans concern themselves with international politics, they are very sensitive towards any threat to national pride or to the myth of American superiority. (According to a poll taken during the Reagan years, only eight percent of the population knew which side the administration supported in El Salvador as well as Nicaragua.) The Iranian debacle, the runaway inflation and a high rate of unemployment set into motion reactionary forces that put into power an actor whose callous banality could not be hidden behind his plastic smile. Unfortunately, his talents, which never made him a Hollywood star, proved more than adequate when it came to deluding the majority of Americans, to the point of earning him the appreciative nickname of "great communicator."

I watched in horror when he – or rather the class whose spokesman he was – began to slash away at welfare, which in our

day is a cornerstone of every civilized nation, while simultaneously granting unprecedented tax breaks to the rich. Or when he filled
posts created for the protection of the environment with people
bent on exploiting rather than conserving natural resources. Or else
when he passed the largest military budget in human history and
increased the arms sales across the globe by a staggering amount.
For every newfound problem his only 'solutions' were military; he
even threatened to shatter the hard-won but nevertheless precarious
understanding with the Soviet Union that was so necessary to
world peace. When all of this began to happen, I set myself the
task of documenting these nefarious stupidities, and went to work
clipping articles from newspapers and magazines as evidence for
another, and possibly better day. But I soon found this to be a
Sisyphean labor, for the bad news was flooding in at such a rate I
would have spent the whole day clipping. I was better off saving
the whole paper, but that was something the libraries were already
doing in my stead.

I realize this is not the place to catalogue the sins of the
Reagan administration; it is enough for me to point to a general
trend. But in the context of this book it would seem a crude
omission to ignore what was happening in Latin America – to
which for obvious reasons I still feel strongly tied. I would be
remiss to ignore the irresponsible establishment and implied
vindication of military dictatorships in Chile and Argentina, or the
partial culpability for the war in the Falklands, or the political,
economic and military aid granted to oppressors of human rights
in El Salvador and Guatemala, or else the incitement of Honduras
against Nicaragua. In fact there was hardly a dictatorship on earth
that was not supported by the Reagan administration, as long as it
claimed to be anti-Soviet – however harshly it may have ruled.

The massive hypocrisy and outright fabrication that accompanied these policies was not their least objectionable aspect. Even
worse was the virtual obsession with weaponry, the acceleration of
nuclear armament to an unthinkable extreme, despite clear popular
opposition on both sides of the Atlantic. After all, while the
continued manufacture and deployment of nuclear weapons is no

guarantee for Western security, it does carry the threat of destruction of life on earth.

While all this continued unabated, American liberalism seemed paralyzed or ideologically bankrupt, either unwilling or unable to stop these horrors. For their part, the wealthy were determined to protect their newly acquired privileges at all costs, and elsewhere benighted fanatics began actively emerging from their hiding places into full public view, to the point of gaining evident legitimization. By the mid-1980s I was convinced that nothing short of an economic crisis would shake the voters into awareness.[6] Meanwhile the more conscious and better informed citizens turned inward, to their private lives; helpless to change the course of events, they evidently sought to maintain their psychological equilibrium by focusing on day-to-day survival.

In view of all this, it is hardly surprising that I am not a more "patriotic" American. In fact, the question arises as to the extent I am American at all. I have my American passport, which is important to me when I travel; there are some American landscapes that I love beyond anything, though that has little to do with nationalism, at least not in my vocabulary. I still find joy whenever I run across some vestige of the democratic spirit I described above, which to this day happens more often here than in Europe. And of course I have very many American friends.

Otherwise I am not particularly American: I take a skeptical if not directly negative view of the political system and most other manifestations of public life – and this reserve does not leave much room for a national identity. But this is simply who I am – or who I am not. Similarly, I am unable to assign a nationalistic meaning to being a Jew, as I have already explained. I am only a Jew insofar

---

[6] While the Savings and Loan debacle, the collapse of the bond market, the question of health insurance and other blatant inequalities did not constitute enough of a crisis to turn things around, they did contribute to Clinton's victorious campaign on economic issues, thus proving my theories. To install true social democracy would require greater upheavals.

as I, having experienced a Jewish destiny, belong to the community of those who shared that fate. But that is probably not enough to establish an unequivocally Jewish identity. Naturally I am not an Austrian either, as should be clear from what I have written in this account. It would probably be most accurate to say that I bear something of all these cultural and psychological configurations within me.

Nor do I mean to suggest I am a citizen of the world – that would be biting off more than I can chew. Even if such citizenship were desirable, it still doesn't exist: whether you wish it or no, you still have to be a citizen of this country or that. But intuitively I tend in that direction, and what I am lacking in an innate or acquired sense of local ties I try to make up for with a kind of thinking that takes into account the populations of the earth in general. This question has ceased to be a problem for me. I am simply there; I am interested in this or that, enthusiastic about this or that; I support this or that political current or enterprise; I have contact with these or those human beings – and that's really all I need.

When I look back to the beginning of my life, I realize that it was stirred up early by the fascist movements in Germany and Austria and that it was because of them that I turned out as I did. To claim that Hitler was good for me would be making a mockery of the murdered millions among whose numbers I could easily have figured at any point in the fascists' destructive crusade through the world. It is nonetheless true that the explosive outbursts of Nazism catapulted me out of the narrow confines of my home to those airy regions where I gained a broader perspective than I would have ordinarily. Some people are profoundly threatened or even destroyed when their roots are severed from that bit of earth they call their own. Nor was this experience exactly a pleasant one for me either, but in the long run it unleashed powers within me that would have otherwise remained forever slumbering beneath the surface. Unlike other refugees who mourn for their homeland, I think emigration is a good thing and I affirm it not because it just so happens that it's something I went through and because people tend to be positive about their experiences, but almost as a matter of principle, as a process to which I owe my freedom and, strange as it may sound, the attainment of a certain inner harmony.

But it is not enough to try to make sense of events in my life from the philosophical perspective of an individual alone – it is the intertwining of that life within a given world that is worthy of note. Looking back, I see that my life has neither been randomly directed nor consciously led; its direction was neither accidental nor willed. Instead, I see how my fate was shaped by historical forces that were beyond any one person's influence or even comprehension – so much so that my own destiny can be calculated fairly precisely as a function of those historical occurrences. Even those decisions that I did make now and again can be shown to be the result of relative circumstances and historically determined possibilities. Whenever times were bad, my life too was in turmoil. And if in recent years I have become more settled, then it is because the particular time and place in which I live allow for a more restful existence. I could have gone under at any point during my passage through the epoch I have described. Even this necessarily abridged account has shown how often destruction seemed at least as likely as survival. Whether in the 'annexed' Vienna, in the no man's land, in the besieged and ultimately occupied city of Prague, or in the impassable terrain of the Andes, the very real threat of physical and spiritual annihilation was constantly present. And had it caught up with me, who could have said it was because of some personal inadequacy? But just as I can't say that defeat would have implied failure, I cannot give myself credit for any sporadic success I might have encountered. In this day and age, as the net of inevitability is drawn ever tighter around us, it makes little sense indeed to apply moral standards to the doings of the individual. Such things are the luxury of an ordered world. We can admire a hero if one comes along, but we shouldn't expect one to show up very often.

I needed to say these things in order to qualify the word "freedom" that I used before, as I examined the questions that first inspired me to write these reminiscences. No one can become acquainted with the ever-changing circumstances of my life and arrive at the opinion that I overestimate the individual's freedom to shape and direct his own development in this world. Sometimes it seems as though we were being whirled about by uncontrollable powers, and were no more able to resist them than a snowflake is able to resist a winter storm. Only in favorable circumstances – this much will I cautiously say – does a person retain a certain freedom of movement according to his particular situation. In that case an encounter takes place between an overwhelming external reality and a given individual, equipped with his own cleverness, vitality and ethical motivation. At the proper moment, when the mix is right, something can come of this encounter. It is necessary to postulate this little element of freedom in order to safeguard the concept of human dignity. Common ideological embellishments – such as that we as humans are inherently free – should be avoided. Normally, statements like that only serve to conceal some dismal truth. Given the present state of the world, one can say that humanity is groping its way forward in terrible darkness. My own experience doesn't leave me with anything particularly soothing to say. I see reason and freedom flickering feebly as they send an occasional ray through the shadows of history. I consider it a human duty to do everything possible to preserve and nourish this little light; indeed, we should regard it as our most meaningful task to keep it from going out. Nevertheless, the assurance that it will one day grow into a high and vital flame is not one that I have gained from the lessons of the past.

POSTSCRIPT 1998

Years have passed since I first published this account. In the meantime there is little new I have to say about the US. I am still living here in St. Louis, still grateful for the enormous chances I received fifty years ago and the career this opportunity afforded me. But I continue to deplore certain aspects of the social system, the ongoing military adventurism in distant lands, the deepening chasm between wealthy citizens and those less fortunate. Recent cuts in welfare, attacks on affirmative action and sporadic bursts of anti-immigrant frenzy have done little to allay my concern.

Nonetheless it is about Austria that I wish to add a few observations; by recounting my more recent experiences with my native country I hope to close the circle described in this book. These renewed contacts have grown more and more frequent over the years: I have already touched upon some of them in the last chapter. At this point I should like to dwell on a particular one of those "returns."

In the mid 1980s I had the opportunity of spending more than just a few days in the Austrian capital – for the first time since 1938. The Ministry of Culture had furnished me with an apartment between the districts of Margareten and Wieden – a section of town I hadn't known very well from before. I set up house and began to move about the city that was my former hometown, although I myself made every effort to remain unmoved by this reunion.

Happily I had every conceivable variety of small shop and service right under my nose, and the *Naschmarkt* – an open-air food produce market – was only three minutes away on foot. I could also walk to the *Nationalbibliothek*, where I was working, in just twenty minutes. This proximity was particularly enjoyable after living so long in the United States, where you have to drive miles to get to the giant supermarkets.

The salutary effects of all this exercise were challenged,

however, by the culinary temptations lurking in every café, *Konditorei* and bakery. My palate reveled in the freshly baked breads, the *Landbrot, Alpenlaberl* and *Wachauer*, and despite the regrettable consequences for my waistline, I renewed my acquaintance with poppyseed *Striezel* and Viennese pretzels, and sundry pastries of my youth such as *Dampfbuchtel, Germknödel, Indianerkrapfen, Topfenpalatschinken* and *Powidltatschkerln.*

Before long I had mastered the reliable public transportation and was fighting for tickets in the Hanuschgasse or at various other box offices. Taking advantage of the numerous cultural offerings, I attended plays, concerts, readings, and operas. In a word, I enjoyed playing the casual tourist, with the notable exception that I knew where things were, and had no difficulty understanding even the thickest local dialect. In fact I could have even spoken it had I not felt so inhibited. But fifty years of speaking in foreign languages had left my tongue a little tied, myself a little wary lest my lapsing into Viennese be read as an inappropriate ingratiation. And all the while I deliberately avoided the more intimate contact with the Landstrasse district, where I knew every side street, even individual buildings – at least many of the ones that were still standing.

But one night was enough to shatter any illusion of being a disinterested tourist. I was taking a limousine from the Schwechat airport to the Hilton hotel, and as we rode along I began to notice with growing emotion that the driver was following with sadistic tenacity a route from my childhood. We passed along the Schüttel until we crossed the Danube channel on the Rotunda bridge, "my" bridge, which I had crossed countless times escaping my schoolwork to play soccer or on my way to my first romantic encounters in the Jesuitenwiese in the Prater park. We crossed the Donaukanal, past the Café Zartl, where my parents had fetched whipped cream on Sundays, and came in sight of the Geologengasse, where I had grown up, then drove down the Rasumofskygasse towards my grade school on the Siegelgasse. What were a measly fifty years compared to the feelings unleashed by this moonlit tryst? Mixed as they were, even hopelessly entangled, they came surging forth from their hidden depths, forcing me to renounce the fiction that I was just another carefree tourist roaming through his "favorite city in Europe," oblivious to present reality and unfettered by historical ties, happily enchanted by the much-admired Lippizaners.

This drive taught me that the Viennese child was still very much alive inside me, despite my sixty-odd years. I realized that you never lose your childhood; it just keeps on existing, albeit buried beneath the years. There was life there after all, still stirring beneath the ruins, like magma deep beneath a cold volcano. And I understood that everything that had happened to me in the span of half a century – and what a one at that! – had had to build on this rubble, hardly a secure foundation, to be sure, but there simply wasn't any other. Just like my childhood home at Geologengasse 8, with its wrought iron French doors, its stone steps and the ornate lantern in the foyer, once so magnificent, then bombed and – according to a tablet affixed outside – rebuilt with funds from the Ministry for Reconstruction. In the interim, however, it has once again grown shabby: an almost identical biography!

I know about this plaque because after that night I gave up trying to resist and searched out all the old places: the Franz-Josefs-Realgymnasium, now known as the Bundesgymnasium Wien I, the streets and squares where my friends had lived, the house with the seventeenth-century stone missile fired by the Turks where my father had kept his workshop, the corner in the Stadtpark where I sat with my first girlfriend, the building in the Löwengasse which had once housed the cinema where I had first beheld the actresses who were my early idols. I even went back to the Rasumofskygasse, where, across from the Geologische Bundesanstalt, is the former home of Robert Musil. For some time I had passed the house every day on my way to school, although all I knew was that people said there was a man inside "who was writing things." Today an inscription informs the reader that Musil lived there from 1921 to 1938, precisely the time I spent in Vienna. It further states that Musil died in exile, and it strikes me then and there that I, too, will die in exile, although with no promise of

226

plaque or inscription, whether my end meets me in St. Louis or somewhere else.

Vienna had the advantage of having come through the second World War relatively unscathed. In fact it is probable that more of the city was demolished after the war, by the fury to tear down and rebuild, than was destroyed by bombs. Less tangible aspects of the city, such as psycho-historical ones, show similar continuities and discontinuities. Today everything is brighter and decidedly more glitzy than in the oppressive, gloomy days of the first republic – at least as I remember it. Facades have been scrubbed clean; the display windows are overflowing with goods; everything seems quite expensive. Still, people crowd the theaters, the concert halls, the restaurants. The Viennese dress well and drive expensive cars, although once more there are also people begging on the streets. Even so, many people are obviously well off and, as a result, less stricken by ressentiment or class envy, less prone to aggression.

Of course vestiges of old behavior remain, such as the traditional Viennese *Schadenfreude*. A few examples: a friend was planning to visit, so I set out to look for a room. It was Pentecost, and I kept running into one rejection after another. Finally a hotel porter explained it to me in his thick Viennese dialect: "You want a room? I'm gonna tell you something: you can search the whole city and you're not gonna find a room at Pentecost any more than you found one here." I ask a woman on the street how to get to the nearest bank: "I don't know about any banks, but there's a post office at the Faulmanngasse." My wife, a German from Westfalen, was dealing with the owner of a small grocery, who evidently felt challenged by her northern German accent:

"Do you want Styrian eggs or Austrian ones?" he asked.
"As far as I know Styria still is part of Austria."
"You're right. The difference isn't very great."

In such situations one feels taken back by decades; psychological structures don't change so quickly. Is there any other place in the world apart from Vienna where you get answers like that?

The political arena has its own share of upheld traditions, as exemplified by the Frischenschlager affair, named after a former minister of defense. This gentleman decided to be on hand to personally welcome back a former SS-officer and war criminal who had been imprisoned in Italy, then pardoned and released. Upon his return the officer was given refuge in the Austrian army – and that was enough to rouse every conceivable political passion Vienna has ever known. Were we going to allow an incident like this to offend our neighbors to the south – still looked down upon, at least unconsciously? Or was this just the naiveté of an inexperienced politician, who was trying to curry favor with the nationalists, militarists and reactionary elements both in the nation and especially in his own party (the FPÖ).[7] In many ways the reactions were more remarkable than the event itself – first there was a flood of jobs loudly offered the pardoned officer, which considering his age and health could have only been meant as provocation. Next came the haggling over what to call him – was he a prisoner of war who had done his duty, or a war criminal who had wrought havoc among the civilian population? Finally Minister Frischenschlager outdid himself by hypocritically apologizing to Israel (!) for what he had done, accompanied by the predictable indignation in certain circles for his having done so. Many people proved incorrigible; no one seemed repentant.

A similar reaction occurred when Reagan attempted to "balance" his visit to the Bitburg cemetery by including a stop at the Bergen-Belsen concentration camp. I recall my own disgust at the search for a "photogenic" concentration camp to serve as a suitable background for the president to pose with his ominous plastic smile. The Austrian popular press, however, reacted indignantly to the minister's apology, to the point of stooping to

---

[7] The FPÖ, ostensibly a party of free traders, is the refuge of old and new "sympathizers," who have to tread warily because any *Wiederbetätigung* or "resumed activity" – i.e., Nazi attitudes – is forbidden and punishable by law.

use that ineradicable old coupling: "Jews and Soviets will surely triumph" warned several newspapers. Was this 1985 or 1935? Evidently anti-Semitism runs so deep that it doesn't even need the presence of Jews.

It's all somewhat spooky, and I'm not using the word metaphorically, but very concretely. Sins of the past will always come back to haunt people as long as they are not confronted and put to rest. The myth that Austria was a victim and not an agent of fascism – a clear fabrication for anyone who was actually there, regardless on which side – has undoubtedly brought certain political advantages. But this invention is ultimately a stultifying one, which has caused and will cause psychological damage to those who have actually begun to accept it as fact. Following the tradition of Karl Kraus, a Viennese wit by the name of Alfred Polgar summed it up very nicely – and not without a hint of *Schadenfreude* of his own – "I have reached the devastating conclusion that Vienna really does go on being Vienna!"

Still, it's clear to me that a lot has changed, especially in the area of personal relationships, gestures of friendliness that I, as a "visitor," found particularly moving. This came out in my meetings with school friends I hadn't seen since 1938, or in my encounters with the cleaning lady who brought homemade pastries to the graying gentleman, perhaps because she saw right through him, or perhaps because she didn't. Or the pains taken by the librarians to find new material for my research. Even the *Nationalbibliothek* went out of the way to accommodate me, although the routines there are enough to warrant their own satirical essay. The same could be said of the General Hospital whose services we were forced to utilize, where a young doctor repeatedly took us under his care, steadfastly refusing to accept any remuneration despite all our clever attempts to offer some. It's amazing how often my efforts to pay for services received were rebuffed. Even the police chose not to fine me for wrongful parking. For my part, I would have been happy to pay, too – at least for everything but the parking ticket; after all I wasn't returning as the penniless beggar I became when I was driven away. Still, in my opinion it is the duty of the state and not certain well-meaning individuals to compensate me for the long deprivation of my youth, as the German state did for those citizens who had been driven out by the Nazis.[8] But I was nevertheless happy that these people didn't want any money from me; their selfless behavior was a good demonstration of Kantian goodwill in this world so given to materialism. And since I'm not so conceited as to suspect that I might have become more charming, sympathetic or otherwise more attractive during the last fifty years, the only logical explanation of this evident change in behavior towards me is that the people themselves have changed, and for the better.

In summing up my present relationship to Vienna and Austria, I realize that passing judgment on what happened to one person is unquestionably a matter of perspective. Things look different from a distance of so many years than they appeared in the close-up of the moment. My immigration was without a doubt fraught with physical danger and discomfort. Nor can one ignore the psychological experience – the loss of human rights, the banishment from the community, the erosion of inner security, of any feeling for homeland, identity and cultural belonging, the fracturing of childhood, the effects of being torn from friends and school and future expectations, and perhaps worst of all the dismal hopelessness of an unbearably long decade. From the psychological and legal point of view there is nothing to be said except that I was the victim of a gross personal and social injustice, which brought me to the brink of annihilation, and which cost many members of my family their lives.

But today, more than half a century later, another point of view is possible. Being driven out of Austria separated me from my *Gymnasium* precisely at a time when I could experience this as a good thing. It freed me – and I say this without sarcasm – from

---

[8] In the meantime the Austrian parliament has provided modest compensation to the few survivors and is contemplating restitution for the thousands of slave laborers from Eastern Europe.

Vienna, from a provincial city ridden with poverty, inflamed with political passion, seething with prejudice and at the mercy of an inhuman government. Painful though it was, after it was over I never really missed all the illusions that were stripped from me in this one fell blow. In fact I later came to perceive the inevitable results of this loss as something positive, this lack of nationalistic, ethnocentric or Eurocentric identity. I often ask myself whether, had it not been for March 11, 1938, I would have ever come to such a thorough understanding of the "underdeveloped" world, which has contributed so much to my own worldview. Or where I would have acquired the historical insight that has so fashioned my way of thinking and become an inseparable part of my personality. When I ask myself – and the question cannot be ignored – what would have become of me in Vienna, the hypothetical answers always compare unfavorably with what I did become. And I don't even mean the concentration camps or death camps where so many of those who stayed behind were imprisoned and murdered. No, I'm thinking of a more normal and less cataclysmic course of events, in a Vienna of my childhood that would have muddled through the years without the Nazis. How would I have fared in such a city, either personally or professionally? The chances of making a career as a literary critic and university professor would have been minute.

My hometown treated me so badly in my youth that simply in order to survive I had to fight any feelings of belonging and devotion, which were once quite strong, until I lost them altogether. But it would be wrong of me not to recognize that the city of my birth also gave me something that proved priceless on the hard road of emigration. The linguistic and cultural impressions it bestowed upon me even before I went to school could never be erased or extinguished. I believe I've made my critical attitude toward my *Gymnasium* all too clear. But I happily admit that in addition to a sizable amount of factual knowledge, it also provided me with a fundamental intellectual orientation. People say that if you're patient enough, you will accomplish something, and this proved true for me.

A few years ago I was invited back to my old school, where the Austrian minister for education honorarily awarded me the diploma I had missed – a little late, to be sure, but even so. The handful of former classmates who showed up to be similarly honored entrusted me with speaking on their behalf – their hair had long since grown gray, and one even became the American ambassador to Austria a few years later. Some of what I said in my speech of acknowledgment bears repeating here: "We do not view states and nations as monolithic structures that speak with only *one* voice or act with only *one* will. By accepting this honor we are allying ourselves with the progressive elements of Austrian society. We cannot, nor would we want to forget the hardships and horrors of the thirties and forties. To forget and so repress such trauma is incompatible with the concept of human dignity, and today we know that such repression can cause great psychological damage. However, this act of remembering is compatible with the spirit of reconciliation and the joy we find in the abundant changes for the better that have occurred over the past decades, both in our country of origin and in the city we once called home."

I made similar remarks when Austria conferred on me the official Medal for Art and Science, and when I received an honorary doctorate from the university I was prevented from attending.

Wordsworth wrote that the child is father of the man, and certainly this is true of me, in looking back on my career. Perhaps now I am able to discern more clearly than before what is specifically Austrian in my intellectual and cultural makeup. Because my life has followed so many different and very winding paths, these initial ingredients have mixed with other forces to create a synthesis sui generis. But it would be foolish to deny their abiding influence. Meanwhile, my periodic returns to Vienna now happen with no more emotion than if I were traveling to Mexico or Australia, which I also do on occasion. Mostly I go back for professional reasons, to deliver a lecture or attend a congress to which I have been invited. And what I enjoy most is seeing the new Austrian friends I have made during these visits, since the old ones have vanished without a trace or left this world entirely.